Giants of Garbage

The Rise of the Global Waste Industry and
the Politics of Pollution Control

Harold Crooks

James Lorimer & Company, Publishers
Toronto, 1993

James Lorimer and Company Ltd. acknowledges with thanks the support of the Canada Council, the Ontario Arts Council and the Ontario Publishing Centre in the development of writing and publishing in Canada.

Cover photo: Thomas Kitchin/First Light

Canadian Cataloguing in Publication Data
    Crooks, Harold, 1943-
    Giants of garbage
Includes bibliographical references and index.
ISBN 1-55028-399-5 (bound). - ISBN 1-55028-398-7 (pbk.)

1. Refuse and refuse disposal - North America.
2. Conglomerate corporations - North America.
I. Title.

TD789.N67C76 1993 363.72'8 C93-093469-5

Distributed in the United States by:
Formac Distributing Limited
121 Mount Vernon Street,
Boston, Mass 02108

James Lorimer & Company, Publishers
Egerton Ryerson Memorial Building
35 Britain Street
Toronto, Ontario
M5A 1R7

Printed in Canada

To T.R.B.
for thirty years of friendship

INSTITUTE OF URBAN STUDIES
THE UNIVERSITY OF WINNIPEG
515 PORTAGE AVENUE
WINNIPEG, MB   R3B 2E9

Contents

Preface

In early 1990, I was contacted by a Philadelphia law firm that was spearheading a class action lawsuit against the world's leading waste disposal corporations. The lawyers hoped to demonstrate that these corporations had achieved the ability to operate as a nation-wide cartel. In building their case, the high-powered legal team had used my first book, *Dirty Business*, as a primer on the workings of the waste industry and wanted to meet to discuss the possibility of my appearance in court as an expert witness in the event of a trial.

Since its publication in 1983, *Dirty Business* has found an audience as diverse geographically as it is ideologically. Throughout North America, aggrieved community groups and businesspeople, grass roots activists, reporters, academics, law enforcement investigators, federal trustbusters as well as antitrust lawyers in government and private practice turned to the book in search of insights into the waste business.

The class action never made it to court. And in spite of the important public policy implications of the lawsuit and the unprecedented size of the defendants' out-of-court settlement payment, the media ended up giving the case short shrift. One of the few instances of a public outcry came from Citizen Action of New York. The consumer-advocacy group, whose membership numbers 2.5 million, called for a public inquiry to "expose the pricing policies of our country's garbage kingpins." But with the prospect of that cry going unheeded (particularly coming as it did during the build-up to the war in the Gulf), and with *Dirty Business* now out of print, I decided to use my earlier book as the foundation for an enlarged and updated study which would re-focus the inquiry.

At the time *Dirty Business* first appeared, many in the environmental movement were made impatient by its preoccupation with issues of political economy and corporate power. But that view began changing as the "voodoo" economics of Reaganism and its companion ideology of privatization came to be seen as a threat even to the most basic forms of public enterprise — the custody of the environment and human health itself. Questions about power and politics came to be recognized as central issues by true environmental conservatives — no matter what their political stripe.

Nowhere was this more true than among grass-roots activists experiencing first hand the frightening depredations that could result from the unchecked bottom lines of corporate polluters.

The Canadian Union of Public Employees, Canada's largest labour organization, financially underwrote the first edition of *Dirty Business*. Recognizing that it served as a public resource and had helped build bridges both national and international between the labour and environmental movement, CUPE readily accepted the need for a new book and agreed to back the second project.

Dirty Business was preoccupied with defining the limits of free enterprise in providing public services. However, as time passed, and the dangers posed by mass disposal practices to human health and the environment became more widely understood, the need grew for a deeper analysis. In *Giants of Garbage*, I have tried to shed light on the uneven contest between ever-burgeoning multinational waste disposal companies and a myriad of beset urban, suburban, rural and underclass communities. By so doing, *Giants of Garbage* adds its own disturbing questions to those already being raised in other quarters about the capacity of the global corporation — and therefore of society in general — for rational waste policy in the face of the extravagant profits being made from current disposal practices.

I thank the following individuals for their generosity in sharing with me their knowledge of the issues: in Ontario, Steven Shrybman, Drew Blackwell, Rhonda Hustler, David McRobert, Doug MacDonald, Richard Gilbert, Michael de Gruchy, Dr. Barbara Wallace, John Jackson, Jock Ferguson, Royson James, Peter Leiss, Jay Switzer and Paul Christie; in Manitoba, Bill Omiucke, R.J. Cooke, Ray Richter, Ed Blackman, Paul Moist, Terry Duguid and Donald Campbell; in Quebec, Andre Bouthillier, Yves Corriveau, Jacqueline Mayrand, Aaron Freeman, Andre Noel, Luc Ouimet, Pierre Morency, Liliane Cotnoir and Alain Rajotte; in the United States, Dave Blow, Ellen Connett, Edwin Cluster, Will Collette, Luke Cole, Pat Murray, Dave Yeager, Charlie Cray, Ralph Haurwitz, Kevin Greene, Jamie Whitten, Velma Smith, Dr. Peter Montague, Chris Manthey, Ragnar Naess, Tom Turnipseed, Jim Zinsor, Douglas Wold, Marina Ortega and Marvin Robinson; and in Great Britain, Adam Kemp and John Plender.

In particular, I must single out Brian Lipsett, former editor of *Everyone's Backyard*, the grass-roots journal published by the Citizens' Clearinghouse for Hazardous Wastes, Inc. of Falls Church,

Virginia. During his years at CCHW, Brian was at the vital centre of a network of 7,000 community groups working for environmental justice across North America. He proved himself to be an indispensable ally.

As well, I wish to express my appreciation to Larry Katz, John Calvert, Jim Lorimer, Diane Young, Bob Chodos and Melinda Tate, each of whom helped guide the project along the path to publication.

Finally, I acknowledge my debt to my wife, Medrie MacPhee, for her love and forbearance during the long year spent immersed in the preparation of this book.

Introduction

... as pollution becomes America's most plentiful resource, Big Garbage seems poised to replace Big Oil as the Republican growth industry of the 1990s.
Bill Gifford, *In These Times*, 27 February 1990

In the summer of 1969 there didn't appear to be much that distinguished Tom J. Fatjo, Jr. from the thousands of other operators in the least glamorous of North American industries — the hauling and disposal of garbage. The twenty-eight-year-old accountant had done well since buying his first truck a few years earlier to haul refuse in a subdivision of his hometown of Houston. Like every other North American city at the time, Houston had its own local hauling industry. Competing with a dozen or so rivals, Fatjo built up his business, adding apartment houses, shopping centres and a few light industries to his fledgling network of accounts. Soon he had four trucks, a million dollars in annual revenues and a partner. Norman A. Myers was an ambitious banking and finance graduate of Oklahoma State University with a reputation as one of the southwest's most successful insurance salesmen. By 1968 their American Refuse Systems had landed a coveted garbage removal contract from the City of Houston and opened a licensed dump.

But if Fatjo's garbage business was still fairly modest, his ambitions were typically Texan. Tom J. Fatjo, Jr. hoped to do for garbage what John D. Rockefeller had done for oil, the industry that was the source of so much Texas wealth. His idea was to turn the fragmented, chaotic garbage trade into an integrated industry that was in step with the modern era of transnational megabusiness.

The garbage industry's new era began with an obscure financial transaction in July 1969, the month all eyes — especially in Houston — were on Neil Armstrong's giant step for mankind. That month Fatjo and Louis A. Waters, a thirty-year-old graduate of Houston's Rice University and the Harvard Business School's M.B.A. program, raised $600,000 and bought a corporate vehicle listed on the New York Stock Exchange. Called the Browning Ferris Machinery Corporation, the company was a Texas-based heavy equipment distributor. Fatjo and Waters merged their hauling business with the public company and changed its name to Browning-Ferris Industries, Inc. (BFI). Now the garbage industry had access to the money markets of Wall Street for the first time. Soon investors were persuaded to gamble on the possibility that a waste systems company operating in a multitude of metropolitan markets *was* a profitable idea. By the early 1980s, the Houston-based garbage-collection company had become a corporate waste empire stretching from Riyadh, Saudi Arabia to Victoria, British Columbia. A decade later, its annual sales exceeded $3 billion and its blue-and-white trucks and dumpsters were a familiar sight in a multitude of countries.

But as spectacular as it was, the growth of BFI was only part of the story. Three other companies — Waste Management, Inc. (WMI) of Oak Brook, Illinois, the Boston-based Service Corporation of America (SCA) and Laidlaw Motorways of Hamilton, Ontario — joined BFI in the ranks of the new waste majors. At the same time technological advances and environmental consciousness changed the way waste was disposed of, making both disposal facilities and waste increasingly valuable commodities. Soon, the biggest waste corporations were engaged in fierce competition across North America and then farther afield for control of disposal sites and waste flows.

As this book reveals, the process begun by Tom Fatjo in 1969 was well advanced but far from complete by the early 1980s. The more sophisticated methods of market dominance and the new forms of waste management introduced by the waste majors — public financing, control of disposal, resource recovery — existed alongside the more familiar features of the old industry — strong-arm tactics, claims of "property rights," environmental neglect. Then in the late 1980s, as we shall see, the top three waste companies (BFI, WMI, Laidlaw) emerged as veritable continental private utilities and a further distancing process from the business culture of the traditional industry occurred. Highly skilled and politically well-connected managers replaced the corporate acquisitors who, in building their purported pollution-control companies, had excelled more as deal makers than as custodians of the environment.

Like the exposés of the oil, railroad, banking, insurance and food-processing industries written during the brief golden age of muckrakers early in the century, *Giants of Garbage* also focuses on a new industry whose power and freedom from economic regulation raises far-ranging questions about our capacity for maintaining democratic control over crucial social issues. What is different, however, is the sense of historical calamity now hanging over our heads as we approach the next century. And in few areas of human enterprise is the ability of society to make rational decisions so thrown into question as in the control of waste.

Readers already familiar with *Dirty Business* will remember that it dealt with what we now can describe as the entrepreneurial phase of the modern waste disposal industry. *Giants of Garbage* illuminates an important new phase and the means by which the leading companies have fulfilled their promise to become continental institutions. It demonstrates how these companies are forced into trying to adapt the inappropriately aggressive business culture of the industry to reflect the public character and environmental consequences of their activities.

Part I looks at the structure of the industry before the emergence of the global waste companies and shows how green legislation and "privatization" ideology set the stage for the local refuse collection business to become a global corporate enterprise supplanting all alternative forms of waste management. It also examines the history of monopolization endemic to the waste industry; the emergence of a municipal-industrial complex committed to mass incineration as the ultimate means of waste disposal; and the birth of a popular North American counter-movement to the notion of for-profit corporate waste disposal. Part II focuses on the four most important waste corporations, one of which was mired in scandal and was eventually taken over by its rivals. It also contains a chapter dealing with the attempts of one former industry insider to expose the predatory nature of many of the pricing and marketing strategies developed by dominant players. Part III consists of case studies tracing the evolution of the multi-national waste industry in three major Canadian metropolitan regions (one of which was seen in the late 1970s by some fairly cloistered Columbia University academics as a possible model for all of North America). It also describes the growing politicization of waste issues and government, and popular responses to corporate domination of the waste trade and policy. Finally, in conclusion, a call is issued for an end to the privatization of the information without which democratic control over waste issues becomes inconceivable.

PART I

The Municipal-Industrial Complex

Chapter 1

The Changing World of Waste

There's always that spectre of making a utility out of the whole business.

Michael A. Oberman, Editor, *Waste Age*, 1976

The more than 12,000 haulers, dump operators and recyclers operating in North America in the late 1960s represented widely varied forms of enterprise — public and private, union and non-union, large and small, old and new, crooked and straight. The industry was in a highly fragmented state. Integration, either vertical (between different aspects of the business) or horizontal (between different geographical areas), was a rare phenomenon. Over half the private haulers possessed no more than three trucks; almost 90 per cent of these one-, two- and three-packer outfits were not engaged in disposal or any other business; and most firms were unincorporated.[1] Each metropolitan area was its own isolated garbage market, and in each of these markets, the garbage industry was based on a *modus vivendi* worked out over the years by municipal governments, local entrepreneurs, trade unions and other interest groups.

As early as the 1890s, in many North American cities waste disposal was a mixed undertaking of public and private enterprise, as private teamster-driven wagons carted refuse to public dumps for burning. As long as contractors were involved, ridding the streets of refuse and debris was more than a simple business proposition. Many municipal politicians saw contracts as a source of supplementary income, cash for slush funds, jobs for constituents and favours for friends and allies. In spite of its association with cronyism and corruption, the practice of contracting-out flourished. By the 1960s, while two-thirds of American cities had publicly controlled disposal systems in some form, the private sector accounted for the larger share of total tonnage and dominated the collection of commercial and industrial wastes.[2] Although half the refuse contractors collected solid wastes from both businesses and households, a significant number were exclusively involved in the commercial and industrial market, a market the municipalities generally avoided.

It was in the postwar period that the industry underwent its first significant experience with technological change. Hydraulically operated trucks took to the streets and back alleys, replacing horse-drawn carts and open dump trucks. With their ability to compact tons of refuse in one swallow, these wheezing and whining packers quickly became the workhorses of the collection industry. The rear-loader became a familiar sight and sound in residential neighbourhoods. Containerized collection was the big change in the commercial and industrial market. Front-loading trucks automatically picked up, emptied and compacted containers holding up to eight cubic yards of garbage; another containerized system, called *roll-off*, was used for larger volumes of industrial refuse.

The disposal side of the business remained highly improvised, especially in the private sector which was the domain of the penny-ante entrepreneur. To bury garbage for profit, all that was required was an exhausted gravel quarry, an empty ravine or a few acres of farmland and a bulldozer — the essential elements of a dump. Thousands of these smouldering, rat-infested burial grounds littered the continent. While the bigger hauling outfits often had access to private disposal facilities, the economic survival of smaller companies generally depended on continued access to municipal incinerators and dumps. As long as the public sector maintained such facilities, the collection industry could — in theory at least — maintain some semblance of competition with its presumed benefits of low prices and good service. A variety of instruments, however, ensured that competition didn't get out of hand.

The fragmented and disorganized nature of the garbage business left most firms extremely vulnerable to the hazards of the open market, and so, like other big-city industries in similar situations, it often resorted to coercive means of self-protection. In offering its good offices to keep established markets free of unwanted rivals, the underworld took an unsanctioned but evidently necessary role. In Brooklyn, for instance, without benefit of official approval, the Brooklyn Trade Waste Association served as the de facto regulatory authority, providing a model of how crime-controlled garbage collection worked.[3]

The entire territory served by the association was divided among the private commercial haulers. Once assigned, the individual business account, called a "stop," became the hauler's private property. (If a commercial building had several "stops," it was divided floor by floor.) When an account was assigned to a member contractor, he received exclusive "rights" to service the account. If he wanted more customers, he paid a fee to the association. The association not only played a role in the assignment of "stops" but assisted in protecting the "rights" of its members against raids by outsiders. It also served as an adjudicator between contractors, determining the sale price of either a single "stop" or a whole hauling operation. Since this underworld "utility" did not have the force of law, various forms of coercion were employed to make customers accept their status as the private property of the association. The legal regulatory authority was ignored and frustrated. Threats, bad service and price-gouging raised the ire of commercial clients, and a resulting sixteen-month undercover investigation led to grand jury indictments in 1974.[4]

Although the enforcement mechanisms involved in this arrangement may have been peculiar to Brooklyn, the concept of "property rights" was not. In 1971 Chicago refuse haulers were charged with dividing the market in violation of Illinois antitrust legislation.[5] In some industries the presence of giant corporations and sophisticated technology helped create stable markets; in others stability was effected through government regulation. As none of these factors yet applied to the garbage industry, contractors imposed their own regulations to ensure predictability and order. They most typically used some kind of "property rights" arrangement.

Across the continent in San Francisco a very different kind of arrangement prevailed. The San Francisco garbage industry was dominated by northern Italians, especially Genoese. Competition had once been unusually intense, with haulers aggressively vying for each other's customers block by block and the typical garbage contractor going about his business with a horse, a wagon and a gun. The endless jousting for market positions demanded some resolution to alleviate the consternation and insecurity. In the early 1920s, for reasons not entirely clear, the incessant garbage wars were called off. The truce took the form of a cooperative sharing of the city's routes by the rival contractors, who styled themselves "boss scavengers." Ethnic solidarity and memories of the tribulations of the competitive era fostered a tight sense of community

among the scavengers. They began to form worker-controlled organizations, which were virtually closed ethnic groups. (One scavenger company had bylaws that prohibited non-Genoese from
admission.) Certain taboos were imposed on each boss scavenger.
Talking to wives about the business was forbidden. Bylaws enforced this rule with fines, warned of "our enemies," and cautioned
against helping "rivals" in "their war on this corporation."[6]

In 1921, the year after the birth of this cooperative movement,
San Francisco City Council followed the scavengers' lead by attempting to bring order to the industry. Municipal bylaws were
passed laying down residential collection districts and legal rates.
By 1939 the cooperatives had won. Two worker-owned outfits were
licensed to collect all of San Francisco's domestic trash and to
charge each householder directly for their services. Like telephone
or electric companies, the cooperatives were regulated, and public
commissions heard from citizens from time to time. Thirty years
later, the system — a hybrid private utility operated by franchised
self-employed garbagemen — was still in place. In 1971 an industry
trade magazine reported that Sunset Scavenger, the leading cooperative, handled domestic rubbish "for what generally is recognized
as probably the lowest charge of any major city in the United
States."

In Toronto, as in most Canadian cities, residential garbage was
collected by an arm of the city government. But commercial and
industrial wastes and suburban residential garbage represented a
rich market for private haulers in the Toronto area, and a former
North York reeve named Norman Goodhead sat atop one of the
largest commercial-industrial waste contractors on the continent,
Disposal Services Limited. In Montreal the city's policy of contracting-out domestic refuse collection spawned one of the continent's largest residential contractors, Sanitary Refuse Collectors.

The Assault

But as different as these arrangements and organizations were, they
all had one important thing in common — they were all vulnerable
to attack from the new, aggressive continental waste disposal firms.
The obsolescence of the localized industry provided the starting
point for the changes of the 1970s. It was at the level of organization
that the old industry first showed signs of its vulnerability. Small,

undercapitalized, cash-poor and with little access to credit, the average independent contracting firm was not in a position to resist an attractive takeover bid. And the conglomerates' typical takeover offer — your shares for ours — appeared attractive indeed in the early 1970s when the prices of waste management stocks were rising rapidly. Once in a market, the waste disposal majors could employ such tactics as predatory price-cutting to force its competitors to heel. The old garbage industry had hardly been a perfectly competitive one, since market sharing (based on the concept of "property rights" in one form or another) prevailed in many cities. The big firms simply superimposed themselves on this already existing system. What had previously been local oligopolies were now continental ones. In all this it was not surprising that the garbage industry attracted the attention of anti-combines authorities from Florida to Manitoba and from Nebraska to New Jersey. Or that the authorities' efforts were largely powerless in the face of economic logic. The march towards concentration continued.

The financial and organizational obsolescence of the older industry (though not necessarily its culture) accelerated as the environment became a leading political issue. Passage of the U.S. Solid Waste Disposal Act in 1965 inaugurated a new age of environmental concern. Thousands of the open dumps and incinerators that were fouling the water and air were eventually closed down. In Canada, Ontario caught the ecological wave first. In 1969 Premier John Robarts announced a major change in government policy respecting solid waste management by incorporating all aspects of environmental and pollution control in the Department of Energy and Resources Management. The 1970 Ontario Waste Management Act's regulations were considered the most advanced in the country.[7]

These new laws decreased disposal alternatives. As society relentlessly spewed out a larger and larger volume of waste, disposal facilities that were still able to pass muster became increasingly valuable properties. In 1968, the U.S. Federal Bureau of Solid Waste Management found that 94 per cent of all refuse disposal sites were improperly and unsanitarily operated.[8] In 1970, a U.S. government program called "Mission 5000" closed 2,200 dumps, and there was mounting pressure to close more. According to *The New York Times*, new U.S. federal rules, combined with various state laws, meant that by 1993 most of the remaining 6,500 community dumps across the country would be forced to close, to be replaced by about a thousand giant modern landfills owned "primarily by a dozen or so companies and intended to serve entire regions."[9]

For the municipalities, the environmental legislation passed by senior governments proved burdensome. The legislated demand for more rational forms of waste management would be costly, and new sources of financing would have to be found. Secure regional sanitary landfills would have to be engineered, constructed and — not unlike nuclear waste facilities — maintained years after being topped off. New alternatives, such as energy-from-garbage stations and recycling plants, represented multi-million-, if not billion-dollar investments. But if reluctant municipalities regarded these prospects as a burden, sharp-eyed entrepreneurs saw them as an opportunity. As an early Browning-Ferris Industries annual report put it, "the resulting increased demand for properly managed disposal methods has, in just a few short years, made it economically practical for free enterprise to provide ecologically sound alternative methods of disposal."

The ambitious Texans and their rivals in Chicago, Boston and Hamilton understood that in its existing fragmented state the industry had no access to the huge amounts of capital needed to meet the demands for properly engineered landfills and garbage recovery plants. The longer the public sector could be delayed from renovating its waste-handling systems, the greater the possibility that large investments in dumping grounds and the development of hauling networks would turn the "garbage crisis" into an extraordinary bonanza.

Thus the new concern for the environment dovetailed with a third factor fuelling the growth of the new corporate waste managers — the ideology of "privatization," whose advocates won the day with the political triumph of Reaganism and the attendant ascendancy of the rich and powerful. The major waste firms came along at a time when the private sector appeared to be gaining the upper hand in its longstanding contest with government agencies for control of public service markets. In this climate (examined in more detail in the next chapter) public institutions had no business making money; profit-making (not to mention windfall profit-making) was designated the sole and exclusive prerogative of private enterprise. The potential waste bonanza, eagerly anticipated by private entrepreneurs, was something of an embarrassment to the municipalities. Civic administrators did not feel they possessed the mandate to balance the enormous cash outlays needed with the considerable revenues that would flow from proper large-scale disposal services. And so the rickety independent contractors were not the only targets. The budding global firms also set their sights on the municipal garbage collection and disposal agencies and presented themselves as the municipalities' chief competitors to manage the new forms of waste disposal.

Chapter 2

Public vs. Private Enterprise

Trash is our only growing resource.
Hollis Dole, U.S. Undersecretary of the Interior,
Houston, 1969

The California tax revolt, which spread through North America in the 1970s, echoed a conflict over public services that goes back to the beginning of the Industrial Revolution. Then, the dispute mainly concerned the means for delivering municipal services and maintaining the poor; eventually it broadened to include all aspects of national economic organization. Left-wing parties, when they achieved office, tended to nationalize industries; right-wing parties to privatize them. Each panacea is rooted in particular social beliefs, its rationale argued in terms of the superior efficiency of either public or private enterprise.

During the Reagan-era swing towards increased contracting-out of government services — a concomitant of tax-cutting and budget-slashing — neoconservative academics provided justifications for privatizing garbage collection. But as the high environmental costs of mass dumping and other dubious disposal practices begin to be understood, the private waste managers' claim to improved efficiency seems more an accounting trick than an actual accomplishment. The scale the newly integrated industry has so quickly achieved has nevertheless provided both public and private planners with new horizons. In a world where diminishing natural resources are the currency of growth and development, garbage is recognized as a resource. And modern means of waste management — the creation of technology and improved organization — have made the actual ownership of trash a critical issue.

Contracting-Out and Public Enterprise

The earliest form of organized local public service appeared in England in the eighteenth century. This was "farming," or contracting-out. A contractor hired a gang of the unemployed poor, who set about repairing highways, scavenging, collecting tolls and dues from parish pounds, manorial cornmills, municipal markets and turnpikes. In their history of English local government, Beatrice and Sidney Webb described an early eighteenth-century contracting-out system:

> The most scandalous of all these forms of contract ... was the farming of the prisons. These, like the workhouses, could be let by contract to the gaolers ... The wretched inmates ... could be fed and clothed by contract, and even physicked by contract. The vagrants were conveyed by contract, fed by contract and also whipped by contract; and when the felons were sent beyond the seas, they were habitually transported by contract, and sold by auction on arrival to those who contracted at the highest rate to employ them.[1]

By the early nineteenth century, the commercialization of public services had contributed to some of the great private fortunes of the time. London had been carved up by five water companies; the most prominent one enjoyed near-absolute control of the city's water service according to the terms of a royal charter initially granted in 1619 (the King had been among the original shareholders). The water merchants had grown immensely rich by supplying virtual sewer water and the contents of slop pails emptied upstream through their pipes and pumps to the soup tureens of the metropolis. In 1810 there was a rush of competition as new rivals boldly flung their pipes into the tangled network sprawling in every direction under the hotly contested streets. Soon the cartel reapportioned London district by district. Each member's share became its private property, and thus was peace restored. The water rates quickly rose to extortionate levels. By the mid-nineteenth century, the public was blaming the recurrent outbreaks of disease on the abominations of the water trade. But it was not until the turn of the century that scandal, combined with the efforts of zealous reformers, statisticians and philanthropists, resulted in the consolidation of the water supply under public authorities throughout England.[2] In Manchester a local consumers' association had fought to supplant a local water company as early as 1809. The consumers lost, but they immediately set their sights on gas-making. Though private entrepreneurs were supplying gas in other cities, in Manchester gas was produced in municipal retorts for municipal use. Writing in the early twentieth century, Beatrice and Sydney Webb saw this public undertaking as the first flowering of what they called municipal socialism: "This incipient Municipal Socialism ... did not fail to be denounced by those who objected to interference with capitalist enterprise; but it proved to be the beginning, in all parts of the country, of an ever-increasing volume and range of 'municipal trading', often in actual supersession of capitalist profit-making, the whole scope of which it is impossible, at the present day, even to forecast."[3]

Utilitarian philosopher Jeremy Bentham, whose views inspired much of Britain's early-nineteenth-century social legislation, argued that the state ought to assume trusteeship of the public interest — a revolutionary idea for the time. The problem of public administration was to formulate artificial means of achieving the greatest good for the greatest number. When necessary the ancient sanctity of the Englishman's home would have to be invaded and coercive measures taken to align private and public interest. Among the Benthamite reforms there emerged two methods for delivering municipal services. One system proposed eliminating pork-barrelling by compelling contractors to submit competitive tenders and public authorities to accept the lowest bid. The alternative involved increased reliance on public works departments to eliminate the monopolistic "rings" and "knock-outs" of conspiring contractors.

An obvious flaw undercut both alternatives. There were far more ratepayers than civic workers. To achieve the greatest good for the greatest number of urban dwellers, the reformers institutionalized cheap labour practices. Whether it was the private contractor or the municipal employer who could most efficiently sweat his labourers, it was all the same to the ratepaying public. Nevertheless, in the delivery of municipal services, public enterprise took root alongside capitalist endeavour. Demands for such urban amenities as a pure water supply and the collective disposal of garbage and sewage were accompanied by increased municipal socialization. The historian of the city, Lewis Mumford, described the process: "In smaller centres, private companies might be left with the privilege of maintaining one or more of these services, until some notorious outbreak of disease dictated public control; but in the bigger cities socialization was the price of safety; and so, despite the theoretic claims of laissez faire, the nineteenth century became, as Beatrice and Sidney Webb correctly pointed out, the century of municipal socialism."[4]

These two alternative models of municipal service — public enterprise and contracting-out — took root in North America as well and continued to coexist through the twentieth century. In the 1960s the private sector mounted a new offensive to increase its share of government service. As early as 1961, in its brief to the Glassco Royal Commission on Government Organization, the Canadian Manufacturers' Association (CMA) declared that "because the Canadian Government should at all times give the strongest support to the private enterprise system, the growth of the private business sector should be favoured over that of government whenever possible. We trust that the Commission will find ways in which the present scope of government activity can be modified with this end in view."[5] The spirit of the CMA brief infused the commission report, though the apostles of privatization had not yet taken to their pulpits. By 1976, however, a Canadian government working paper, *The Way Ahead*, was calling for increased contracting-out. Three years later the Progressive Conservative government of Joe Clark, misreading public sentiment, proposed privatizing Petro-Canada, the country's largest domestically owned petroleum firm.[6] It also envisioned returning to private hands two aeronautical firms, Canadair and de Havilland, which had been resuscitated with infusions of public money. Only the abrupt end to the Tory interregnum stopped this trend — at least for a few years.

In the United States the conservative onslaught on the public sector began in earnest with the signing of a two-page memorandum by the director of President Gerald Ford's Office of Management and Budget on 18 October 1976. Under the terms of OMB Circular No. A-76, hundreds of millions of dollars worth of services previously provided in-house were farmed out to contractors. Implementation of the memorandum, however, was too slow to satisfy conservative New York congressman (and later Housing Secretary) Jack Kemp. He complained that everything from janitorial services to weapons systems research were not yet contracted-out, and in the meantime, "Capital has lost. The adequacy of capital investment has been impaired. The private sector has lost part of the capital base it needs for facility expansion and employment ..."[7] An administration fully committed to privatization would soon be elected, and would dominate Washington for the next twelve years, putting much of its program into effect.

The Advocate: E.S. Savas

In the waste management industry, privatization found its academic voice in E.S. Savas. An urban systems manager at IBM until the late 1960s when he moved to New York City Hall as first deputy city administrator in the mayor's office, Savas foresaw the fiscal crisis that eventually almost bankrupted the financial capital of the West in the mid-1970s. Much of the responsibility for the crisis, he reasoned, rested with civic administrators and with "the municipal monopolies" that delivered fire, police, transit, education and sanitation services.[8]

In 1970 Savas directed the first of a series of garbage collection analyses. This was not the first time the industry had been examined. Sociologist Stewart Perry looked at San Francisco's garbage workers' cooperatives as an example of how dirty, dangerous work could be combined with pride of ownership, just income distribution and workplace democracy. Peter Reuter of the Center for Research on Institutions and Social Policy examined the obvious monopolistic tendencies of the private refuse carting industry in New York and New Jersey. But the Savas studies, which were to gain wide currency, focused solely on the question of cost, and only for the collection side of the business. They ignored one critical fact — the increasing interdependence of collection and disposal economics as the new waste management industry integrated the two functions. Taking as the basis for its comparison the relative performances of the New York Department of Sanitation and a private carter in adjacent neighbourhoods, both consisting of single-family homes, the original November 1970 refuse collection report claimed the private firm did the job better and cheaper. In a 1971 article in *Harper's* magazine, Savas made some generalizations:

> The comparison is instructive: it costs Sanitation almost three times as much to collect a ton of garbage as it costs the private entrepreneur. Furthermore, the average Sanitation truck is out of commission more than 30 per cent of the time; the private truck is out only about 5 per cent of the time. The explanation is obvious: if you own a mere one or two trucks, as most

cartmen do, and your livelihood depends on them, you make sure they stay in working order.[9]

Without any comparative examination of the working conditions of these employees, Savas used these findings to prescribe solutions for the ailing city's problems. Among his cures was "reprivatization" — a return to the competitive bidding by private carters that had been practised in parts of New York City until the Depression. But his findings were controversial and dismayed students of the garbage industry who refused to reduce the issues to the narrow question of costs. Stewart Perry described Savas's assumptions as "questionable."[10] Also critical of his approach was John DeLury, the leader of New York's Uniformed Sanitationmen's Association. For more than forty years, DeLury had concentrated on gaining a living wage with pension benefits, early retirement after twenty years and job security. He had succeeded in making the sanitation worker's job attractive, despite the hard and dangerous nature of the work. The year before the city's 1975 crisis budget with its "horror list" of drastic cuts in city services, 68,845 people took the civil service exams to qualify for the few job openings for New York City sanitation workers.[11] But such considerations did not carry any observable weight for Savas.

Perhaps the most serious weakness of the Savas study was its failure to come to terms with the real nature of the city's private carting industry. A year after the *Harper's* piece appeared, a Brooklyn district attorney investigating the industry secretly bought a compactor truck and went into the garbage business. His endeavour was not a commercial success. Even with rates 30 per cent below the prevailing scale, only 19 of some 2,000 businesspeople he approached signed up. The district attorney soon understood that the merchants whose business he solicited feared reprisals from the carting industry. A day after complaining about his $15-a-week carting bill, one merchant discovered that he had a new carting company and a bill of $86. Another cancelled his garbage removal contract and started hauling his own waste at night. The next morning he found his garbage returned with a note warning that his business would be blown up if he did not renew the contract.

The sixteen-month Brooklyn undercover investigation in the early 1970s produced evidence showing that most of the refuse collection industry in this New York City borough was dominated by criminals and "operated essentially as a monopoly."[12] Fifty-five refuse haulers were eventually caught in the net of the district attorney's charges. Collusive practices were yielding an estimated $20 million a year in overcharges. To one reporter's query about whether the private refuse hauling business throughout New York City was controlled by mobsters, the Brooklyn district attorney replied, "That's a fair assumption."[13] E.S. Savas suggested, in effect, that the private firms whose practices in the commercial collection business had been exposed in the investigation should be allowed into the residential market as well. The grand jury in the Brooklyn case reached exactly the opposite conclusion. It recommended that the Department of Sanitation's operations should be not only maintained but extended from residential pickup to include the lucrative commercial markets. The grand jurors saw that in the economic jungle of the real world, the department was the only institution that could "drive out the private monopolizers who were restraining trade."[14]

The pressure to farm out household trash pickup mounted. Desperate for relief from the financial crisis, many New Yorkers appeared to adopt the attitude that if the Mafia could do it cheaper, then let the Mafia have it. Savas claimed the city could save at least $75 million annually by turning half its routes over to the private sector.[15] In 1980 city officials announced their intention to test Savas's claim by experimenting with private refuse collection on a limited basis. Mayor Edward Koch, however, balked at the plan. Significantly, in considering privatization, the administration talked not to local refuse haulers but to national firms. Recognizing how dimly the flame of competition flickered in the local industry, New York solicited bids from the continental majors trading on the Big Board of the New York Stock Exchange. As one close Savas associate put it, the local carters were bypassed "to get around any major territorial problems."[16]

Following his stint in the mayor's office, Savas moved uptown to Columbia University. With a research team and a $560,000 grant from the National Science Foundation, one of the government's main funding agencies for scientific research, he undertook a continent-wide analysis of the various institutional arrangements for collecting garbage. Eleven major surveys between 1902 and 1974 had examined the organization of refuse collection in American cities, but the Columbia researchers found them conceptually defective and difficult to interpret.[17] What Savas wanted to establish was the relationship between different forms of organization on the one hand and efficiency and effectiveness on the other. Because garbage collection was carried out in a variety of ways, it seemed to offer a "superb focus" for studying the basic policy questions.

The National Science Foundation survey gathered data in more than 2,000 communities with populations of 2,500 or more (excluding 15 of the largest American cities). The cost per household of collection by a municipal agency was compared with the cost per household of collection by a private firm under contract or franchise with the municipality. For cities with more than 50,000 inhabitants where data on tons collected were available, municipal collection was 29 per cent more costly than contract collection; for cities with more than 50,000 inhabitants where data on cubic yards collected were available, municipal collection was 37 per cent more costly than contract collection.[18]

In a word, the policy conclusion was privatization. The permanent monopoly of municipal collection was considered an anathema. While acknowledging that continuous competition was inefficient, the Savas group prescribed a system of what it called temporary monopoly or periodic competition, "as exemplified by contract collection."[19] The study suggested dividing cities with populations larger than 100,000 into districts of about 50,000, with most districts contracted out to private firms. With this system and a small municipal agency servicing one or a few districts, a large city "could best assure a continued competitive environment and protect itself against possible collusion by its contractors or its employees."[20]

It was with some satisfaction that, a few years after the study's results were published, Savas wrote:

Montreal created such a system for this reason as long ago as 1955, but in the United States it was not until 1977, following the release and widespread reporting of the above-mentioned findings concerning the greater efficiency of contract collection, that a number of large cities started shifting to competitive systems. Oklahoma City, New Orleans, Phoenix, Nashville, Tampa, Newark, and Washington, D.C. were among the cities following this course of action since then. As of this writing, the number of such cities continues to increase, in an apparent trend.[21]

The private sector made much of the Columbia study's conclusions. They were worked into full-page, four-colour glossy ads. The National Solid Wastes Management Association (NSWMA), voice of the private garbage companies and especially of the majors, helped publicize the findings. A trade magazine carried the headline "Columbia Study Says Communities Save With Private Contract Collection." But all the publicity didn't change the fact that the Columbia study, like the earlier Savas study, was out of touch with important aspects of the real world.

Despite the mass of statistics they collected, the Columbia researchers' actual contacts with the industry were brief and detached. This was most conspicuous in their treatment of such issues as monopoly and the underworld presence in the industry. In their view some economic activities were natural monopolies, but garbage collection was not one of them. They believed that competition was structurally feasible, but that territorial agreements, price fixing, mergers and alliances resulted in monopoly. For small communities with populations under 50,000, the Columbia analysts concluded that a single collector "may be the most efficient arrangement."[22] For larger cities, however, they claimed that economies of scale vanished. At a time when small trash haulers were giving way to the majors in many metropolitan markets, this was, to say the least, an unexpected finding, which did not go very far towards explaining the changes the industry was experiencing.

As for the issue of organized crime, Savas and his fellow investigators raised it only long enough to let it drop. Unlike holders of the "property rights" theory of behaviour for the refuse collection industry, the Columbia researchers took the position that there was nothing intrinsic to the economic fabric of the business that made an underworld presence inevitable. Wherever collusive arrangements and underworld penetration occurred, it was the role of the judicial bureaucracy and the police to deal with them. Don't tamper with the private market system; leave crimes against the market to the police and judiciary, they argued. A key member of the Savas team, Dr. Eileen Berenyi, admitted that "we never go into a company's background. We obviously assume a legal operation."

She did, however, acknowledge a strong interest in the question of whether the presence of the underworld in the industry was a predictable economic phenomenon or only a historical accident. Unfortunately, when the researchers tried to interest the National Science Foundation in this question, their previously beneficent patron was decidedly unenthusiastic. "We were hooted out," Berenyi reported. "They said, 'cut it out. We don't want anything to do with it.'"

But the Columbia study's most serious omission was its failure to measure the costs of refuse removal in terms of both collection and disposal. This represented a severe limitation on the study's applicability at the curbsides and in the back alleys of urban North America. For it was the disposal side that was undergoing the most extensive changes as the garbage business was transformed into the transnational waste management industry, and it was there that the most significant battles between the public and private sectors were fought.[23]

As the chief advocate of privatization in the garbage industry, Savas soon found a place in Ronald Reagan's Washington, where he became an assistant secretary for policy development and research in the Department of Housing and Urban Development.

Landfill — The Key to the Business

Every working day the debris of modern life is buried in flat or rolling farmland, canyons, ravines, worked-out or abandoned quarries, sand and gravel pits, and marsh and tidal lands. The sites are the scenes of ceaseless movement reminiscent of an insect colony. At the working face of a landfill cell, dump trucks and packers disgorge paper, cans, bottles and cardboard boxes; plastics, lumber and metals; yard clippings, food waste, washing machines and furniture; construction rubble and hospital wastes; dead birds, cats, dogs; industrial liquids, semi-liquids, films, sheets, granules, turnings and powders; defective products, paints, dry-cleaning fluids, magnesium shavings, fly ash and dewatered sewage sludges. The equipment operator spends his shift trying to develop the working face on an incline between twenty and thirty degrees, spreading the refuse against the slope while moving a steel-wheeled crawler dozer up and down, tearing and compacting the waste and eliminating voids. He makes passes across the slope, depressing the surface until it rebounds as much as it is pushed down. As construction of the cell progresses, the earth-moving equipment spreads and compacts cover material which has been excavated by dragline nearby and transported to the site by dump trucks. At day's end the cover is graded to prevent erosion and to keep water from ponding.

Beneath the surface, decomposition takes place at various rates. Rainwater percolates into the myriad of cells, and the wastes absorb it like a sponge until they can hold no more. Then whatever rainwater enters from above forces an equal volume to leave below in the form of a malodorous liquid called *leachate*, which carries substances of unknown toxicity.

Soil characteristics determine how fast and far the leachate flows. Blue clay, for instance, has far better attenuation properties than sand, gravel, cracked limestone or fractured shale. While the hydrogeological issues involved in leachate control are complex, typical landfills are known to leak liquids that can easily eat their way through thick concrete. Once free of the dump, the vile fluid can migrate in dark plumes into the water table and poison the groundwater. According to a 1981 Ralph Nader study called *Who's Poisoning America*, "from the nation's 18,500 municipal landfills alone, an estimated 90 billion gallons of leachate enter the groundwater annually. How much leachate from industrial dumpsites has reached groundwater is not known, but with as many as 50,000 chemical dumps nationwide, the amount may be prodigious."[24]

Since most landfills have some kind of hydraulic connection with natural water sources, there are environmental costs tied to waste disposal that have traditionally been sloughed off by people with vested short-term interests in cheap dumping practices. Large parts of the population, especially in rural areas, draw their drinking water from underground aquifers, and as the lakes grow more and more unpotable, groundwater becomes an increasingly valuable resource.

As horror stories about indiscriminate dumping of solid and liquid wastes surfaced, public outrage had some positive effect in altering the accounting principles underlying landfill economics. Inevitably the process played into the hands of the garbage majors. With authorities forced to improve the standards of dump sites, the increased engineering costs meant that only the most highly bankrolled players could remain in the game. A significant portion of the sites shut down were those operated by municipalities or small-time undercapitalized firms. Perhaps not untypical was the fate of a landfill owned by Les Enfouissements Sanitaires de l'Est of Ste-Julie, Quebec, located on the south shore of the St. Lawrence near Montreal. The site lost its licence in 1979 after the company — which was owned by Lucien Rémillard, the son of Léo Rémillard (a garbage contractor with a notorious past) — totally lost control of it. Lagoons overflowed toxic liquids; domestic garbage lay uncovered atop industrial wastes. The site was extremely contaminated and would require years of surveillance and public expense to keep in check.

For those who had the financial resources to weather the storms of public opposition to corporate landfill practices, the rewards for owning licensed, accessible dumps were enormous. The biggest contractors had already begun to show signs of integrating collection and disposal services in the early 1970s. A U.S. Environmental Protection Agency study indicated that the more trucks a hauler had on the road, the more likely the firm also did its own dumping. Of the 5,084 establishments surveyed with three trucks or fewer, only 2 per cent were engaged in a related disposal business. By contrast, 39 per cent of the 141 companies with 50 trucks or more were engaged in disposal. In 1972 the top eight American garbage companies operated 119 landfills, and the Big Three — Browning Ferris, Waste Management and SCA — accounted for nearly 80 per cent of them.

During February 1981 a wholly owned American subsidiary of Laidlaw, the Canadian entry in the big leagues of waste management, acquired three approved landfills in Massachusetts by purchase and long-term lease and obtained an option on a fourth site in New Hampshire. In addition to the 52 million tons of new dumping capacity this gave the firm, the dumps opened up collection markets in Massachusetts and bordering states. The cash flow generated by these acquisitions was potentially staggering. Not long after Laidlaw set up shop in a suburb of Chicago, Illinois, trustbuster Sandra Rasnak observed that "whoever controls the landfills will control the industry." Referring to the majors, she added: "They perceive it that way. We have to start looking at landfill acquisition over the next fifteen, twenty years or we'll have a natural monopoly and there'll not be much we can do about it."

Spokesmen for the companies confirmed this view of their strategy. "In the final analysis ... the key to the business is the place to dispose of it," said a Laidlaw executive. "He who controls the landfill situations can also control the means of disposal."[25] And the Canadian firm's guiding genius, Mike DeGroote, explained that "a landfill site is like an oil well in reverse. With an oil well, the more you take out, the more you make. With a landfill site, the more garbage you put in, the more you make. A few years ago, it cost about $3.50 a ton to dump garbage at a site. Now it ranges up

to $15 a ton, and this does not include the pickup charge."[26] A WMI
official told the Toronto *Globe and Mail* in 1974 that "it's always
been our operating philosophy at Waste Management to be in
control of our destiny," and went on to explain that the way for any
refuse company to control its destiny was to own its own dump
sites.[27] And the 1979 annual report of SCA expressed a similar view
of the industry: "Disposal service is our most profitable business.
As with our collection business, the key to further margin improvement is maximizing the revenue which ... is generated by each
disposal facility. Landfill operations ... are characterized by high
fixed costs and low variable costs, and the receipt of additional
tonnage at a site which already has sufficient volume to cover its
fixed costs will produce a dramatic increase in profit and margin."

Garbage as the Last Resource

With the new conservation consciousness of the 1970s, the stakes
in the struggle for control of waste disposal increased. As the public
envisioned a world depleted of its non-renewable resources, only a
few took note of a corollary phenomenon — the growing importance and value of wastes. A science fiction writer based a story on
the idea that a group that controlled garbage in twenty-first-century
America would exercise enormous power. An undersecretary of the
Interior told a waste management seminar in Houston in March
1969 that "trash is our only growing resource." The budding waste
management industry — along with other elements in the private
sector — not only saw the future in similar terms but was also
conscious of the potential for profit in the coming era of recycled
materials consumption. The transition to this era was not an entirely
smooth one. Garbage energy and resource recovery plants were
risky undertakings requiring a wizard's capacity for putting together very complicated pieces of a financial puzzle. The dealmak-
ers faced not only staggering capital costs but also highly unstable
markets for recovered cardboard, organic fibres, compost, glass and
ferrous metals. Consequently, resource recovery facilities were usually so in name only. They were simply mass incinerators whose
giant stacks let millions of dollars of potential revenues go up in
smoke for want of customers for their steam. In 1970 Montreal
began to burn much of its municipally collected trash at the Des
Carrières incinerator. Some years later the Commission d'initiative

et de développement économique de Montréal estimated that because neighbouring markets for steam had never been developed, the municipal treasury had been losing nearly $8 million a year. It was not until early 1983 that the City of Montreal announced plans to sell steam from the incinerator to a corrugated box plant and other enterprises.

The imperatives to develop more environmentally sound methods of waste disposal were real. As the U.S. Environmental Protection Agency noted in its *Fourth Report to Congress on Resource Recovery and Waste Reduction*:

> There is considerable evidence and theory to indicate that certain national government policies, institutional shortcomings, and failures in our market system of resource allocation have all contributed to a situation where waste generation is too high and resource recovery is too low ... By failing to control pollution and other forms of environmental degradation, as a society we have implicitly subsidized the material and energy sectors. By allowing cheap, environmentally damaging waste disposal, we have caused alternative waste reduction and recycling options to be undervalued ... *Conventional accounting systems and financing methods generally lead to understatement of the true costs of solid waste management* [emphasis added].[28]

By the 1970s each big-city dweller was throwing away about 600 kilograms of garbage yearly, only 7 per cent of which was recycled. What was left overflowing from the continent's dumps, a "crisis of capitalism" in the eyes of some social critics, was seen by some businessmen as an investment opportunity.

Garbage Energy

As early as 1970 a private-sector group, the National Center for Resource Recovery (NCRR), envisioned high-tech "hard-path" solutions to the garbage crisis. NCRR's visionaries were advocates of giant energy stations of Rube Goldberg complexity, like the 700-ton-per-day facility they designed for WMI in New Orleans. Several senior staffers had come to NCRR from the National Aeronautics and Space Administration, and among its directors were executives from industries that produced much of what was carted off to the dumps. Coca-Cola, Pepsico, Dow Chemical, International Paper, packaging industry unions and the U.S. Chamber of Commerce were all represented.[29]

In 1974 Dun and Bradstreet predicted that, after agriculture, the recycling industry would be the country's biggest by the year 2000.[30] As big business came to realize that it would have to depend more and more on North American consumers for its raw materials, the giant paper, aluminum, glass and rubber companies began to integrate recycling activities into their overall operations. At Downsview, Ontario, a garbage factory operated by BFI called the Ontario Centre for Resource Recovery occupied an eighteen-acre site. The sprawling structure, whose gates were officially opened in August 1978, was designed to shred, air-separate, cyclone, separate magnetically, tumble, air-clean, bale and load 900 tons of refuse for transportation to waiting markets — all in two eight-hour shifts. And as if to create some elbow room for itself beside the biggest corporations, BFI also replaced Grumman as the North American licence-holder for a West German garbage energy system. In April 1980 BFI signed an agreement with Vereinigte Kesselwerke, a member of the Deutsche Babcock group, for an exclusive licence in the United States and Canada for energy-from-waste technology. According to reports, the Kesselwerke power plant was being used in fifty cities in Europe and Asia.

While the garbage majors and other large companies jockeyed for position in the new industry, doubts were expressed about whether the "hard path" was the best one to follow and about whether the private sector — which had after all created much of the mess in the first place — was the most appropriate agent to ensure efficient use of North America's wastes. Community activists saw the new garbage energy plants as too costly, too centralized and on a scale incompatible with democratic control. Richard Goodacre of the Recycling Council of British Columbia pointed out one of the contradictions of the new energy stations:

We arrive at one of the inherent dilemmas of an expensive energy recovery operation: all other things being equal, the more garbage there is, the cheaper the operation. A problem arises if a recovery facility is running at optimum efficiency but there is not enough garbage to feed it; costs per ton automatically increase. This is precisely the situation that has evolved in Quebec City. The recovery plant there produces steam for a nearby paper mill, which requires a steady supply of energy. The incinerator cannot guarantee a regular supply based on waste firing alone because waste supply is not constant, and auxiliary oil burners have been installed to take up the slack.[31]

An article in *Barron's* noted that a $50 million mass-burner in Saugus, Massachusetts, was undermined financially until a competing landfill closed.[32] And in *The Progressive,* authors Janet Marinelli and Gail Robinson reported: "As citizens of Saugus found out, enough garbage has to come in to make the plant cost-effective. And so resource recovery gives local governments a vested interest in encouraging lots of garbage and discouraging recycling."[33] Writing about the American experience with its slender public-enterprise tradition, Marinelli and Robinson equated the "hard" energy path with the machinations of big business. They looked to "soft" paths controlled by communities — combinations of local recycling, unified community action, disposal user fees, litter taxes, "bottle" bills or deposit legislation, packaging laws and some small mass-burning facilities.

But even among those who agreed with the basic "hard path" approach, important issues of control remained unresolved. If garbage was now a resource, there were bound to be competing claims on a finite supply of refuse. Municipalities, oriented towards providing a service rather than managing surplus revenue flows, were slow to see the potential in the trash generated within their limits. But when they did, they could hardly avoid coming into conflict with the private sector. In the late 1970s, the industrial town of Akron, Ohio, became the battleground where these issues were fought out.

The Battle of Akron

Like many other metropolitan areas, during the late 1960s Akron faced a garbage crisis as its own dumps filled to the last sardine can. At the same time the local utility, Ohio Edison, was threatening to cut off steam sales to downtown businesses. So the city decided to go into the energy and scrap business by building the Akron Recycle Energy System (RES) in 1973. The idea involved recovering ferrous metals from wastes and producing steam by burning what was left. The incinerator was supposed to meet its costs by charging a tipping fee and selling the ferrous metals and the steam. Financing would come from RES bonds issued by the Ohio Water Development Authority, and investment bankers were engaged to underwrite the sale of the bonds. As responsible bankers, Dillon, Reed & Company had to look at the potential for success. They realized that the profitability of RES, and thus the marketability of the bonds, depended on obtaining sufficient supplies of garbage to run the plant around the clock. What if the supply collected by the municipality, as well as that voluntarily delivered by contractors, was insufficient to keep the fires alive? Dillon, Reed insisted the risk be covered, and urged that a supply somehow be guaranteed.

Local authorities agreed to take "all available action" to ensure that all solid wastes generated within the city and surrounding Summit County would be delivered to the garbage factory. And Akron City Council enacted its controversial Ordinance No. 8411976, which required haulers to deliver to the plant whatever portion of their refuse was needed for steam generation and materials recovery. On top of not being paid for the value of the wastes they delivered, contractors would be charged a tipping fee. Contractors who violated the ordinance faced loss of their licence and criminal penalties. It was this ordinance that became the subject of controversy and landed the City of Akron in the courts.

In February 1978 members of the Ohio chapter of the National Solid Wastes Management Association (NSWMA) challenged the constitutionality of the ordinance, contending that it amounted to the confiscation of valuable property and violated antitrust law by creating a disposal monopoly and eliminating competition with private firms. The Fifth Amendment to the Constitution guaranteed that private property could not "be taken for public use without just compensation." Through its trade association, the industry took the position that "even waste material not purchased but which is discarded and abandoned by its owner becomes the property of the person who exercises control and possession over it."[34] Whatever garbage fell into the hands of private industry was private property, argued NSWMA's lawyers. Though the court battle had all the outward appearance of an unseemly struggle over a heap of rubbish, the legal issues went to the heart of capitalist organization. The courts were asked to rule on the extent of municipal sovereignty and on the right of locally elected governments to interfere with trade patterns determined by national market forces.

Behind the legal issues lurked economic ones. Which sector — public or private — would come out on top in this new era of recycled resources and energy from garbage? "Make no mistake," read a NSWMA trade journal advertisement, "resource recovery is coming. The question: Can haulers and landfill operators survive? Ambitious politicians want the credit for resource recovery. They often choose the 'easy' path of 'flow control' — legislating monopolization of the waste stream."

When the U.S. District Court of Northern Ohio ruled in favour of the ordinance, deciding that by virtue of its sovereignty the city was immune from antitrust law, NSWMA appealed. The industry anticipated that the federal department of justice would join NSWMA in opposing the ordinance because it interfered with interstate trade and raised important antitrust issues. However, the justice department adopted a different view of where the public interest lay. In its *amicus curiae* brief before the Sixth Circuit Court of Appeals, the department argued: "The City of Akron's ordinance promotes the development of a resource recovery facility which is both in the interest of the residents of the city and the entire nation." The NSWMA organ, *Waste Age*, commented: "The government decision to support the ordinance is interpreted by one close observer as a possible response to pressure from the Environmental Protection Agency and/or the Department of Energy or Justice to go on record in support of substitute fuel benefits."

Yet, though the ordinance did stand, much of the initial enthusiasm for garbage energy waned. Like nuclear energy, garbage energy demanded massive subsidization, and private waste managers were unwilling to pay for new technology out of their own funds. Under the Reagan administration in the early 1980s, public subsidies for environmental matters were drying up, and the envisioned forest of garbage factories planted in every city had to await some more distant future. Of the twenty-five existing plants in the United States in 1980, only three operated at design capacity. Canada claimed only three such plants. "Four or five years ago everybody was looking for alternatives to landfill," said Ian McKerracher, Metropolitan Toronto's refuse disposal director. "Now it's back to landfill and mass burning. [The Italian firm] Cecchini tried to sell one [recycling plant] to Miami. It didn't fly. I keep coming back to the fact that landfill is the basis for solid waste disposal."[35]

Surveying the waste land, an article in *Barron's* in July 1980 cast doubt on the future of mass burning in a capitalist economy. Without reliable supplies of garbage, sufficient demand for the energy produced and technical reliability, the plants stayed on the drawing boards. "The eminently sensible, perhaps even historically inevitable idea of turning waste into productive fuel has, so far, been a great flop," said the Wall Street business organ. The second coming of these new energy systems, it concluded, would have to await the greater direct involvement of bankers. As corporate tax-payers the banks — unlike the municipalities — were eligible for the necessary tax-based federal subsidies. As if to signal the end of the first tentative era of garbage energy, the National Center for Resource Recovery closed its doors in September 1981.

Rush to Burn

The return to cheap oil meant that the garbage majors had to modify their gospel. No longer was the dragon in need of slaying a cartel of shifty foreign oil potentates. Now the enemy was within. The latest threat to our consumerist throw-away lifestyle was the emergence of a growing environmentalist critique of the economic system, and more immediately, the disappearance of landfills.[36] Between 1980 and 1986 the number of landfills decreased from 20,000 to 6,000. What once had been dubbed an energy crisis now had a new name. As the chief executive of Wheelabrator, a leading incineration company, put it to the business magazine *Forbes* in 1988, "the driving force behind this company is the garbage crisis."[37]

Supremely contemptuous of the questioning of their logic of burning trash only to create more toxic by-products, a powerful nexus of incineration technology vendors, boiler makers, merchant bankers, bond underwriters, intermediaries and political fund raisers continued crystalizing their incineration plans. Because profits from burning tend all to be upfront, which is to say before the first green bag is consigned to the flames, deal-makers rushed to exploit the social paralysis over what to do about an economy as much based on waste as it is on oil.

For, before anything else, burning billions of kilograms of garbage spells one thing to promoters: bonds. And for the privileged few who raise and manage them, bonds offer access to vast pools of cash. *Newsday* reported that between 1982 and 1989 alone, Wall Street floated $13.5 billion worth of tax-exempt bonds to build garbage incinerators.[38] For the investment bankers involved, the take was estimated to be near $200 million in fees.[39]

As well, faced with doldrums in the nuclear reactor business, especially after the Three Mile Island meltdown in 1979, engineering and construction firms like Westinghouse, GE and Combustion Engineering (responsible for building the controversial Detroit furnace) began looking to billions of dollars in incinerator contracts as a salvation. And as far as the major waste haulers were concerned, by the mid-1980s, as they quickly evolved into global cash flow machines, it became less and less necessary for them to fight city hall to prevent profits being diverted out of their private dumps and into public trash furnaces.

As Brian Lipsett of the Citizens' Clearinghouse for Hazardous Waste discerned, the whole flow control issue, once significant enough to provoke the war of Akron, "had become a moot point, as garbage companies themselves got into incineration in a big way."

Browning-Ferris entered a partnership in a waste-to-energy firm called American Ref-Fuel. Waste Management, which was positioning itself to become the leading disposal company, purchased a stake in Wheelabrator Technologies, which was America's second most important builder and operator of municipal incinerators after Ogden Martin.

In return for the exclusive right to site its incinerators in the vicinity of Waste Management landfills, WMI agreed to provide Wheelabrator space for the toxic ash whose ultimate disposal was proving to be an intensely divisive issue. In fact, the ash residue (the incinerators' equivalent of spent radioactive fuel) was becoming one of the poles around which public opposition was rallying in resisting the kind of capital-intensive pollution control methods being pushed by an emerging waste management oligarchy.

Speaking at St. Lawrence University in 1988, anti-incineration activist Professor Paul Connett explained that "more than any other issue, the ash presents us with concrete evidence that incineration is not the answer to the trash crisis. It doesn't make either economic or environmental sense to convert three tons of trash into one ton of toxic ash."[40]

An anecdote Connett recounted illustrates the emergence of grass roots mobilization as a potent counterforce in the politics of waste in the mid-1980s. A ship with 15,000 tons of Philadelphia incinerator ash set sail for Panama. In response to warnings by Greenpeace and the U.S. Environmental Protection Agency about the ash's toxicity, the Panamanians rejected the cargo, as did various Caribbean, Central American and West African ports of call.[41] Finally, eighteen months later, the pariah ship redocked in its home port only to have its pier burn down as Philadelphians awaited an injunction they sought to ban the ash's unloading. The ship sailed again, changed its name and its flag, and finally disappeared somewhere in Asia. Some say the ash's ultimate destination was the bottom of the Indian Ocean.

By the time the scorned ship departed from the City of Brotherly Love for the second time, municipal solid waste incineration had begun to generate a high level of social tension. Successful incinerator sitings had tripled in the U.S. and Canada to more than 170, with Greenpeace estimating that another 300 could be on stream by 1992.[42] However, *Rachel's Hazardous Waste News* pointed out that as a result of grass roots activism, the incineration industry was hitting the same kind of wall that the nuclear business had hit: "In 1987, for the first time in recent memory, more [incineration] capacity was canceled (33,656 tons per day) than was ordered (20,585 tons per day)."[43] Unlike comparably divisive issues such as abortion or nuclear arms, the pro-incineration forces were hard-pressed to find anyone willing to come out into the streets to counteract the broadly based and ever-growing opposition movement.

Louis Blumberg and Robert Gottlieb observe in *War on Waste* that "with conflicts over incineration spreading rapidly from community to community, the focus of debate around solid waste management shifted from the question of the best technology and the role of industry to the policy-making process within the public sector."[44] Yet the ability of public administrators to debate rationally and act independently was increasingly limited by the incineration lobby itself, which laid siege to municipal government everywhere. In the crisis atmosphere surrounding not only waste but municipal finance in general, public officialdom believed that the aggressive schemes of incinerator vendors promised the least threat to the status quo. After all, who could say with absolute assurance that if the only choice was between burning and burying, spewing toxic metals into the air was any more or less deadly than leaching poisons into the water tables?

The Municipal-Industrial Complex

No better illustration of the corporate will to burn urban garbage can be found than in the political gamesmanship surrounding the long-nurtured plan to build the world's biggest municipal garbage burner.

Between 1978 and 1986, New York City's sanitation commissioner Norman Steisel's most important goal had been "his plan to build an incinerator in each of the [city's] five boroughs."[45] He awarded the contract to build a 3,000-ton-per-day incinerator in the Brooklyn Navy Yard (worth nearly $600 million in 1992 dollars) to the company soon to become known as Wheelabrator and end up as part of the WMI group.

However, in the face of public opposition which was stalling construction, New York City Council in 1988 passed by a vote of twenty-nine to one a law mandating solid waste recycling. Curiously, the only dissenting vote was cast by the council's most outspoken recycling advocate. The dissident councillor as well as such activist organizations as the Sierra Club and the New York Public Interest Research Group were dismissive of a law which they regarded as a "watered-down commitment to recycling" and a blatant public relations smokescreen to facilitate the city's real agenda — mass incineration.[46] Events soon confirmed their suspicions.

In 1989, David Dinkins, running as the environmental candidate for mayor of New York, distinguished his candidacy from his rivals' by pledging to study recycling and other options before moving ahead with new incinerators. This won him crucial support from environmentalists as well as from the Satmer Hasidic community residing in the precincts of the site of the proposed incinerator.

But no sooner was the new Mayor Dinkins ensconced in Gracie Mansion than he found that one of the prices to be paid for the support of Wall Street was his appointment of Norman Steisel, now installed in the major investment bank Lazard Frères, to the powerful position of first deputy mayor. Lazard had a multi-million-dollar stake in the burner deal. "In effect," wrote Matthew Reiss in *The Village Voice*, "Dinkins handed over the future of New York to one of the country's foremost incineration lobbyists."[47]

Steisel had travelled the U.S. championing incineration as founding president of the now defunct National Resource Recovery Association, whose waste-to-energy lobbying function had been obscured by the fact that it also happened to be an arm of the U.S. Conference of Mayors. Steisel went on to help set up California Waste-to-Energy where "he openly pushed incineration with other members, among them Lazard clients Westinghouse, Wheelabrator, Browning-Ferris Industries, Waste Management Inc., as well as regional and multinational incineration consulting and engineering firms like Bechtel."[48]

Before revolving out of his office as New York's sanitation commissioner into a suite at Lazard Frères, one of Steisel's final acts as a public servant was to sign a contract that "makes it all but impossible for the city to successfully recycle."[49] The bondability of the Lazard-backed burner had been assured by a city guarantee (like the one in Akron in the 1970s) to deliver to Wheelabrator's gate a king's ransom in garbage. In the case of the proposed Navy Yard deal, that was going to amount to at least 18 million tons of municipal waste.

In addition to raising the world's greatest trash burner, the incinerationists seemed set to accomplish something equally remarkable: they were provoking an alliance between Brooklyn's medieval-garbed Hasidim and its projects-dwelling inner-city blacks, who came together in opposition to the plans. It was a coalition of groups not typically noted for marching to the same drummer.

By the early 1990s, with the face of waste management radically transformed, Professor Savas's prescriptions had taken on the quaint aura of academic artifacts. Savas had sought to reform municipal finances through privatizing waste collection. His vision had depended for its logic on the existence of an infinity of competing contractors who asked for no more than a decent living in return for decent service. But what had evolved in its stead were multinational waste companies whose size, aggression, global ambition and ability to exercise a degree of power made them private enterprises of a very different kind than he had envisaged. As for reforming municipal finances, the emerging financial interest in incineration had created what *Newsday*, in an exposé of New York incineration politics, described as "the municipal-industrial complex."[50]

The Recycling Component: Urban Ore

Another effect of ever-widening hostility to burying refuse in anyone's backyard had been to shift the emphasis from disposal to recycling and reuse. During the 1970s, while the multi-national waste managers generally concentrated on burial and burning and ignored recycling, a community-based multi-materials recycling industry grew out of the 1970 Earth Day experience.

By the early 1990s, thirty-eight American states had enacted a variety of product bans, mandates, taxes and tax incentives to promote recycling. This burgeoning interest in recycling efforts, the mandating of waste diversion and the availability of public monies to underwrite such activity set into motion a new round of corporate concentration. But now the acquisition and co-venture pattern reflected something approximating an identity crisis on the part of the major haulers. They had grown powerful serving a throwaway-and-flush society and were faced with having to fashion a role for themselves in a budding conserver society.

WMI, the world's biggest waste collector, and Du Pont, the world's largest maker of plastic products, briefly ventured into a joint paper and plastics recycling effort in Chicago. WMI also arranged to provide a steady supply of discarded paper to Jefferson Smurfit Corporation of St. Louis, the world's largest recycler of waste paper. Other links were established between WMI and such major players as U.S. Recycling Industries and Stone Container Corporation. BFI, in conjunction with Dow Chemical, signed an agreement with Weyerhaeuser Paper to supply old newspapers in the Pacific Northwest, and another with Alcoa Aluminum to sell it used beverage cans.

But the corporate marriage best typifying the dawn of a new epoch in industrial evolution was the take-over of one of the waste majors not by another waste multi-national but by a resources and railway conglomerate. Canadian Pacific, in buying Laidlaw from Michael DeGroote, now had its own continental provisioner of used materials. The waste hauler had an exclusive contract to feed used newspapers to newly converted pulp mills in Thunder Bay, Ontario, and Gatineau, Quebec, both of which were operated by another CP subsidiary — Canadian Pacific Forest Products Limited.

Thus, while burial, burning and treatment continued to be the major source of industry profits and control, the biggest firms were paying far more attention now to "urban ore" or — to use the jargon of the hour — the middle of the waste hierarchy. A waste management hierarchy can be imagined as an inverted triangle, with treatment and disposal at the bottom-most tip and, higher up in the middle area, the three R's of recycling, reuse and reduction. Faced with this political thrust forcing waste disposers out of the tip of the waste triangle, the Big Three began elbowing aside existing recyclers in much the same way as, twenty years previously, they had set out to supplant the myriad of mom and pop operators, cooperatives and public collection systems.

Throughout the 1980s consumer and recycling groups, fearing that the franchising of recycling would severely handicap both private and non-profit recyclers and help oligopolize the business nation-wide, fought off attempts by local and state authorities to award exclusive contracts. But by the early 1990s, the major waste haulers were asking cities to give them commercial and industrial recycling franchise agreements along with their refuse pickup contracts. And with such contracts in hand, they quickly moved to exert their publicly sanctioned territorial imperatives.[51]

In late 1991, for instance, BFI's legal counsel wrote a warning to the Independent Recyclers' Association in Oakland, California. The lawyer pointed out that BFI now possessed a franchise not only for garbage but for recyclable materials as well from all properties in thirteen service areas of San Mateo County. He insisted that his client would not tolerate incursions by any other company which might have a contract to remove recyclables within its exclusive jurisdiction.

BFI was not the only waste major that was trying to supplant all public forms of waste management control. A Wall Street analyst, Drexel Burnham, claimed WMI, which in 1988 operated in 325 North American metropolitan markets, intended to be active in 500 by 1991.[52] In fact, so far had such companies gone in supplanting competing systems of public and private waste management that one alarmed U.S. senator concluded the disposal industry was becoming a "shadow government" whose leading members helped regulatory authorities write regulations, lay down rules for enforcement and train agency employees in writing and awarding contracts.[53]

We now turn to an examination of how — in the course of barely two decades — a small number of corporations evolved out of the lower depths of the corporate world to end up being convincingly portrayed as a shadow government.

PART II

Big Garbage — The Globalization of the Waste Trade

The process that transformed so much of the economic system into megacorporations swept through the garbage business in the 1970s. Solid wastes joined most other basic commodities of modern life — oil, precious metals, natural resources and even information — as objects of corporate control. By the 1980s so overpowering was this general tendency that one merger specialist nervously glanced at contemporary French history and lamented (on the op-ed page of *The New York Times*) that supergiant companies were not only a challenge to democracy but also a temptation for some American Mitterrand, perhaps already waiting in the wings for an invitation to curb these private corporate dictatorships by government take-over.

Beginning as a continental phenomenon, by the early 1990s the waste disposal industry had burgeoned into a global one. Browning-Ferris and Waste Management, the two largest American waste companies, both developed substantial interests in Canada as well as in South America, Europe and Asia. In the 1980s, much of the expansion of Canada's waste giant, Laidlaw, was in the United States. Only the scandal-wracked SCA of Boston remained confined within the borders of its home country, and by the late 1980s its nation-wide assets would be divided up between WMI and Michael DeGroote's Laidlaw, one of Canada's most voracious corporate acquisitors. In its turn, Laidlaw, now North America's third largest solid waste and second largest hazardous waste company, would end up under the control of Canadian Pacific, one of Canada's bedrock private economic institutions.

The next four chapters trace the growth of each of these companies, as well as the public resistance that arose largely as a reaction to the unrelenting efforts of the new waste industry to keep on expanding the market for its services. The last chapter in this section deals with Canadian and American government and private lawsuits against the front-rank waste companies during the early 1990s. These cases offer compelling evidence that in transplanting the *modus vivendi* of urban trash haulers to the continental level, the major waste companies are perforce evolving into an ever more deeply entrenched private cartel.

Chapter 3

BFI: The Pathbreaker

... BFI is indeed and seems destined to remain ... 'a company building an industry.'
Michael A. Oberman, Editor, *Waste Age*, 1972

BFI was the first of the waste majors to indulge in continental expansion at a hitherto unimagined pace and scale. It sent teams of deal makers to buy out the competition in one city after another across North America until in 1980 it had subsidiaries in thirty-six states and six Canadian provinces, not to mention six other countries. On the way it managed to hurdle the obstacles of public- and private-sector competition and increasing environmental regulations — using methods that often generated controversy and unease. By the late 1980s BFI had attempted a major "cultural" re-orientation, adjusting its leadership and corporate ethos to square with its avowed mandate as a custodian of the planet. With the company grossing more than $2 billion a year, senior government bureaucrats with environmental experience were being lured into positions atop its executive tree. But since unbridled expansion and environmental protection do not sit easily in the same institution, this new tack ultimately got BFI in trouble with its most important allies, the stockholders. This chapter chronicles the path BFI took to maintain its position as king of continental waste.

Although the process of concentration had not yet really begun in 1969, its potential was there. A number of contractors in different parts of the country had built up substantial local or regional firms that were a departure from the one- or two-truck operations of the past. If a mastermind merged some of these noteworthy local operations, they would have the basis for a continental empire. And it was a group of young entrepreneurs in Houston who saw that potential most clearly.

Houston imbues its favourite sons with a schizoid personality. The metropolis grew up on the ethic of cowboys and grew rich on the ethic of oil kings. Shaped by these influences, Tom Fatjo was part lone ranger, part empire-builder. He started his small garbage business with the self-reliance and the solitary independence of the frontier hero; with the shrewd confidence and ambition of John D. Rockefeller, he and his associates launched Browning-Ferris Industries in the world capital of the oil business. His monolithic models were hardly havens of frontier independence, and their legacy was symbolized by the city's reigning heroes, the astronauts, the foot-soldiers of a highly regimented corporate colossus.

In her 1902 muckraking classic about Standard Oil, Ida Tarbell quoted Rockefeller as saying, "You see, this scheme is bound to work. It means an absolute control by us of the oil business. There is no chance for anyone outside. But we are going to give everybody a chance to come in. You are to turn over your refinery to my appraisers, and I will give you Standard Oil company stock or cash, as you prefer, for the value we put on it. I advise you to take the stock. It will be for your good."[1] Similarly, BFI had one eye on takeover prospects all over the continent and the other eye on the New York Stock Exchange. As its price rose, BFI stock was increasingly attractive bait for the struggling independents the Houston entrepreneurs were trying to entice with takeover offers. And the more companies BFI took over, the higher the stock rose.

Building the Chain

BFI executives jetted into cities as close to Houston as Lake Charles, Louisiana, and as distant as Thunder Bay, Ontario. Local haulers and landfill operators were offered big salaries if they agreed to sell out and stay on board under the flag of the continental chain. They were persuaded to exchange their assets and accounts for the inflated stock, whose paper value was being pushed to new highs. They would be instantly richer, the acquisition team informed them. The response was spectacular, and during late 1969 and 1970 BFI penetrated twenty different urban markets, buying firms in each. Among its acquisitions were five companies owned by Harry Phillips, a University of Mississippi dropout who hauled garbage in Houston, Memphis, and San Juan, Puerto Rico, and who was hired as the newly merged company's chief operating officer.

The chain-building process was now underway, and the pathbreaking BFI was soon dubbed "the company that built an industry."

But the Houston-based company was not the only bidder in this new game. By the end of 1971 the three other newly formed waste managers — WMI of Chicago, SCA of Boston and Laidlaw of Hamilton — had also gone to the stock exchange. WMI had bought 75 businesses by late 1972. By 1973 SCA possessed a network of 130 formerly independent firms. And Laidlaw had swallowed 33 trucking and waste hauling firms by 1973. These fledgeling enterprises were greeted with considerable enthusiasm by a rising stock market. In March 1972 *Business Week* described Wall Street's attraction as the "tinge of glamour that surrounds companies that can claim to be helping the environment."

The National Solid Wastes Management Association was an early booster of the revolution in the garbage industry, and the trade magazine *Waste Age*, which later became the association's in-house organ, sought to coin a new term which could convey what was unique about these new companies. In a 1972 issue, the magazine explained its choice of the word "agglomerate" in the following terms:

> The tendency of many in the solid waste field has been to call these new companies "conglomerates". Reality shows, however, that the process of fusing the best local enterprises in the industry into several national firms is, indeed, a far cry from the traditional interpretation that society has placed on the meaning of the term conglomerate. In contrast to this WASTE AGE prefers to regard these companies as "agglomerates" — a term we feel is much more consonant with the realities of the situation. The dictionary defines agglomeration as the process of forming, gathering or growing into a mass. The adjectival form of the word means clustered densely; and what better term could be used to describe what is currently taking place ...[2]

This was the industry's aggressive expansion phase — the years in which financial muscle replaced the physical kind which had always been associated with the garbage business. But despite the new wholesome aura, evidence of the persistence of the industry's traditional character lurked not far below the surface. *Business Week* expressed some niggling doubts about the industry's glamorous image. The magazine wondered whether the business might prove unresponsive to excessive amounts of computerized centralization and worried about an obstinate crime element that might refuse to stand aside for the advancing chains. It noted that though "garbage chain executives deny they have run into organized crime, the denials are sometimes less than convincing." One contractor was quoted as saying: "One of my operations in Cleveland was blown up last summer, but that was purely a competitive battle and had nothing to do with the Mafia." Soon afterward the contractor sold out. The new owner was murdered, and a competing local, independent garbage hauler was charged.[3]

Not only did criminal enforcers have a regulatory role, as we have already observed, in serving to stabilize precarious markets, but there were other opportunities connected with garbage collection. The large cash flows offered opportunities for skimming and laundering funds. In large city ports, marine refuse haulers were well placed to move contraband on and off ships without arousing suspicion.

Yet the day was coming when the new chains would entirely supplant the Damon Runyon types. The mobster was obsolete in garbage. As highly capitalized oligopolists, the majors looked forward to sharing their markets with a small number of like-minded rivals, and as public companies they were accountable to securities commissions, who did not appreciate the companies they listed being chronicled by crime reporters. However, the complete disappearance of crime figures from local refuse markets didn't happen overnight. In the meantime, the big waste corporations and the underworld coexisted and — as we shall see in later chapters — sometimes met.

The concerns expressed by *Business Week* didn't appear to worry anyone at BFI's head office in Houston. In 1971 BFI combined with the National Disposal group of companies. This acquisition gave it access to the lucrative Chicago markets and kicked off a period of extraordinarily rapid growth. By the fall of 1972 BFI subsidiaries were hauling trash in ninety cities. In addition to its takeovers of local trash haulers, BFI acquired a liquid waste facility located in Louisiana near the oil refineries and chemical plants along the Gulf Coast, and Consolidated Fibers, Incorporated (CFI), one of the three largest scrap paper dealers in the United States. With these moves, BFI's underlying ambition — to manage the nation's waste streams — began taking concrete shape.

Between 1971 and early 1973, investors drove the price of BFI common stock from under $10 to $37 a share. Most of the shares issued in exchange for acquired firms stayed in the hands of the once independent contractors, who remained as local officers. Directors, officers and key employees throughout their network were harnessed to BFI's fortunes by a potentially lucrative stock option plan. They, and they alone, were permitted to buy new shares over time below market value, a right they would exercise only if values continued to rise. Thus it was in senior management's personal interest to push hard for local sales and earnings growth, which would be directly reflected in the future price of shares.

The acquisition of National Disposal Service was a notable step in BFI's growth. Forged in the tough Chicago school of trash hauling, National Disposal was one of the largest private American contractors. It had $13 million in annual sales, operated 11 landfills, and ran 375 trucks in 6 states. Its 18 residential contracts added municipal service to BFI's primarily commercial and industrial operation. And the former president of the National Disposal group, John Vanderveld, who was chairman of the public affairs committee of NSWMA, joined BFI as a key executive.

BFI's entry into the Chicago market also had its dark side. Local trustbusters had uncovered evidence that Chicago's garbage markets were governed according to the monopolistic laws of "property rights." In April 1971 a lawsuit brought by the Illinois attorney general's office revealed a massive price-fixing scheme. Some two hundred firms — including National Disposal — and a trade association were accused of having conspired to carve up the huge Chicago market. According to the charges (see Appendix), the companies had rigged bids on government contracts, prohibited one another from soliciting the customers of other association members, refused to deal with customers wishing to switch their business from other member contractors and, in some cases, bought and sold among themselves the exclusive rights to service "stops."

The charges were denied. Nevertheless the association was handed a $50,000 fine, and the defendants consented to a judge's decree prohibiting them from engaging in monopolistic practices for the next ten years. A year after the consent order was signed, a newspaper columnist, without identifying any specific company, cast doubt on the sincerity of the industry's efforts to adhere to the consent order. "The companies that dominate this enormously profitable industry," wrote Mike Royko in the *Chicago Daily News*, "have a long history of price-fixing, collusion, squashing small competition, muscle, threats, and other unsportsmanlike conduct. Much of this was supposed to stop a year ago, when their powerful trade association was fined $50,000 and told to knock off the fancy tricks, but sources in the industry say things have changed very little."[4] Nor would the new, giant private waste managers do much to improve competition as they expanded their market shares throughout the 1970s.

In these early years, BFI common shares (an initial public share offering was floated in 1971) were trading off speculative perceptions about future earnings. Wall Street and the company's bankers expected BFI to become a force in a continental garbage handling system. Before the day of reckoning arrived, the task of Tom Fatjo, Lou Waters, Harry Phillips and the company's other officers was to deepen and widen its newly acquired networks. More contract haulers had to be added, more customers billed, and more landfill banks assembled. Alternative forms, such as workers' cooperatives and municipal authorities, had to be eliminated. And to complete the whole process, a position had to be established in resource recovery.

Recoverable paper and fibrous material represented 60 per cent by volume of the solid wastes BFI hauled, and with its Consolidated Fibers division the so-called agglomerate (a coinage which would seem to fly in the face of revelations dealt with in Chapter 7) intended to recover these materials. Consolidated Fibers (CFI) provided paper recovery facilities and market outlets in Dallas, Phoenix, Los Angeles, Buffalo, Toronto, Montreal and a half dozen other cities. It was a marriage of moneymaking and ecological ideology on a new scale. From late 1972 through 1974, key executives in BFI's head office in Houston's Fannin Bank Building were obsessed with their vision. After the CFI acquisition, they were reportedly devoting nearly all of their attention to resource recovery, seriously contemplating the arrival of zero industrial growth and of the day urban garbage would become valuable. "We feel that these commodities are at some point going to be scarce," said Board Chairman Waters, "and we want to have access to all the material we can get, so that we can continue to supply the markets we develop in conjunction with the Consolidated Fibers people."[5]

BFI signalled its new-found consciousness by commissioning a medallion struck in recycled metal, which carried the words of a prophet of the new age:

Since the beginning of time each generation has fought nature. Now in the life span of a single generation, we must turn and become the protector of nature.

Jacques Cousteau

BFI and the San Francisco Scavengers

BFI was hardly ignoring more basic aspects of the business. The company's buying spree continued all over the continent. While certain features were common to all of BFI's acquisitions, there were also variations based on the characteristics of a new market and the company's situation at the time of the takeover. As a result of a combination of such circumstances, a BFI acquisition in the San Francisco Bay area in 1973 was a particularly interesting instance of the company's progress.

With this acquisition BFI encountered the unique system of waste management built by the Bay area's Italian boss scavengers. The hybrid franchise/cooperative structure guaranteed that dirty work was properly respected and rewarded. Its labour methods were not designed to suit the purposes of distant speculators. Hoodlums were kept at bay. And for such a hazardous industry, workers' compensation rates were low. This was not the kind of structure that was readily accepted by corporate America. As sociologist Stewart Perry observed, the cooperative idea — despite the deeply democratic structure it fostered — was considered "un-American," an alien transplant.

The largest cooperative, Sunset Scavenger, was just another corporation to the Internal Revenue Service. The tax department refused to grant the company the more favourable tax rates paid by agricultural cooperatives. Following a bitter dispute, Sunset Scavenger drew up a set of bylaws which captured the spirit of the cooperative:

At no time have the stockholders regarded this corporation as an entity separate or distinct from its stockholders or as anything other than their tool or servant ... We feel, insist, and claim that the term "stockholder" or "shareholder" misrepresents the true relation existing and which has ever existed between the owners of the stock of this corporation and this corporation and the relation of the so-called stockholders among themselves, and that the term "member" truly represents and describes that relation, for this corporation was intended to be ... from its very inception an association solely of boss scavengers and decidedly not for the benefit of drones or speculators; in other words, they were an association of workers who intended to form and carry on a cooperative corporation where every member did his share of the work and expected every other member to work and do his utmost to increase the collective earnings.[6]

In an interview Sunset president Lenny Stefanelli told Professor Perry that "of course, there's a lot of them like a bunch of old ladies, but on the other hand, thank God, the majority of the stockholders take pride in their company. It's theirs. *E cosa nostra* — it's our thing, it's ours."[7] While the Italian phrase for "our thing" has become associated with a criminal organization, in this context it simply reflected the garbagemen's deep sense of involvement with a structure that had always remained free of underworld penetration.

The burly boss scavengers knew their trade intimately. Their skills, however, were of little use when the worker-owners of San Mateo County, south of San Francisco, encountered BFI. When it came to deal-making and talk of price/earnings ratios, secondary offerings and unlegended stock certificates, the boss scavengers were no match for the fast-talkers from the Fannin Bank Building.

BFI wanted to buy two of the boss scavengers' companies, San Mateo County Scavenger and San Mateo Disposal. The acquisition team held extensive discussions and negotiations. Letters were exchanged with executives in Texas. The basic offer delivered to the cooperative's directors was the standard one — our shares for yours. Attached to BFI shares, however, were certain restrictions on how and when they could be sold.

At two meetings the directors explained their understanding of the deal to the assembled owners. If they agreed to sell out, they would be able to cash in some of their new BFI certificates during a promised secondary offering, which Houston intended to float in May 1973. This public issue would give the garbage workers an opportunity to liquidate a portion of their holdings. They also understood that BFI would try its best to make it easy for them to resell their shares, although the stock they could sell at any given time would be limited. The company agreed to have fully registered, transferable shares available for delivery to the cooperative members, and to instruct its transfer agent to exchange the non-negotiable BFI shares for marketable ones at the times set forth in the agreement.

One week before the 31 January 1973 deadline on BFI's offer, the Italian-American garbagemen gathered for a special meeting. It was a momentous decision for all of them. They had close ties from working together, from marrying into each other's families, from a common immigrant experience. Many had been raised in the company. But it was as businessmen rather than family men that they approached BFI's forty-page proposal. The stock transfer would instantly make each of them a couple of hundred thousand dollars richer — on paper. The deal represented their confrontation with remote forces that seemed to be reshaping American life, and they did not feel able to resist. They signed over their companies, and the San Mateo cooperative was finished.

No sooner had the San Mateo companies become BFI subsidiaries than the stock market turned bearish as deteriorating economic conditions wiped billions of dollars off the value of publicly held corporations. Speculative enterprises — the new waste managers among them — were hardest hit by the decline. BFI's waste paper recycling venture further complicated matters for the pioneer agglomerate. A down business cycle always seriously affects the scrap industry, and Consolidated Fibers was being very badly buffeted. Thus 1973 was not the year for BFI to go back to the stock market for new capital. The worst thing for a new public company is to have a secondary offering delayed or withdrawn. Once perceptions about the company's future are altered, significant price erosion follows. Existing shareholders, including all of BFI's top managers, naturally wanted to avoid this.

Instead of going to Wall Street, BFI went to the banks. Within three months of the San Mateo takeover, it raised its indebtedness to banks from $65 million to $140 million. These were hardly auspicious times for very recent BFI shareholders to realize the anticipated profit on their stock. This was not the former cooperative members' idea of what BFI's proposal had been; they had not realized that the Houstonians might go to banks rather than investors for additional capital.

At various times after 1 May 1973 when they tried to sell their new shares, the boss scavengers came up against what they took to be "untoward and extraordinary delays" by BFI in facilitating the resale. They suspected BFI was not being entirely forthcoming and felt that it was taking unnecessarily long to provide them with marketable certificates. As the share values declined, they assumed that the delaying tactics resulted from a simple motive — Houston was trying to stanch the wound opened by a steep decline in the stock market. The quantity of BFI stock traded had to be kept to a minimum to maintain the value of the outstanding shares.

The boss scavengers eventually launched legal action, alleging that they had been defrauded of their companies as a result of BFI's misrepresentations and non-disclosures. During the discovery phase of the lawsuit, a new revelation heightened their sense of having been had. A BFI employee gave a deposition stating that during the negotiations the boss scavengers' own legal counsel — who had been advising the San Mateo garbagemen about the wisdom of the deal — was also being employed and compensated by BFI.

The boss scavengers asked the courts for their companies back. Alternatively they sought millions of dollars in damages. In a 1980 court-signed settlement (which bound the San Mateo garbagemen and their representatives to secrecy) the plaintiffs agreed to BFI's express denial of any guilt or wrongdoing; for its part, BFI paid the aggrieved scavengers $700,000.

But the deed was done. BFI held onto its corporate assets, and its blue and white colours flew in the Bay area. The area's remaining boss scavengers faced the future with growing uncertainty. As early as 1973, the year of the San Mateo takeover, Sunset Scavenger had decided that its only defence was to brave the new world of waste management by turning itself into a mini-conglomerate called Envirocal. The presence of BFI just south of San Francisco was a victory for the drones and speculators the original boss scavengers had found so abhorrent.

North to Canada

During the same period of aggressive acquisition in which BFI entered the Bay area and dozens of other metropolitan markets in the United States, the Houstonians also rode north into Canada for the first time. Near the top of its shopping list in 1971 were haulers working the Edmonton market, for while the Alberta capital was climatically light-years away from the arid tablelands of Texas, economically and politically it was inviting territory. Alberta was already in the corporate orbit of oil company head offices in Houston and Oklahoma City. It was on the verge of an oil and natural gas boom, and that meant new highways, stores, plants and office buildings. So in Edmonton's forty-below weather, the members of BFI's acquisition team clutched their cowboy hats and moved about town seeking contractors to buy out.

By year's end they had found three, which were consolidated and which immediately began experiencing annual profit increases topping 30 per cent. Collection vehicles were soon hauling everything from the refuse of the fabrication and manufacturing sector of the oil industry to chicken feathers. And Calgary and Lethbridge joined Edmonton as districts of BFI's Arrowhead Region, which was to take in the Upper Peninsula of Michigan, Wisconsin, parts of Illinois, Iowa, Minnesota, North and South Dakota, Nebraska, Colorado, Wyoming, Montana, Alberta, Saskatchewan, Manitoba and part of Ontario.

In Winnipeg BFI took advantage of intense warring among the local Ukrainian and Mennonite contractors for hauling business. "It's not a two-bitter's game any more," observed one marginal front-end operator. After BFI took over the three largest local firms, some new and more substantial rivals joined the fray, and the ensuing severe competition proved worrisome to Houston's head office managers. (The resulting campaign to control the Winnipeg market and the related legal complications are the subject of Chapter 8.)

With its entry into Winnipeg, BFI immediately became the second largest waste removal contractor in Manitoba. The largest was the City of Winnipeg, a municipality whose view of urban administration was somewhat removed from the prevailing ethos in Texan cities where the level of public services was low. Since 1911 Winnipeg had been firmly committed to the principle of municipal ownership of essential public utilities. The private waste managers, however, saw the public sector as an area in which further corporate growth could be achieved, and BFI was soon chipping away at the underpinnings of the municipally controlled waste management system — its collection routes and the authority to regulate tipping fees at landfills — that not only accounted for the long-term maintenance of these sites but also made possible the financing of more desirable disposal technologies.

In Windsor BFI bought out Patrick and Joseph Sasso, who stayed to direct the company's local affairs. Thunder Bay, with its grain elevators, harbour, shipbuilding and drydock facilities, also beckoned the company, and BFI set up shop at the Lakehead. Then London, the metropolis of southwestern Ontario, and Sarnia, with Canada's greatest concentration of petrochemical industries, were added as depots of operation.

In 1972 Metropolitan Toronto's private business was almost swallowed whole by BFI and its sister agglomerate, Waste Management Incorporated. BFI picked up several firms, including a paper recycling plant and Bulk-Lift Systems, a major independent. The remaining small fry were nervous. "People in the business are scared," said the president of the Canadian Refuse Haulers Association. "These two companies have the money and the disposal sites and they're going to squeeze a lot of people out of business." "Private Waste Disposal Becoming U.S. Preserve," read a *Globe and Mail* headline. Between them, BFI and WMI had captured 70 per cent of the private sector. Only Superior Sanitation Services, part of Mike DeGroote's budding Laidlaw empire, remained a serious rival.

With its hundred trucks collecting in more than a dozen Ontario cities, towns and townships, Kitchener-based Superior Sanitation was definitely an asset worth coveting. Its chief executive, Ralph Carter, received the same lavish treatment that had been used on contractors all over North America. "BFI have their own jet, two or three of them, I think," said Carter, "and they come wheeling in here in alligator cowboy boots and with cases full of money. They put on quite a show, I can tell you." But Canada's mini-agglomerate had expansionist designs of its own, and the Texans failed to seduce Superior Sanitation.

Rolling onwards, BFI landed in Montreal. It was the stamping ground of Sanitary Refuse Collectors, one of the continent's largest residential contractors. (Quebec law didn't insist that suburbs go through the motions of calling for tenders on garbage collection contracts, and by the early 1970s accommodating civic administrators had more or less guaranteed Sanitary Refuse the status of a local private utility — without the encumbrance of public regulation.) An obvious prize, Sanitary Refuse was courted by BFI and somewhat more seriously by WMI. But Belgium Standard, a company based in Waterloo, Ontario, which had pretensions of becoming a waste manager in the style of the new multi-nationals, made

Sanitary Refuse an even better offer. The American major's interest in a large-scale Montreal venture waned. One reason was that most of the city's significant disposal sites were out of their reach; the other was Belgium Standard's bidding higher than they were willing to go. Sanitary Refuse accepted the offer from the Canadian company. (The activities of Sanitary and Belgium Standard after this point are discussed in Chapter 10.)

In 1973 BFI acquired Raicek Refuse Removal, a 9-truck outfit with 5 of Montreal's 180 garbage removal contracts. Raicek had taken over collection in the east-end suburb of Pointe-Aux-Trembles when it was first farmed out in June 1965. In buying a small operator and not Sanitary Refuse, BFI had, in the words of Frank White of Metropole, Montreal's second-largest hauler, "made a mistake coming here. They bought poorly. They overpaid and got a pig in a poke." Nevertheless, the Houston company's blue and white garbage hampers began appearing throughout the Quebec metropolis.

In three short years the structure of Canada's garbage industry was revolutionized. BFI subsidiaries dotted the map from Quebec to British Columbia, and WMI was a strong presence in southern Ontario. Laidlaw was building an empire of its own, and Belgium Standard was trying to imitate it. Only one major family-owned solid waste contractor now remained — Smithrite Disposal Ltd. of Vancouver. By late 1974 it too was feeling the pressure as the majors moved into British Columbia. From the east came the Canadian interloper, Laidlaw, with two subsidiaries pushing their way into Smithrite's Lower Mainland market. Owner Ascher Smith, who had introduced containerized pickup in western Canada, wanted to remain his own man. When BFI moved into the province, establishing a beachhead in Victoria, Smith prophesied: "We are the last big company in the country that's independently owned — if they get us, they've got the whole country."[8] In the end, it was Laidlaw that bought out Smithrite, in 1983.

While Smith managed to hold out on the mainland in the mid-1970s, BFI captured much of the market in Victoria, picking up customers while the Foreign Investment Review Agency (FIRA) — the Trudeau government's effort to control foreign investment, later abolished by Brian Mulroney's Conservatives — dithered over whether to allow it to buy Cypress Disposal, the largest local hauler. One small Vancouver Island contractor who watched the struggle for control of the provincial capital observed: "They like to cut the other guy's throat until they sell out. I don't know whether BFI has been doing this with Cypress [but] if you can't cut prices you work until you almost go bankrupt." However, righteous indignation over BFI's price-slashing tactics was somewhat undercut by the fact that the local operation itself had held a three-year monopoly. BFI did not eliminate Cypress Disposal then, but by the spring of 1975 it had about 50 per cent of Victoria's garbage business, including the University of Victoria and the weather ships *Quadra* and *Vancouver*.

BFI was also the first of the multi-nationals to establish itself on Canada's east coast. FIRA permitted BFI's takeover of Shore Disposal of Dartmouth, Nova Scotia, in August 1978 and four years later of its chief local rival, Commercial Refuse. This gave the company access to residential, commercial and industrial contracts in the Halifax area, including the business of the Department of National Defence.

By 1979, a decade after the Houston entrepreneurs established BFI as a public waste management company, they could be well pleased with their progress in integrating the Canadian market into their system. Their front-end packers hauled from the Alberta parliament buildings, from the Kapyong Barracks of the Princess Pats and Canadian Light Infantry in Winnipeg, and from the Man and His World fairgrounds in Montreal. They operated a provincially funded experimental resource recovery facility north of Toronto. The day was still a long way off when BFI and its sister waste companies fully controlled Canadian municipal solid waste flows from pickup through transfer, disposal, reprocessing and energy extraction. But in dealing with these companies, even the largest Canadian cities were facing institutions whose revenue was comparable to, and in most cases exceeded, their own. BFI's sales revenues in 1979 totalled $457 million; WMI had revenues of $382 million. In the same year total revenues for municipal services amounted to $352 million in Edmonton, $278 million in Toronto, $256 million in Winnipeg and $201 million in Vancouver. Only Montreal, with municipal revenues of $750 million, was still larger than the garbage majors.

The Big Leagues

The stock market decline of 1973 and the recession of 1974–75 did not seriously set back the big waste firms. The increasing trend to privatized waste management in the United States and President Jimmy Carter's strong stand in favour of environmental and energy conservation measures rekindled investors' interest in the big waste companies. Being "rediscovered" by Wall Street allowed BFI to push for further market penetration. In 1978 its acquisition team brought BFI blue to Alabama, Idaho, Indiana, Oklahoma and Utah, and up the Atlantic coast from South Carolina to Halifax.

Tom Fatjo, the man who started it all, left the company in 1976 to devote more time to Criterion Capital Corporation, an investment and consulting company which acted as a consultant to BFI and other clients. A share of the Fannin Bank (with assets of more than $300 million) and a lavish, secluded hotel, conference centre and spa called The Houstonian were among his other interests, and in 1980 Carter appointed him to the President's Council on Physical Fitness and Sports. Harry Phillips and Lou Waters continued the work he had begun, and when BFI stockholders assembled in Houston for the company's 1980 annual meeting, they could be proud of the empire the company had built. It had 3,200 trucks stationed in 150 locations. It had subsidiaries in 36 states, 6 Canadian provinces, Puerto Rico, Spain, Kuwait (where BFI had a subsidiary, Al-Mulla Environmental Systems, W.L.L.), Australia, Bermuda and Saudi Arabia. It had 250,000 steel dumpsters scattered throughout North America, and heavy earthmoving equipment sitting at 65 landfills. This sprawling operation was manned by more than 8,000 employees. And the future seemed bright. President Harry Phillips confided to the stockholders that he expected BFI to double its revenues during the 1980s: "Looking down the road several years, we expect Browning-Ferris to become a billion-dollar company in terms of revenue during this decade and to reach and maintain a return on common stockholders' equity of approximately 20 per cent."[9]

Although its aggressive Chicago rival passed it as the world's largest private garbage company, by 1982 BFI appeared to have recaptured the initiative. In March BFI spirited away one of WMI's most prized jewels — the sanitation services contract it had signed in 1977 with the city of Riyadh, Saudi Arabia. "Property rights" were evidently not yet a factor in Middle Eastern garbage and city cleaning markets. With the fantastic returns on equity anticipated from the Saudi contract, BFI had gained "a bit of a psychological edge," according to one financial analyst.

A district manager, who had pitched for the St. Louis Cardinals before ending up in the minor leagues, was quoted in a BFI annual report as saying: "When I left baseball in 1972 and joined Browning Ferris, I was determined not to be in the minor leagues of business. I definitely am not in the minor leagues now." Perhaps most impressive was BFI's accumulation of expensive physical property — trucks, compactors, incinerators, landfills, transfer stations — which, as the waste companies' founding fathers correctly perceived, was the key to the business. In 1969 BFI reaped $28 million in sales on $13 million in gross properties. By 1977 sales were up elevenfold and gross properties had multiplied twenty-two times.

Limits to Growth: The Public Sector

But even if the garbage majors' big-league status was assured, there was still a crucial difference between these firms and the oil companies that had inspired them. The oil companies had mastered nature with feats of engineering and chemistry as they established and maintained their dominant position in an expanding market. At the heart of complexes like Exxon stood chemical engineers. The garbage companies were merely triumphs of salesmanship and organization. While these attributes had brought BFI and its sister company a long way, they still faced serious obstacles in their drive to become international waste managers. These obstacles were, at bottom, political. For, by the late 1970s, the public sector had replaced the independents as the prime opportunity for continued growth. The frontier between private and public sector activity would have to be drawn according to the ideological climate of each particular jurisdiction. An economic consultant writing in *Waste Age* pointed out the utility character of the business: "Residential waste collection and disposal has, to the economist, several striking features. It is a 'natural monopoly', meaning it is cheaper if one entity, public or private, performs the service for a given area."[10] Would government authorities allow themselves to be supplanted as natural monopolists by private contractors? And, if they stepped aside, how much of a role would they play in providing financial backing for the civic systems the contractors would operate?

Although favourable financial treatment by governments played a role in the growth of the oil multi-nationals, big oil was willing to finance a substantial proportion of its exploration, refineries, ocean-going fleets and filling stations out of profits from foreign crude. For the garbage majors, however, public money would be crucial. As long as the role of the public sector was uncertain, financing regional dumps or energy-from-waste plants was a risky affair. Capital had to be matched with garbage to ensure a return on investment, and neither money nor refuse was available in unlimited quantities. Not only did the industry have to be wary about public control over where wastes might flow but it was heard to complain early on about the unfair advantage public agencies had in raising funds by granting tax exemptions to bond buyers. For the big waste corporations the solution to this problem was public-private collaboration, which could let in the back door what competition law wouldn't let walk in the front. Authorities could sell tax-exempt bonds and hand over the proceeds to the firms to develop facilities. Between 1975 and 1980 BFI was the beneficiary of such arrangements in Pennsylvania, Ohio, Illinois, Kansas and Alabama. In addition, the experimental resource recovery centre it operated north of Toronto was financed by the Ontario government through a five year, $10-million contract. Maintaining the goodwill of governments would be the key to future growth of BFI as it entered the 1980s.

Limits to Growth: Environmental Standards

A second set of political problems for the waste companies arose out of questions about their ability (as highly centralized, profit-maximizing corporations) to manage wastes in a way that satisfied local community standards. Horror stories arising from BFI'S waste disposal practices led *The Clarion-Ledger* of Jackson, Mississippi, to conduct a ten-month investigation and to suggest that "BFI's purring Cadillac could be more hearse than limousine." The newspaper concluded:

> As a corporate body whose blood is cash, Browning-Ferris Industries need never fear anemia. BFI's per-share earnings

annually reach new summits. Waste disposal is a growth industry because Americans fervently accept Du Pont's maxim
that chemistry provides better things for better living ...
Americans hire BFI and companies like it to push the brooms
and spread the rugs — then presume the problem solved ...
A people that equates BiC's, Baggies and Saran Wrap to life,
liberty and happiness cannot expect Earth to be Walden Pond
— and Audubon its landlord. Thus, BFI and its analogs offer
essential services. BFI's role is not at issue: its performance
is.[11]

Most questionable were the company's chemical waste disposal
practices. In 1980 BFI and three other firms accounted for 45 per
cent of the chemical waste disposal in the United States. So when
tougher disposal standards came into effect in November of that
year, investors figured that the existing facilities were like gems in
short supply. The waste companies' shares were hit by a wave of
speculative buying far greater than the first one in the early 1970s.
In just six months, the three American majors experienced a total
rise in market capitalization of $1.9 billion. But BFI and WMI —
although not SCA — invested heavily in secure-landfill techniques
for hazardous disposal just when such facilities were becoming
obsolete and unacceptable. *Forbes* watched the stock market interest in the private waste managers with arched eyebrows. It suspected that the chemical industry would win the race to find new
disposal methods. Its 8 June 1981 issue quoted one analyst who
observed that the multi-nationals "are selling themselves as the
definitive answer to the chemical waste problem. But they stand on
the technological bottom rung."[12]

In 1976 BFI was selling oil to be sprayed on subdivision dirt
roads near Nederland, Texas, in the heart of the state's petrochemical region on the Gulf coast. The oil smelled like shoe polish and
it made the locals cough. After the Texas Department of Water
Resources rebuffed citizens' complaints about respiratory problems, a BFI chemist, who allegedly was forced to resign in November 1978 when he complained about the mixing of cyanide and
nitrobenzene with the road oil, took his concerns to a local newspaper. The allegations drew the attention of politicians who made
a special visit from Washington. BFI and state officials were questioned about the handling of the road oil, which turned out to be a
dangerous mix of industrial waste sludge.

At 1979 congressional hearings in Houston a Texas congress-man, Bob Eckhardt, publicly questioned the company's ethics, claiming that "BFI was led to allegedly dispose of the road oil by the profits it could make. Instead of making only enough money to cover its expenses by properly disposing of the cyanide and nitro-benzene wastes ... BFI could clear between $800 and $1,500 per 200-gallon truckload by dumping it on the subdivision roads."[13] Ontario activists fighting a BFI project in their province learned from the Texas attorney general's office in May 1980 that "during the House of Representatives Oversight and Investigation Subcom-mittee hearings, evidence was presented that Browning-Ferris was taking road oil, some of it contaminated with poisons such as nitrobenzenes and cyanide, to unlicensed, fly-by-night reprocessing companies in Louisiana. These companies were then selling the reprocessed oil as fuel oil." From Houston, BFI's chief counsel, Howard Hoover, acknowledged that after several deliveries in 1978 and 1979 a contamination of road oil occurred, caused by the presence of nitrobenzene, and that the company had taken steps to remedy the problem. He also noted that the unfortunate incidents in East Texas and Louisiana had resulted in "no allegations of bribery or intentional conduct on the part of company officials and no suggestion whatsoever that any criminal charges have been or were being considered." But whether or not there was any deliber-ate wrongdoing, the impression remained that BFI was in less than absolute control. (A BFI subsidiary spent about $3.5 million clean-ing and resurfacing local dirt roads, setting up a health monitoring system and veterinary referral program. While nitrobenzene was found to be present in the spray, no cyanide ever was found. Finally, in late 1982, the state and the company reached an out-of-court settlement over charges brought on behalf of the Texas Department of Water Resources. While continuing to strongly deny all allega-tions, BFI paid a $200,000 statutory civil penalty as full and final satisfaction of all claims.)

The Liquid Waste Mountain of Kent County

When the southwestern Ontario farmers who had formed Citizens Rebelling Against Waste — CRAW — learned about BFI's dis-

posal practices in the company's backyard in Texas, they were wary
of the company's plans for their own area. BFI had been dumping
wastes near their fields of soybeans, wheat, corn and summer fruit
since November 1972, when its newly acquired subsidiary, Sasso
Disposal of Windsor, had established a landfill position for itself
by purchasing all the shares of Ridge Landfill Corporation. As
prime agricultural land not subject to undue flooding, the Ridge site
(located in Kent County just east of Chatham airport between Highway 401 and Lake Erie) was well suited as a waste cemetery. It
possessed a provisional licence, and there was no indication as to
what might be buried there. Year by year the dump grew and the
locals dubbed it "the Mountain." The farmers believed the large
tankers heading there were carrying sewage sludge.

In late 1978 and 1979 one farmer saw trucks circling on top of
the completed and capped cells as shiny black liquid poured to the
ground. Another neighbouring farmer reported that water from
three wells had become oily and impossible to drink. And another,
whose land was 1,798 feet from the BFI property line, witnessed
fish going "berserk" and jumping out of the water in a drain that
crossed his fields. He asked the Ontario Ministry of the Environment to have autopsies performed on ducks that died at a stream
on his farm, but he was told that he should have kept the ducks in
the refrigerator if he wanted them examined. Other farmers in the
area also became suspicious of their water, but no one yet knew the
truth.

In 1979, in response to a government request for private-sector
proposals to construct a liquid waste solidification facility, BFI
submitted a plan for its Ridge site, and Ontario Environment Minister Harry Parrott announced that his ministry would be a co-pro-
ponent with the Texas agglomerate. But liquid waste management
in Ontario, a jumble of primitive practices and ineffective supervi-
sion, was becoming an increasingly hot issue. The local farmers
decided to resist the BFI-Ministry of the Environment proposal.
During the controversy that followed farmers found out that the
tankers were actually bringing millions of gallons of unclassified
industrial waste liquids, and the local dump was the largest of its
kind in Ontario. A former heavy equipment operator at the site
remembered how "in the summer of 1978 one of the new pits we
dug was on the west corner of the existing used site. That pit was
dug to a depth of thirty-four feet and we would have dug deeper
but we didn't have time because we couldn't keep ahead of the

volumes of liquid industrial wastes. Liquid industrial wastes were always the first thing we put in the pits and then a layer of garbage."

In March 1980 the county federation of agriculture called a meeting, which led to the formation of CRAW. "The sound of the group's name," said secretary-treasurer Dianne Jacobs, "is completely in keeping with the spirit of protest that lay behind its inception." Funds were raised by means of an auction, a Christian music festival, a beef supper and dance, and the sale of T-shirts and bumper stickers. Information about BFI was obtained from Texas. After a giant demonstration in August 1980 when 690 floats, pickup trucks, cars and tractors surrounded the dump, and a subsequent blockade, the provincial government withdrew from the planned facility.

BFI's next move was an offer to give up liquid waste disposal in exchange for permission to expand its solid waste operation from 100 acres to 215. The quid pro quo offered by the company appeared to represent a substantial sacrifice, since between August 1979 and July 1981 Ridge Landfill buried 5,223,827 gallons of liquid wastes. However, it turned out to be an academic issue. In October 1981 three judges in the divisional court of the Supreme Court of Ontario ruled that the company had never been legally licensed to bury liquids and ordered it to stop immediately.

Whatever the obstacles to BFI's corporate growth, however, the company kept expanding. The Rockefeller adage was now as true for the small-time waste operator as it was for oil: "The day of the combination is here to stay. Individualism has gone, never to return." Surviving independents across the continent could only view the future with trepidation. Aggressive salesmanship had brought BFI and its sister conglomerates to a dominant position in North American garbage markets. In the absence of any significant resistance, momentum could be counted on to take care of the rest. Groups which sought to halt the juggernaut of the refuse disposal megacorporations would only succeed by discrediting the idea that laissez-faire ideology is a sound basis for waste management.

BFI Takes on Hazardous Waste

One group unlikely to debunk disposal for-profit (at least not until the challenges of the 1990s sent shareholders into shock) was Wall Street. Its investment houses were busily bestowing a special mystique on the major dumpers and had primed investors to expect earnings to grow at an annual clip of 20 to 30 per cent. Portfolio managers of pension and investment funds and insurance companies paid out massive sums for waste company shares, multiplying share values to high ratios of per-share earnings. And for their part, front-runners like BFI were fulfilling in spades the projections of the brokerage firms, becoming larger and more far flung, buying hundreds upon hundreds of companies selling at earnings multiples lower than their own.

This aura of rising expectations demanded above all else that the new waste managers be deal-makers, for they had obligated themselves to transmute fevered promotion into self-fulfilling prophecy. E.F. Hutton (the firm which had taken BFI public) and its brother brokerages constantly had to be reassured that growth and record profits would be forthcoming — ad infinitum.

So news of what analysts were saying at a 1983 Wall Street roundtable must have seemed to BFI like the throwing down of a gauntlet. The consensus among these industry watchers was that Waste Management Inc. was beginning to surpass BFI, the path-breaker supposedly destined to be the model for what the industry might become.[14] BFI may have out-manoeuvred WMI in Saudi Arabia, won away its Riyadh contract and brought in cheap Sri Lankan labour to reap better than 20 per cent pre-tax profit on no capital investment, but analysts were more bullish on WMI. It was proving to be the one company which "has always been at the right place at the right time."[15] Dean Buntrock, chairman of WMI, was leading the charge not only into foreign markets but also out along the waste spectrum, into such politically (not to mention environmentally) risky areas as ocean incineration (the MS *Vulcanus*) and low-level nuclear disposal (Chem-Nuclear).

Later that year, BFI, as if to prove itself no less agile, foresighted and capable than WMI, raised the ante by paying a group of beleaguered Buffalo entrepreneurs $85 million worth of BFI shares for CECOS International Incorporated. With CECOS, a company in the hazardous end of the waste spectrum, BFI was rushing into an area where even the grand acquisitor Michael DeGroote of Laidlaw feared to tread. In the late 1970s, CECOS had been a prime contractor for a Love Canal cleanup and controversy surrounded the company. A state civil lawsuit against CECOS's former owners charging bribery and false billing was to knock around the courts well after those proprietors, in return for their BFI shares, signed a non-compete agreement and bequeathed BFI its major position in hazardous waste.[16]

The gods of growth were mollified only temporarily, however, because CECOS's dumps near Niagara Falls, in Williamsburg, Ohio (where it operated one of the U.S.'s largest hazardous waste landfills), and at Baton Rouge on the Gulf Coast, all had problems and would test to the fullest BFI's capacity for moving beyond its pursuit of the next hot deal to something approximating credible ground pollution control.

Poor operating practices and strained relations with regulators plagued each of the CECOS sites.[17] Between 1982 and 1985, thousands of permit infractions were issued at the Louisiana site where suspicions arose that it might prove geologically unsuited for hazardous waste. Contaminated water pumped from its Ohio waste facility into a tributary supplying water to a town had led to criminal charges; and in time, as the Niagara Falls facility reached capacity, the company was faced with the grave (and well-founded) doubts of regulators and citizens about BFI's expansion plans.

There was perhaps no limit to how far Houston might go in trying to extend attention spans on Wall Street beyond the next quarter's financials. But a different strategy was required for managing the outrage of guileless-sounding citizens' groups such as the Society to Prevent Pollution in Towns and the Ecumenical Task Force of the Niagara Frontier, grass roots organizations that couldn't care less about BFI's blithe promises and its shareholders' expectations.

By the late 1980s, a badly performing CECOS continued to drag down earnings — in direct violation of the cardinal rule of glamour stocks. Chief executive officer Harry Phillips Sr. had to surmount severe problems with the regulatory authorities if BFI was to stand any chance of renewing its dumping ground permits. So, in what at first was taken by some company insiders as a stroke of genius, Phillips offered his job to Bill Ruckelshaus, the former Environmental Protection Agency administrator whom one *Wall Street Journal* reporter described as "one of the nation's most famous Republican bureaucrats." In doing so, whether wittingly or not, Phillips acknowledged his company would have to become something other than what it had been. Moreover, implicit in the changing of the guard was the recognition that more than ever waste management was, as Louis Blumberg and Robert Gottlieb had said in *War on Waste*, "a matter of politics."[18]

Before seeing how BFI was to fare under Ruckelshaus, it is useful to reflect on how stressful environmental law and regulation was proving to be on companies who were seeking to expand the limits of the private waste market as well as their own share in it.

Fighting Dirty in Pennsylvania

The solid waste business, given the low barriers to entry, tended to be most revealing of just how predatory the culture of the waste industry was. As the new era in enforcement standards increased the ferocity of the struggle, few waste wars matched the one waged by up-and-comer Chambers Development Company in Philadelphia.

For Chambers, the contest to survive in its home market was a baptism by fire. Founder John Rangos and a partner had bought themselves a landfill in Monroeville, Pennsylvania, in 1971 — five years before BFI's arrival in Allegheny County. From the outset, Rangos dreamed of going national and, with his long experience building fly ash monofills, the Greek-American knew what rich rewards would go to those who managed to wrest a commanding position in privately controlled disposal.

However, in the mid-1970s, before Rangos could act on his ambition, his partner sold out his interest in Chambers to BFI. Rangos bought that share right back but had to agree not to haul commercial and industrial garbage in Allegheny County for five years. Then in 1982, Rangos struck back, winning away a City of Pittsburgh garbage contract from BFI. Two years later, believing that his company had been the victim of a conspiracy orchestrated by BFI employees with the connivance of head office, Rangos filed a federal civil lawsuit which one analyst later described as being a part of Chambers's business strategy.[19]

The 1984 suit targeted the highest-ranking local BFI official, a Canadian named Bill Curtis who had been with BFI in Winnipeg and later was sent to manage its Pittsburgh office. According to Chambers's civil action, BFI had dispatched Curtis to Pennsylvania to acquire Pittsburgh waste haulers and landfill operators as well as to push for the establishment of a waste-to-energy incinerator project called the Pittsburgh Allegheny Corporation for Energy Recovery (PACER).[20]

Chambers charged Curtis with being at the centre of a scheme involving agreements between "surrogate" hauling companies and landfills which "were to be kept secret in order to create the false appearance of competition to insulate BFI, and BFI of Pa. from anti-monopoly action by the Justice Department and private party victims and to assist BFI and BFI of Pa. in price-fixing and bid-rigging schemes. The 'surrogate' companies would be made to appear independent even though they would be controlled by BFI and BFI of Pa."[21]

The lawsuit listed other landfilling companies which it alleged BFI also had set out to destroy. One of the named firms, an alleged victim of BFI's, was run by William Fiore, a wealthy self-made businessman who as a survival strategy would resort not only to court action but also to violence, and end up caught in the web of his own machinations.[22]

As a result of having to enforce some of the U.S.'s strictest disposal laws, the Department of Environmental Resources' (DER) officials found that as a direct consequence of their authority they had the power to shift the competitive balance among rival contractors. Merely by requiring millions of dollars in upgrading (as they did in the case of Chambers's landfill) or closing dumps they deemed to be in non-compliance, regulators unavoidably became arbiters of economic fates. This power (in a chaotic or "free" market with many millions of dollars at stake) made public officials targets for bribes, false allegations of corruption, threats and, failing all else, physical violence.

Rumours circulated of secret slush funds generated by false disposal billing and intended as pay-off money for officials. According to Ralph Haurwitz of *The Pittsburgh Press*, Chambers had two off-duty police officers watch the DER's Charles DuRitsa as part of its effort to prove BFI was receiving favourable treatment.[23] Persons unknown sprayed DuRitsa's car with gunfire, and his family was held at gunpoint while masked men worked his hands over with a hammer. To add insult to injury, Fiore ended up accusing DuRitsa of taking bribes.[24]

The level of paranoia was screwed even higher by a double (and never solved) murder on Memorial Day in Pittsburgh's North Side. The victims once had been in the employ of an alleged BFI "front" landfill whose principals later gave sworn testimony about their involvement with Curtis in bid-rigging schemes.[25] Jewellery found in the murdered men's van had been stolen from DuRitsa's home.

At a DER meeting to discuss allegations of bribery, one official admitted he was on the take from Fiore and claimed Fiore intended to kill DuRitsa if he did not get a hazardous waste landfill expansion permit. When DuRitsa shut the landfill for non-compliance, Fiore became convinced that the state agency was acting on behalf of his rival contractors and he was being singled out unfairly.

Reality, however, had been turned on its head. Generators of waste were paying a ransom in disposal fees. By Fiore's own estimate, the shut-down was costing him $300,000 monthly in pure profit. But, in spite of his considerable resources, Fiore preferred not to be encumbered by a staff of high-priced PhDs and experts on huge retainers to design and monitor a state-of-the-art facility. As a consequence, his means for coping when things began to go awry were what one regulator called "a last frontier approach."

Leachate accumulating in Fiore's impoundments was pumped into the nearby Youghiogheny River. Monitoring systems were rigged. Bribes were paid to the only DER official ever to be found guilty of being on the take. And, along with another disposal contractor, Fiore proved that he was not a man given to idle threats. He hired a former police officer and an accomplice to gun down DuRitsa.[26] The would-be killers bungled their assignment.

BFI's promotion of the PACER burn plant was seen by Chambers to be part of a conspiratorial design to control the garbage burning facility and in the process send up three-quarters of the garbage of Allegheny County in flames. To succeed in doing this would be to ruin not only Chambers's but also everyone else's business, and Chambers expended much effort and money, hired consultants and launched a public relations campaign to combat the incinerator. Chambers also charged Curtis with bribing officials to hassle the company over the off-site migration of methane from its landfill. And there was far worse in the hair-raising catalogue of alleged ruthless behaviour for which Chambers sought damages and relief — enough to ensure that by the time a sheriff got around to serving a copy of the Chambers' complaint, BFI's Curtis had vanished.

BFI denied all the charges and counter-sued. It accused Chambers of being the guilty party, alleging antitrust and racketeering activities with the "specific intent to destroy BFI of Pennsylvania." The transnational firm asked U.S. District Court Judge Gerald Weber to dismiss Chambers's frivolous and baseless complaint for lack of evidence.[27]

But Rangos's lawyers fought on, spending years in the discovery process, and pressing BFI for answers and documents which the defence attorneys repeatedly denied possessing. Weber declared the case "a nightmare of discovery arguments."[28] He accused BFI's counsel of deliberately withholding a certain highly critical document.

As the trial approached, Judge Weber was overcome by doubts about his ability to remain objective. For the first time in twenty years on the bench, he decided to bow out. In July 1987, declaring his own judgement could be influenced by his "view of the lack of credibility and veracity of [BFI's] counsel," Weber recused himself.[29]

However, in spite of BFI's stonewalling, Chambers's overall success as a waste disposal company was such that it became less and less credible to portray itself as anyone's victim — even BFI's. By 1989, no doubt with the help of the publicity surrounding the court battles and the plethora of investigations they had spawned, Rangos had succeeded in holding on in Pittsburgh, and had managed to establish footholds in eleven states.

Having long ago read the trend which would see North Americans forced to discard their refuse into a small number of regional facilities scattered around the continent and controlled by a few companies, Rangos was beginning to reap the benefits of his foresight and endurance. Landfilling was making Rangos super-rich, "one of the elite handful of western Pennsylvanians who are self-made cente-millionaires."[30]

That John Rangos was licensed to carry a gun "in at least a dozen states" and was reported rarely to travel without an armed former FBI agent is no wonder. He told one magazine writer, "I would not advise anybody who doesn't have a strong constitution to even remotely think about this business because it's very, very tough."[31] Like Laidlaw's DeGroote, Rangos branched out into the security business. His firm was aptly (if somewhat ominously) called Security Bureau Incorporated.

By 1989, Chambers felt confident enough to end what had become "one of Western Pennsylvania's highest profile legal battles." Its Washington, D.C., lawyer called the decision a business one whereby Rangos agreed to swallow more than $1 million in legal fees and walk away from his lawsuit.[32] As for BFI, the firm dropped its counter-charges without, as the *Pittsburgh Post-Gazette* reported, "claiming victory."[33]

As for Fiore, he eventually was arrested, and dropped his lawsuit alleging BFI had tried to fix prices with rival landfill operators. After a series of trials and convictions, he ended up in Western Penitentiary. DuRitsa, who had had to endure the ordeal without strong support from the state capital, got a promotion. As for Curtis, he never did return to cleanse his name of the dark stains left by the allegations. There were rumoured sightings of the former BFI of Pennsylvania vice president in Las Vegas and Saudi Arabia, but Chambers's lawyers never found more than traces of the disappeared garbage man.

Mr. Clean

Fiore's incarceration fittingly symbolized the ending of an era in which the free enterprisers had not yet accepted the ascendancy of environmental regulators, the big waste firms and a new and important force, the grass roots movement which drove forward the lawmakers and regulators. The coming phase would assume the more civilized guise of global corporations (quasi-utilities in all but name) interlocked in a multitude of ways with the upper reaches of political power and corporate finance.

The waste majors had no need to kill regulators. On the contrary, as wealth and success gave the business a new-found patina of glamour, they could offer far more sophisticated inducements to respecting their point of view than the gross machinations that characterized the Pittsburgh market in the 1970s and early 1980s. Increasingly, the lure they held out to public officials and regulators was that of a job.

As if to mark their exit from commerce's lower depths, the multi-billion-dollar waste companies began recruiting in the highest echelons. By offering public officials salaries often ten to twenty times higher than what they earned as bureaucrats, the leading companies filled their ranks with well-connected insiders, many of whom had written and overseen enforcement of the regulations governing their new employers.

These offers were so lucrative that a 1987 U.S. General Accounting Office survey estimated fully one-third of the EPA staff administering the multi-billion-dollar U.S. federal Superfund program to detoxify thousands of chemical dumps across America were looking for employment with the waste companies.[34] The following year another Congressional study could see "no likely letup in high Superfund staff turnover at E.P.A."[35]

Leading the pack into the executive suites, for an annual remuneration in excess of $1 million, was William Ruckelshaus. Nothing in Ruckelshaus's background smacked of the street-wise shenanigans which had marked the business from its earliest days. The road that led Ruckelshaus to BFI's headquarters rising over the suburban plains of West Houston was a political insider's avenue. That Ruckelshaus should be sought out to be chief executive of a garbage company illustrates how all-encompassing a societal issue the management of waste had come to be.

Ruckelshaus was born into the Republican party, as grandson of an Indiana prosecutor and Republican county chairman, and son of a man who for forty years helped write the Republican national platform. In 1966, as a young Princeton- and Harvard-trained lawyer, he won election and shone in the state House of Representatives. Two years later, on losing his bid for a U.S. Senate seat, Ruckelshaus's credentials as a party stalwart earned him a fateful invitation. The thirty-six-year-old was invited by President Richard Nixon's Attorney General to head the civil division of the Department of Justice.

From his first arrival in the besieged Vietnam-era capital, Ruckelshaus showed himself to be what British prime minister Thatcher later would derisively describe as a "wet." In contrast to his hawkish peers within the Nixon-Agnew administration, Ruckelshaus approached negotiations with anti-war protestors opposed to the Cambodian invasion as a conciliator. He mediated with demonstrators during a controversial Black Panther trial, and on college campuses he sought common ground with students.

In 1972, environmentalism threatened to be part of a Democratic strategy for capturing the White House and, in reaction, Nixon established a billion-dollar super agency, the Environmental Protection Agency. Ruckelshaus, who once had prosecuted polluters under the Indiana Air Pollution Control Act, was appointed as the EPA's first director.

Here again, the Hoosier Republican proved himself a man of independence. He earned respect for the vigour with which he pursued major cities that dumped raw sewage into interstate waterways and such obdurate companies as Union Carbide whose ferroalloy plant had been proven to be damaging lungs in the surrounding towns of Ohio and West Virginia.

After Nixon's re-election, as Watergate began unfolding, Ruckelshaus temporarily directed the Federal Bureau of Investigation before returning to the Department of Justice. It was here in his resistance to Nixon's "Saturday Night Massacre" that Ruckelshaus was famously to prove himself a republican in the more ancient meaning of the term. White House Chief of Staff Alexander Haig, a four-star general with a despot's bent, told Assistant Attorney General Ruckelshaus that he had to fire the Watergate Special Prosecutor who had rejected the President's compromise on the tapes. "Your Commander-in-Chief [Nixon] has given you an order," threatened Haig. "You have no alternative [but to obey]." Ruckelshaus, not mistaking himself for an enlisted man, refused and resigned.[36]

Then in 1983, another Republican administration awash in scandals brought back Ruckelshaus. This time it was to rebuild morale at an EPA damaged by what *Forbes* magazine blithely called "the stormy reign of Anne Gorsuch Burford."[37] For environmentalists, there was much to find fault with in Ruckelshaus's second term, but he did acquit himself with standards more appropriate to the former Indiana Jaycees Man of the Year he had been than those rampantly corrupt ones which passed muster on the previous Reagan-appointee's watch.[38]

Dubbed "Mr. Clean" by the press, Ruckelshaus later confessed never liking the "white-knight characterization." As he explained, "If you refer to yourself as "Mr Clean" — or anyone else does — you're bound to disappoint people."[39] Those disappointments were not to be long in coming.

Ruckelshaus returned to private law practice in the midst of fighting over what public participation and polluter liability standards should be written into upcoming Congressional amendments to the Superfund toxic clean-up legislation. As well, there was intense disagreement over who would pay for cleaning up thousands of toxic dumps — the actual polluters or a more generally derived tax fund. Not surprisingly, powerful interests preferred the latter public works method, which amounted in some eyes to a form of state socialism for corporate shareholders.

The outcome of the political struggle was favourable to environmental groups like the Natural Resources Defense Council which had fought mightily against a public works approach. The NRDC viewed the principle of polluter pays — that is, strict, joint and several liability on the part of responsible parties — as the essential pre-condition for timely clean-ups freed of the political gamesmanship it associated with public works arrangements.

"The beauty of the Superfund program is that it is off budget," explained the NRDC's Douglas Wolf. "Most of the money that's spent on Superfund clean-ups comes from the private parties, they do the clean-up themselves and the liability standard has a tremendously beneficial effect on business behaviour. People are so scared that they are going to get tagged for liability at their sites or because of their behaviour that they are going to change the way they do business."

However, no sooner had far-reaching new liability clauses been passed in 1986 than a consortium including such insurance firms as Aetna and Crum & Forster and manufacturers like General Electric (a company at the top of the EPA's list of companies with the most Superfund toxic waste sites) and Ruckelshaus's old nemesis Union Carbide formed a Task Group to demonstrate the unworkability of the newly passed amendments that they considered so threatening.

In the summer of 1987, Ruckelshaus (who joined BFI's board of directors that year) travelled to the St. Louis corporate headquarters of Monsanto to discuss marrying the Superfund Alternative Task Group with a coalition he was seeking to establish. A letter on Union Carbide stationery summarized the meeting. Ruckelshaus Associates, for a flat rate of $120,000 to be paid by participating companies for the year 1987, was proposing to develop studies to demonstrate how "seriously flawed" the newly amended Superfund law was.[40]

At a subsequent meeting hosted by Ruckelshaus's partner, a Washington tax lobbyist, a comprehensive draft for proposed major research was laid out. The research was to provide a coalition of insurance, chemical, petroleum and electronic companies, who all had significant Superfund liability, with the analytical raw material with which to co-ordinate public relations efforts, build alliances and demonstrate "that the law is failing because of its structure." One central target was the government's power under Superfund to bring its full resources to bear to identify "potentially responsible parties" and order whichever ones it could identify to clean up a site or, in event of failure to act, sue for treble damages.

Documents concerning this new Coalition on Superfund were leaked to an alarmed NRDC which saw in them evidence of powerful interests dismissing out of hand a "carefully considered Congressional judgement, barely a year old." Furthermore, they feared the Coalition was seeking, through what it assumed would be a series of well-financed, heavily biased studies, to create a self-fulfilling prophecy.[41] For the NRDC, Ruckelshaus's involvement seemed to be the most blatant illustration of the "revolving door" phenomenon. Here was the man they described as "one of America's leading environmentalists," who had "been correctly credited with saving the Superfund program," now appearing to be consorting with the likes of Union Carbide to attack that very program.[42]

In publicizing the documents, the NRDC reaped a harvest of headlines assailing the former EPA chief for trying to soften Superfund law. The Union Carbide vice president (whose leaked memo revealed the Task Force's willingness to join Ruckelshaus's Coalition on Superfund) denied any subversive intent. He portrayed the budding alliance's motives as purely contingent, claiming the program being organized by Ruckelshaus was merely meant to gather information "in case" the Superfund program failed. "We have a two-track approach. One is that Superfund is going to be here forever, so let's make it work, and that's what we're trying very hard to do. The other track is, assuming it doesn't work, let's be ready."[43]

Whatever else it did, the controversy showed that the ultimate decisions about waste management were now being made at the highest levels and that public waste policy was more than ever a by-product of the struggle between powerful vested interests and their political and environmental adversaries.

Fittingly, in the federal election which followed directly on the Coalition on Superfund affair, BFI founder Tom Fatjo and BFI director Ruckelshaus ended up advising George Bush. Fatjo's involvement began when he and Bush were jogging at Fatjo's Houstonian hotel spa, which served as Bush's Texas home. When the presidential candidate suggested his host turn his ideas about small business into a memo, the Texas entrepreneur did. Then, in an effort to raise his own profile, given that he was said to be entertaining parlaying his connections into running for governor of Texas, Fatjo had a ghost writer turn the campaign memo into a series of editorial page opinion pieces which were placed in a number of Texas newspapers.

Fatjo lobbied and won approval from Bush's son for a campaign fund-raiser held at his house with the soon-to-be president in attendance. And, according to *The Houston Post*, he helped orchestrate a video attack on Bush's opponent, Democratic candidate Michael Dukakis. After Bush's triumph, and not long before founding a new waste company called Republic (soon to be taken over by the ubiquitous Canadian Michael DeGroote), Fatjo and an Arab financial backer hosted a series of inaugural functions in Houston and Washington.[44]

As for Ruckelshaus, he advised Bush on environmental policy in 1988, recommended the appointment of William Reilly to head the EPA and, in the month before the election, moved to Houston to take over as chairman and chief executive officer of BFI.

His ascension to the cockpit of a waste monolith mirrored a similar move forced by events on its main rival, WMI, which had sought to give itself a new public persona in the face of accusations of mismanagement, a wide variety of violations of federal and state law, coverup of illegal activities and EPA favouritism in permitting its ocean incineration ship.

Coming fast on weeks of allegations in the regional media, articles in *The New York Times* and *Wall Street Journal* in March 1983 had "created major anxiety in the financial markets."[45] WMI's market capitalization, the value of its total outstanding shares, had dropped $1 billion. [16] Forced into a kind of evolutionary adaptation to the ever changing political situation, WMI had begun placing on its payroll the likes of Joan Bernstein, EPA general counsel under President Carter, and other high-ranking former Department of Justice and EPA officials. The company was seeking a better balance between its drive for global conquest and a purported commitment to making pollution prevention and the enhancement of the environment "the fundamental premises of the company's business."

By retaining (rather than, as others had, trying to kill) regulators, the big two were re-fashioning themselves into enterprises unlike anything the world had known. Ruckelshaus moved to impose his stamp on BFI and, by extension, on the industry. Not unexpectedly as he did, in-house tensions emerged. The culture in which 'Mr. Clean' had been raised and thrived collided with the one in which his subordinates had been formed and made their spectacular mark. As befits a company grossing more than $2 billion a year to perform a service in the public interest, he experimented with zero defect quality-control programs, gathered together for ethical uplift all 350 district managers (employees who filled the same shoes once worn so controversially by Bill Curtis in Pittsburgh) and made the seemingly obvious (but under the circumstances, perhaps revolutionary) innovation of tying bonuses to compliance with environmental laws.

One former executive complained to *Business Week* that Ruckel-shaus's reforms were "goofy" and confided that the only way BFI had grown was "by acquisition, not keeping customers happy."[47] Resistance to the new regime was not only in-house. The company — as we already have seen — faced severe compliance problems in three states and in the words of Chicago Corporation analyst Kay Hahn, BFI "was already too far behind when [Ruckelshaus] arrived."[48]

The former EPA administrator struggled to prove himself a brilliant management tactician. But, for all his stroking of officialdom and local communities, not to mention his bringing on board two of his former EPA chiefs of staff, Ruckelshaus failed to overcome years of accumulated ill will and mistrust. Regulators remained chilly. There was going to be a price to be paid for so many years of obsessive concentration on growth at all costs.

By early 1990, as BFI was faced with the departure of two-thirds of its regional vice presidents and a $3.5-million agreement to settle criminal violations of Ohio's hazardous waste laws, its highest priority was its rating among investors. For once having been admitted to what emeritus professor Abraham Briloff (in his warning about WMI's hazardous accounting practices) had dubbed the Pantheon of growth stocks, failure to keep on fulfilling investors' inflated expectations would not go unpunished.[49]

Under Ruckelshaus, BFI finally conceded failure and, seven years after having acquired CECOS, put the whole misbegotten enterprise on the block, along with its newest acquisition, the aptly named Last Chance, Colorado, hazardous waste facility. By doing this, the firm gave proof, for those for whom proof was necessary, that selling oneself as the solution to industrial pollution was no guarantee that one was not part of the problem.

Company president John Drury joined the exodus of key BFI executives in early 1991, citing "philosophical differences." The editors of *Everyone's Backyard*, the grass roots journal of Citizens' Clearinghouse for Hazardous Wastes, speculated as to whether Ruckelshaus was distancing himself from a private class action lawsuit spearheaded by a Philadelphia law firm charging that BFI and WMI — with the witting participation of senior executives of both companies — had conspired to divide markets between themselves nationwide (see Chapter 7).[50]

Meanwhile, BFI also faced diminished prospects. Such was the forecast that two insiders — the firm's general counsel and its chief financial officer — decided to unload 75,000 shares of their own in August 1991 before Wall Street got word of BFI's anticipated decreased profit levels.[51] On 3 September 1991, when BFI's financial figures were made public, the dismal profit projection finally broke the illusion of ad infinitum growth, sparking a selloff. A nearly $1-billion plunge in BFI's market capitalization provoked a chorus of grousing by analysts. Ruckelshaus and his company — they said — were adrift. *The New York Times* reported "rumblings among analysts that investors would welcome the dismissal of ... William D. Ruckelshaus."[52]

The day after the financial results were released, Bruce Ranck, whose name had surfaced in the class action lawsuit, was appointed to succeed Drury as president. But the profiteering insiders who had got the jump on the company's tumbling share values were less fortunate. Other regional BFI employees were angered by what they saw as an act of disloyalty, and they cannot have been heartbroken when Ruckelshaus had both the senior officers cashiered.[53]

In changing his recommendation from a buy to a sell, Vishnu Swarup, a Prudential Securities' analyst, may have been more right than he realized when in September 1991 he noted that "clearly, there is something beside the economy — something internal — that's causing problems [at BFI]."[54] All the grousing in the world would not change the fact that a bedeviling waste crisis was demanding far more profound solutions than could be provided for by the creation and conquest of a global waste market by a small group of entrepreneurs.

Other analysts saw that BFI, in spite of its chinked armour, would remain a force. Its core business remained "still very, very strong."[55] So long as privatized dumping represented the main option it could not be otherwise. BFI had had an unused landfill capacity of 600 million cubic yards in 1984. By the year 2000, in readiness for another round of regulation-induced shrinkage in available dumping capacity, the company planned on having a U.S. landfill bank of three billion cubic yards, a sufficient supply to meet the entire country's needs for a decade.[56]

Ruckelshaus's dilemma was not unlike the one he had faced during Watergate. This time, however, instead of the commander-in-chief expecting him to do his duty, it was Wall Street. The conundrum his career now posed was inherent in the perverse logic of the waste-profit equation. How does the chief executive officer of a global waste company manage vast waste flows so as to maximize shareholders' investment and, at the same time, fulfil his obligations as a citizen to the future well-being of the planet?

Chapter 4

WMI: The Global Empire

Garbage collecting is the only business we know.
Dean Buntrock, Chairman, Waste Management, Inc., 1977

What is Waste Management: This company is the dominant force in the global waste management industry ... this juggernaut is the leading factor in what is viewed as one of 'the' growth industries of the 1990's ... a happy combination of a cash-flow machine and substantial opportunities.
J. Stanley, Investment Analyst, October 1990

Like BFI, Waste Management, Incorporated fanned out aggressively in every direction and, in becoming the largest waste corporation in the world, led the way in making pollution a major source of profit and growth. In its thirty-year history the company has had to confront repeatedly accusations of asserting its "property rights" over an ever-burgeoning customer base and of environmental depredation by an ever-growing grass roots opposition. Its latest challenges, however, are philosophical and political, and go right to the heart of the American dream. For if hazardous waste is an article of commerce protected by the highest court, then individual states and communities have no right to limit dumping, and WMI, with its friends in the highest federal quarters, can keep profitable charge of the effluent of industrial America.

If BFI was the hare of the garbage race, WMI was its tortoise. While BFI was launched in the 1960s by parvenu Texans, WMI evolved out of a venerable Chicago firm. It never shared BFI's enthusiasm for resource recovery or the tendency of third-ranking Service Corporation of America (SCA) to dabble in other service industries. Its advance was essentially a product of its devotion to the basics of the garbage business — collection and disposal. Yet within a decade of its going public, the Chicago-based waste manager overtook BFI as the world's leading garbage company.

Never a great centre of international finance, Chicago has gained world stature by attending to life's necessities. From rural America flow in the huge quantities of agricultural produce that are the basis of the country's wealth. Chicago transforms them and ships them onwards. It is a world leader in railway transportation, grain trading, livestock and meatpacking. During the day tens of thousands of animals file out of its five hundred acres of stockyards to be slaughtered. Carcasses of cattle and hogs are sent on as lard, fertilizers, glue, margarine and soap. With one foot in the offal of urban life and the other stepping out across the globe, Chicago was an appropriate home for a transnational garbage empire. Indeed, in later years an expanding Laidlaw, and even the hapless Belgium Standard, would establish bases here as well.

WMI could trace its lineage back to the nineteenth century. An old Dutchman named Huizenga travelled by horse and buggy into Chicago every day. On his way home people would ask if he would mind picking up some trash and dumping it at the edge of town. Deciding there might be a good business there, Huizenga purchased another wagon and converted it into a trash buggy. Thus did Chicago get its first garbage company in 1894. Sixty-three years later, an insurance salesman from Boulder, Colorado, came to Chicago to assume the leadership of the family garbage business after the death of his father-in-law. With yearly revenues of $750,000, Ace Scavenger Service operated on a scale typical of the pre-agglomerate era. But Dean Buntrock, who as a teenager had managed his own family's farm implement business in South Dakota, would not be a typical trash collector.

In 1959, two years after arriving in Chicago, Buntrock expanded into neighbouring Wisconsin, starting with the state's largest city and chief industrial centre, Milwaukee. This was a market greatly coveted by Chicago contractors, a number of whom came in with the intention of taking over. The competition became so intimidating that the whole business ended up before the courts. In 1962 a Milwaukee judge found that some Chicago firms were using a mixed bag of monopolistic tricks, including threats and violence (not uncommon in such situations), and ordered a halt to these goings-on. That was also the year Buntrock expanded into Madison, Wisconsin's capital and another market that would involve legal entanglements. An investigation by state trustbusters led to bid-rigging and price-fixing charges, and Buntrock's company engaged the state attorney general's office in a judicial battle that would drag on for years.

By 1965 Dean Buntrock found himself perched at the apex of his business. As founding president of the new trade organization for the country's private refuse collectors and landfill operators, the National Solid Wastes Management Association, Buntrock was now the industry's leading spokesman. He had a voice in Washington where the new waste management laws were being written. His own hauling operations had spread into Florida where H. Wayne Huizenga, his father-in-law's nephew and a descendant of Chicago's original garbage entrepreneur, was driving his own garbage truck. Together Buntrock and Huizenga caught the first swells of the ecological wave. Teaming up in 1968 with another Chicago hauler, Atlas Refuse Disposal, they formed a company whose name quite simply stated their intentions — Waste Management, Incorporated. The next year Tom Fatjo and his Houston associates were trying to corral America's top independent contractors, and a number of major independents — Harry Phillips of Memphis, Ed Drury of Minneapolis, John Vanderveld of Chicago and others — made common cause with them. Dean Buntrock was courted in the offices of E.F. Hutton, the New York stock brokerage firm that brought BFI public. But Buntrock found the Texans' proposal resistible, and his company went on to teach them some lessons in how to build a corporate refuse empire.

Chicago Plan

From the very beginning of WMI's life as a public corporation, its subsidiaries were embroiled with government antitrust lawyers. The continuous, systematic patterns that market conspiracy lawsuits reveal suggest that criminality is not really the issue in these cases. As a Rockefeller biographer pointed out, the struggle against his movement for industrial consolidation was not against criminality but against destiny itself. The garbage business exhibits a similar inevitability, and market conspiracy lawsuits almost always have the quality of futility about them. They do, however, offer the student of the industry a unique opportunity to examine its innermost workings.

The most significant case in which WMI was involved in its early years concerned the massive price-fixing scheme uncovered in the company's home base of Chicago. In 1971, the year Buntrock and Huizenga took WMI public, the Chicago and Suburban Refuse Disposal Corporation was charged with orchestrating a continuing agreement to carve up the greater metropolitan market among its two hundred members. Like National Disposal — BFI's prize acquisition in the Chicago area, as we saw in Chapter 3 — both Ace Scavenger and Atlas Disposal were affiliated with the trade association, and therefore entangled along with dozens of other trash haulers in the net of the state's antitrust complaint. According to the complaint, the conspiracy had been in effect at least since 1965. Since the association's members comprised more than 95 per cent of the local contractors, controlling among them more than 90 per cent of non-public dump sites, in effect the behaviour of the whole private sector was being described.

The most interesting aspect of the state's lawsuit was its description of how contractors engaged in private-sector planning, supposedly an anathema to believers in free enterprise. Apparently the local contractors conspired to fix prices, allocate customers and territories, obstruct, threaten and intimidate non-member contractor, rig predatory pricing and intimidate customers. The price-fixing and customer allocation agreements were perpetuated through privately enforced rules (see Appendix). Besides these rules to implement the "plan," various manoeuvres were undertaken by certain unnamed contractors to block non-members' entry into the greater Chicago area. Attempts were made to influence locals of the Teamsters' union to do what they could to keep outsiders from participating.

What was uncovered was a natural invention allowing contractors to fashion a sound and predictable business. To ensure that a hauler's main asset — his contracts — were not only measurable but transferable it was necessary to conceive of each customer served — each "stop" — as a piece of property. A "stop" was much like a monetary standard in a primitive economy. As oxen and elephants were used as a basis for comparing the wealth of persons or tribes and thus became the standard for measuring the value of other things too, so had "stops" apparently become a measure of comparative value. The Illinois authorities found that "stops" were actually sold or exchanged among certain contractors, with an agreement not to compete being part of the deal. By making sure that entry into each contractor's bailiwick was forbidden, the value of the "stop" was maintained. Competition for contracts would have the effect of lowering the return on a "stop" and thus undermining its value as a transferable and permanent asset. If a business was to be made of collecting garbage, where there was really nothing to distinguish one hauler from another, then the law of "property rights" was an inevitable consequence.

The defendants denied all the substantive allegations, but to avoid a trial the association signed a ten-year consent order agreeing not to violate the Illinois Antitrust Act. A nineteen-page agreement stipulated the specific activities that were prohibited.[1] The association was also fined $50,000 — a piddling sum when measured against the potential gargantuan profits of such self-conferred price-fixing powers.

In the decade covered by the consent order, the whole focus of the industry shifted. Disposal control rather than collection cartels had become the key. That WMI fully understood this new reality was demonstrated not only by its disposal facilities in Chicago but also by its activities at the other end of the Great Lakes, in Metropolitan Toronto.

The Toronto Coup

During the 1970s, the affairs of WMI in the Ontario metropolis were intertwined with those of Norman Goodhead, the former reeve of North York Township and unsuccessful candidate for the chairmanship of Metro Toronto in 1962.[2]

As North York reeve, Goodhead presided over a hectic era of wheeler-dealer real estate development during which his township burgeoned into a full-fledged borough. He was considered by some to be a buccaneer in tailored suits. When he ran for re-election as reeve in 1964, his relationship with the development industry emerged as an issue and he was branded "the darling of the developers." Another issue was his involvement in a business he had worked in since the age of sixteen — garbage.

Soon after his election as reeve in 1959, Goodhead went into partnership with Max Solomon, a big, cigar-smoking man, and other members of the Solomon family in a garbage company called Disposal Services Limited. A Disposal Services subsidiary was awarded untendered contracts to dump refuse at a disposal site owned by the company near the village of Maple, eighteen miles north of Toronto. During the 1964 campaign, the Toronto press raised the question of Goodhead's failure to declare early on in the campaign his personal interest in these council votes.[3] "Mr. Goodhead's duty, we believe, is plain," said *The Toronto Star* in a November 1964 editorial. "He should either dissociate himself entirely from the two companies or they should cease doing business with the township. If he cannot make either sacrifice, he should withdraw from North York politics."

Goodhead answered the charges by portraying himself as the victim of McCarthyite witch-hunters. Nevertheless, the voters of North York unexpectedly refused to re-elect him as reeve. The political career of the small, fast-talking former slum kid from Cabbagetown was over (except for offstage activities as a riding delegate and fundraiser for the Ontario Progressive Conservative Party, then in the midst of its four-decade reign at Queen's Park). From then on he devoted his energies to the garbage business, and it made him rich. Along with the Solomons, he built Disposal Services into one of Metro Toronto's two major haulers. In 1972 the high-flying American agglomerates came into Toronto looking for takeover prospects. BFI acquired Bulk-Lift Systems, Disposal Services' chief rival. And Goodhead and the Solomons accepted an offer for their firm from WMI.

WMI had been on an aggressive buying spree since going public in June 1971. By late 1972 the Chicago company had issued 3,146,137 common shares, and these certificates were used to acquire local subsidiaries all over North America. Both Buntrock and WMI executive Harold Gershowitz, a former executive director of the National Solid Wastes Management Association, were well known in the industry. They knew where to seek out leading operators, and likely prospects were offered the usual deal. In a little over a year, they acquired some seventy-five companies. In taking over Disposal Services, they reckoned that they had acquired one of the continent's premier operations. It was among the largest industrial-commercial waste contractors anywhere, and — given WMI's goal of supplanting public agencies — Goodhead's political connections were not the least of its assets.[4] Thus the value of their prize was enhanced when Goodhead and the Solomons agreed to stay on board.

If WMI had merely bought Disposal Services in 1972, local independents might not have been overly alarmed. But they could foresee that neither the metropolitan nor the provincial government had the will to cope with an approaching garbage crisis. Public dumps were fast approaching their topping-off points. The independents knew that they would be denied access to these sites as municipalities sought to conserve the remaining capacity, and that eventually the public sector would have no space left for itself. In the absence of a public solution, authorities would accept a private one with great relief. And they saw that WMI and its allies were assembling their own landfill capacity.

In line with the statement by one WMI executive that "it's always been our operating philosophy at Waste Management to be in control of our destiny," by the end of 1972 the company had gained control of the few privately owned landfill sites within eighty kilometres of the metropolitan area. Even more ominous were developments relating to the Maple pits, a moonscape of exhausted gravel quarries. The Disposal Services dump, which had embroiled Norman Goodhead in controversy a few years earlier, was one small part of the vast expanse. In September 1972 Goodhead and some partners purchased 683 acres in the Maple pits. A royalty arrangement made the newly acquired space part of Waste Management's potential landfill bank. The Maple pits, according to estimates, was capable of holding some 60 million tons of garbage. Once the entire site was assembled, engineered, permitted by provincial authorities and all the public sites closed, WMI and the Goodhead partnership could look forward to becoming the keepers of all of Metro's wastes for at least a quarter-century.

It was a scheme to rival the great water supply and burial monopolies through which some of the notable English fortunes of the nineteenth century had been accumulated. The dumping fees the consortium of WMI/Goodhead could charge — under the existing unregulated conditions — held promise of enormous windfall profits. And since haulers dumping at another's site do so at a considerable financial disadvantage, success of the strategy would mean that the remaining independent haulers would exist at the sufferance of the consortium. A paramount concern was attracting large enough garbage volumes into the system. Alternative plans, public or private, could only be viewed with hostility. Rearguard actions by the remaining private operators would have to be fought off, and efforts would have to be made to strike a favourable deal with public authorities. The controversy over the Maple pits would drag on for years. Meanwhile, as they endeavoured to establish their control of Metro Toronto's garbage, the waste managers in Oak Brook, Illinois — the Chicago suburb where WMI had installed its corporate headquarters — were also turning their attention much further afield.

The Imperatives of Expansion

Oak Brook was the hub of an increasingly centralized control system. Raw information flowed to the centre from remote terminals. Eyes in the Chicago suburb tracked a far-flung fleet of 2,100 trucks as they wheezed their way along the back alleys and highways of the continent. Each packer's monthly revenues and yardage of hauled refuse were recorded. The local autonomy of company line managers, many of whom had once been their own bosses, was becoming heavily compromised. Men who had been freewheeling independent contractors now lived in the limelight of the computer age. Since many local managers resisted raising prices, head office scheduled the increases and checked incoming data to ensure that recalcitrant field staff obeyed orders.

WMI's ceaseless search for markets dovetailed with the rising clamour for privatization of state-run activity. In many parts of the continent, embryonic forms of municipal enterprise were being nipped in the bud as the profit potential of waste management became increasingly apparent. During 1977 new municipal business was farmed out to the giant contractor in Illinois, Michigan, Wisconsin, Washington state, Arizona, Louisiana, Georgia and Florida. A WMI subsidiary obtained a garbage disposal contract for the Algiers section of New Orleans, comprising 10 per cent of the city's population, and its Recovery 1 plant began extracting ferrous metals from the waste stream for sale to customers. In Milwaukee, a city that had been pounced on by Chicago contractors more than a decade earlier, WMI began transferring municipally collected garbage for processing at a privately operated materials recovery/supplemental fuel plant. With more takeovers of trash collection companies in Missouri, Mississippi, Alabama and the Carolinas, the company further expanded its base.

New legislation concerning liquid and hazardous waste disposal induced the men from Oak Brook to build a network of seep-proof landfills to handle the vast markets the regulations would create. Good sites were as rare as discovery wells. Like oil men before them, Buntrock and Huizenga of WMI bought up sites after others had done the hard work of discovery. Once the sites were located and permitted, the money men and accountants moved in. One 900-acre showcase site they bought in Livingston, Alabama, had been engineered in 1977. The original partners were modern-day wildcatters who stumbled on a government report identifying western Alabama, with its 550 feet of impermeable clay, as one of the country's ten best areas for hazardous waste disposal. One month after they buried their first load, WMI arrived with an offer to purchase, and the landfill site was added to a growing network of burial grounds the agglomerate controlled in Ohio, Louisiana and Texas.

In the mid-1970s, driven by the imperative to keep growing, WMI began looking overseas. New milestones awaited them in improbable corners of the globe. By decade's end they had secured the two largest civic systems contracts ever awarded, both of them farmed out by political regimes free from the pretensions of trust-busters and of pressure from public employees opposed to privatized service delivery.

Riyadh: The Golden Opportunity

In the 1970s there was probably no better place to observe the power money holds than Riyadh, the desert capital of Saudi Arabia. At one time old King Saud and his 125 wives, their houses and their allowances had been a serious drain on the royal exchequer. But when the petroleum-producing states and sheikdoms forged a successful counter-cartel to the oil companies, all that changed. The House of Saud grew wealthier than any other family in history, and the world beat a path to Riyadh. The backwater capital, which the Saudis had long ago captured from a rival tribe, became a boom town. A veritable Middle Eastern Houston arose, a city with government buildings designed by Texans where religious police still patrolled the streets. Limousines flashed by veiled Bedu women. Amid the construction cranes, minarets equipped with loudspeakers announced the call to prayer. From neighbouring Arab countries and as far as India and Pakistan, migrant Moslem labourers streamed in seeking jobs. And from the West came an endless procession of corporate carpetbaggers — banks, munitions companies, giant builders such as Bechtel of San Francisco, aerospace companies such as Boeing and United Technologies, service firms, racing car manufacturers. Each petitioner had a scheme to recycle petrodollars, and by extension help stanch a badly haemorrhaging western financial system.

In a tribal society bound by Islamic law, with neither press nor parliament, those pursuing contracts had to be finely tuned to the nuances of palace politics. More than a thousand princes swelled the king's progress through the court. The supplicants searched for clues that might help them answer the crucial question: Who are the favourites? Only the right princes could guide the humble contractor through the mazes to drink at the royal money fountains. An American consortium submitted the low bid on a billion-dollar telephone deal, but the contract was awarded to Dutch and Swedish interests. The enraged Americans reportedly had the wrong prince as agent. Commissions for delivering the contract were said to total hundreds of millions of dollars.

The Chicago garbage men came to Riyadh in 1977. By then the capital was flowing in every direction from the royal palace, located in the centre of the old town. At the end of the Second World War, the old walled town had held 30,000 souls. In 1977 the wall was gone, and there were 850,000 people living within earshot of the muezzins' cry. Saudi technocrats desired a western-style sanitation service befitting a modern metropolis. If their chaotic capital was to be as clean as the white starched *thaubs* worn by Saudi men, a migrant labour force had to be assembled, put into uniforms, handed brooms and sent forth daily into the streets. Here was the golden opportunity for the agglomerates: Riyadh wanted to establish a private sanitation utility. The Saudis were cash-rich and reportedly prepared to invest $140 billion in new social services.

In the face of Saudi requirements on foreign contracts, WMI entered into a joint venture. Its junior partners were a British service company and the requisite prince of the realm. It was only a decade since Buntrock and Huizenga had established their company firmly in the Illinois and Florida markets, and this new game was heady stuff. "His Highness," WMI informed its shareholders, "consults with and advises the Joint Venture with respect to such matters as conducting operations in Saudi Arabia, personnel and purchasing." Prince Abdulrahman Bin Abdullah Bin Abdulrahman Al-Saud was evidently a prince worthy of WMI's confidence. The partners secured a five-year, $240-million deal. WMI's share of the profits was 60 per cent, while the courtier took 24 per cent for his troubles.

Such was the high price of doing business in the Kingdom of Saudi Arabia.

The project itself was in the best tradition of the English absentee plantation owner, arranging for indentured Oriental labourers to be transported to his Caribbean sugar estate. WMI threw together a functional city on a thirty-acre site at Riyadh. In a marshalling yard in Beltsville, Maryland, thousands of pieces of equipment were gathered — Heil Mark IV rear-loaders with Detroit Diesel engines, cesspool pumpers, tanker trailers, pickup trucks, dump trucks, fuel trucks, wrecker-tow trucks and containers of various kinds. From Baltimore all was shipped to Saudi Arabia's east-coast port of Damman. Meanwhile, a work force was assembled from the urban poor of Bombay, where newspaper employment ads brought tens of thousands of responses. More than 2,000 workers sailed from India to the joint venture's Main Public Cleansing Center.

The WMI partnership's duties involved building the maintenance and repair depots, landfill improvements, transfer stations, the housing, health and recreational facilities for the labourers, and attending to daily street cleaning and refuse collection and disposal. In April 1977 various princes assembled for a brief ceremony at the thirty-acre Cleansing Center. The Governor of Riyadh Province cut a ribbon. And soon afterwards the 2,500-man work force went into action. It was all quite revolutionary for many locals. Few of their parents had ever seen a car. Now hydraulically operated garbage behemoths were making daily rounds. Supervisors and crews, often speaking through interpreters, had to explain the use of a garbage can to many householders.

Far from the desert capital, WMI's shares received a fillip with news of the Saudi deal. Chicago's waste managers had now established themselves as the industry's trend-setting frontrunners. From a low of around $7 in 1976, WMI's shares rose to $17 by the summer of 1977, significantly ahead of broad-based measures of stock market performance. Observing this renewed interest in WMI, one investment banking firm's vice president wrote: "Waste Management, smaller than BFI in total revenues and net income, has established itself as the industry's premier company in the opinion of many Wall Street analysts ... Perhaps the most challenging opportunity is its joint-venture contract to provide sanitation services for the city of Riyadh ... [The] contract is the largest of its kind." Stock market analyst Roland Williams, a close observer of the industry, said that WMI "made a ton of money because a lot of the money was paid up front" and invested profitably back home. But direct financial gain was only part of the benefit the company derived from the Riyadh contract. In Oak Brook the Saudi Arabian deal was seen as "the leading edge of expanded international activity." WMI now had a privatized model it could sell to other municipalities, wherever in the world garbage contracts came up for bidding.

Two years after it won the Riyadh contract, WMI landed another plum in the different but no more democratic political climate of Argentina, then under the control of a ruthless military junta. Again with a local ally, it secured a deal to operate a municipal waste transfer system in Buenos Aires, and like its penetration of Riyadh this deal was greeted enthusiastically in the industry. Adding his voice to the chorus of approval was Senator Jennings Randolph, a Democrat from West Virginia and chairman of the Senate Committee on Environment and Public Works. A picture in an industry news organ showed the jowly seventy-seven-year-old senator beaming as Dick Hanneman of the National Solid Wastes Management Association introduced him to two Argentine officials. Well primed to the far-reaching significance of the Buenos Aires contract, Senator Randolph noted for posterity, "Buenos Aires joins a growing number of communities throughout the free world which are turning to a public/private partnership for the management of their solid wastes. This development parallels similar conversions from municipal to contract collection ... in U.S. communities from coast to coast."[5] Since all political parties in Argentina were officially banned at the time the senator was making this assertion, to what extent this new model represented the popular will is not recorded.

Staking out Territory

Having become the world's largest garbage company by putting into practice a total-systems approach to refuse removal in distant corners of the world, WMI now looked forward to introducing similar systems back home. It remained an open question, however, whether this approach would be applicable to North American municipalities. Thus, throughout the 1970s and early 1980s, WMI continued to rely on more familiar forms of market dominance in its American operations.

The consent decree signed by 200 Chicago haulers and their trade association in 1971 did not end matters as far as Illinois antitrust officers were concerned. They continued to monitor the industry even as it was transformed by the agglomerates. In 1975 the state attorney general's office investigated WMI for possible monopoly activity, though it did not find sufficient evidence to file a formal complaint. In early 1979 it reopened its investigation on a broader scale, looking at the company's activities in both solid and liquid wastes. Though its staff economist determined that a lawsuit against WMI based on a theory of monopolization or on an attempt to monopolize would not be successful, the antitrust division received a number of calls from rivals claiming that WMI charged discriminatory prices to unaffiliated haulers for the use of its dumpsites. The calls were checked out by the antitrust division, and no action was taken.

As the 1970s progressed, the Big Three American waste managers increasingly came to dominate the Chicago market. The attorney general's office held out the possibility that WMI had restrained trade through temporary predatory pricing policies in various submarkets throughout northern Illinois. By 1982, when Laidlaw joined the major American waste firms in the greater Chicago area, one Illinois trustbuster concluded that if left unchecked, the struggle of the giants over future market shares could result in the creation of a natural monopoly through the control of landfill banks.

In May 1980 a grand jury in Atlanta, Georgia, added to mounting evidence of the exercise of "property rights."[6] An indictment was handed down alleging that all three American majors were treating their accounts — which were worth millions — as private property. According to the indictment, an agreement between the defendants and unnamed co-conspirators for allocating customers and regulating prices had been in existence since 1974. BFI, WMI and SCA were charged with not competing for each other's business, discouraging established customers from changing contracts by means of intentionally high bids or quotations, and using identical price lists for certain potential customers. While such activity made perfect economic sense and was in the best interests of the companies' shareholders, it flew in the face of both free market principles and competition law. After company lawyers successfully challenged the indictment, on the grounds that the jury selection process had unlawfully underrepresented minorities, an appeal court put the case back on the rails again.

Meanwhile in fast-growing Gwinnet County, eighteen miles from downtown Atlanta, independent contractor Ed Grove was feeling the majors' squeeze. To defend his franchise he was building his own political base, with the avowed intention of countering the base established by WMI. A year after the major waste corporations were indicted, he described the relationship prevailing among the big three in the following terms: "They don't compete against each other. I think it's a basic understanding. They don't bother each other."

In January 1983 BFI and SCA pleaded *nolo contendere*, thus giving themselves up to the court. Each received a $350,000 fine, and SCA's local manager and BFI's former manager were sent to jail. The accused WMI subsidiary chose to stand trial, but was no more successful in parrying the charges. After a two-week trial, a jury found against both the company and the executive who had joined with the others in the carve-up conspiracy. A fine and a prison term were handed out in late February 1983.

Ed Grove's words didn't do justice to the complexity of the majors' territorial behaviour. As corporate creatures trying to consolidate as they grew, they each only had so much energy. Whatever was expended butting against sister multi-nationals was not available for going after independents. So peace was often as good a tactic as war. On a North American scale, the industry was being shaped by major waste firms into an oligopoly with a fringe of lesser players, but there was as yet no final agreement on its ultimate form. As in other fields of corporate endeavour, even very big companies were occasionally takeover targets for still bigger ones. In 1977, for instance WMI made an unsuccessful run at third-ranking SCA; a year later BFI picked up the fourth-ranked company, Brenner Industries, with operations mainly in the Carolinas, Virginia, and West Virginia. And for the right offer, eighth-ranked Theta Systems — which later sold out to Canada's Laidlaw — was available.

In 1973 a senior WMI executive was asked whether his company looked upon any one section of the country as its preferred hunting grounds. "To put it more directly, would you raid the henhouse in Texas, near BFI territory?" the interviewer wanted to know. The answer in so many words, was yes. It was soon backed up in deed. By the early 1980s WMI was Dallas's leading hauler of containerized refuse, and possessed a large market share of BFI's stamping ground, Houston.

With their national perspective, Washington's competition overseers watched how the industry was daily becoming more concentrated. Since 1971 WMI had been growing by 48 per cent a year. At the end of 1980, when WMI proposed to buy another big hunk of the business, the Department of Justice was roused to action. A civil antitrust suit was filed, and a temporary injunction was sought prohibiting WMI's acquisition of the New York City-based EMW Ventures and its subsidiary Waste Resources Corporation. With a presence in ten states and sanitary landfills in Pennsylvania, Missouri and Texas, Waste Resources had succeeded Brenner as the fourth largest garbage company in the United States. Even without this merger WMI, now calling itself the world leader, was doing over half a billion dollars of disposal annually.

The federal lawsuit to prevent the takeover focused on the Texas markets. Claiming that the deal would substantially lessen competition in Dallas and Houston, it estimated that WMI's buying of EMW would have two specific results. The newly merged company would command 67 per cent of the revenues in both submarkets — front-end and roll-off — of the Dallas pickup trade, and a tight oligopoly would be established not only in commercial refuse collection in Dallas but in Houston's front-end markets as well. However, the restraining order was denied, and in February 1981 WMI acquired EMW/Waste Resources for 957,312 of its common shares.

By now, not only had the new scale of the industry begun to push it far beyond the pale of strong-arm types, but it was providing the majors with new means to elbow aside regional rivals. Following WMI's acquisition of Chem-Nuclear Systems Incorporated — a transporter of liquid industrial, radioactive and PCB wastes — a Chicago-based hauler, Mr. Frank Incorporated, launched a private antitrust lawsuit alleging the control of Chem-Nuclear's landfills in Michigan and Indiana would have a "chilling" monopolistic effect. The majors' utility-like dominance was portrayed in Mr. Frank's litany of the forms of discrimination experienced by the independents. The complaint claims that WMI "has forced or attempted to force major generators [of liquid wastes] to enter into 'national contracts' for the disposal of wastes before Waste Management would dispose of any of their waste at all. Since certain of their wastes had to be disposed of by Waste Management, there was great pressure to sign the national contracts." The complaint goes on to allege that once national disposal contracts were signed, WMI salesmen used them to pressure the client's local divisions to have WMI handle their hauling needs as well. Two years later, WMI settled with Mr. Frank, agreeing to pay the independent contractor $750,000 as well guaranteeing the company an equal amount of business annually during a four-year period.

Wall Street had good reason to be bullish about Waste Management in 1981. The company was about to open the world's largest landfill facility north of Toronto. Company packers were already working along the five miles of interlocking basins and docks that made up the great port of Buenos Aires. With Getty Synthetic Fuels, WMI was mining one of its Illinois dumps for methane gas. A contract had been secured in Caracas, and low bids were in for others in Cordoba, Argentina, and the Saudi Arabian port city of Jeddah, where WMI's packers supplanted the goats and pariah-dogs that had been sovereigns of the local refuse streams. Although the Saudis choose BFI when the Riyadh contract came up for renewal in 1982 — influenced, according to one Wall Street analyst, by the extent of WMI's profits on the original deal — they allowed WMI to console itself with the contract for the port city.

The Toxic Garbage Business

In New York City, investment analysts recommended continued accumulation of WMI stock. Its premium-priced shares — selling at twenty-one times earnings — were sufficiently alluring to tempt major rivals into mergers. The big EMW/Waste Resources deal was quickly followed by an attempt to take over Rollins Environmental Services, the country's fourth largest hazardous waste manager. Had the proposed $53-million buy-out materialized then, it would not only have provided Waste Management with a hedge against the possible obsolescence of its own landfill sites for toxic materials but would also have given it more than 40 per cent of the hazardous disposal capacity in the United States.

But close observers of the industry had doubts about the garbage majors' potential in the field of hazardous wastes. *Chemical Week* found WMI's recent acquisition activity noteworthy, but it still had misgivings. Even the Rollins takeover would not have provided WMI with the latest technology. The ocean-going incineration ship *Vulcanus*, which the men from Oak Brook bought to burn PCBs (industrial chemicals suspected of causing cancer and birth defects) in the Gulf of Mexico 370 miles south of Mobile, could be rendered obsolete (though never soon enough for certain environmental and community groups) by new detoxification developments. New forms of bacteria being cultivated to consume toxic compounds and new reduction processes to clean up the production of polypropylene plastics would inevitably compete over the longer run with WMI's antediluvian sites. In hazardous waste handling, the originators themselves rather than rival haulers were what the waste majors had to fear.

Chemical waste management was subject to a further unpredictable element — the public's opinion. In spite of worries about unemployment and plant closings, polls suggested increasing popular support for tough environmental laws, a sentiment the new Reagan administration misread. Environmentalism was hardly Reagan's strong suit, and his policies could only exacerbate mistrust for the waste disposal industry. Ironically, a pro-business government bent on wholesale deregulation could only undermine a business that was the child of regulation.

Having endorsed President Jimmy Carter in his 1980 re-election bid, the leadership of the big eight environmental groups moved to the opposing camp when he lost. No olive branches were offered. And as the number of enforcement cases which the Reagan Environmental Protection Agency filed with the Department of Justice fell, the environmentalists went to the courts and used their newsletters to mobilize opposition. The media adopted the environmentalists' views in their coverage of the agency.[7] On network television and the front pages of important dailies, local protest stirred the political process into furious activity. EPA administrator Anne Gorsuch Burford, a Reagan appointee, found herself the object of ridicule as she veered too far from the bipartisan consensus favouring strict environmental protection. When she refused to hand over to Congress files which the president had ordered withheld, she was cited for contempt.

The new dispensation of the Reagan era was interpreted as a deliberate attempt to give industrial polluters a break, but the poisoning of America had hardly begun with Ronald Reagan. The common ecological heritage had long suffered from industrial abuse. In the post-Watergate era, however, the waste disposal problem emerged as a pre-eminent issue, even providing one dramatist with a metaphor for the country's psychic state. Along with several

congressional committees, the press inquired into possible mismanagement and manipulation of the Superfund, the program for cleaning up abandoned toxic dumps. For many the spirit now prevailing
behind the agency's battlements was contained in a memo uncovered in a senior EPA official's computer file. It accused the EPA's
general counsel of "alienating the primary constituents of this Administration, the business community."[8]

Further inquiry begat greater paranoia. Subpoenaed EPA documents were shredded. Appointment calendars and telephone logs
contained apparent erasures. One congressman, with a sense for
historical analogy, dubbed the spreading scandal "Sewergate." To
what extent Reagan's EPA appointees had been sent in as a wreck-
ing crew remained a matter of partisan controversy. But what
seemed incontestable was that few issues were less suited to the
president's free enterprise prescriptions than hazardous (or, for that
matter, any) waste burial. Even libertarians would agree that this
was a problem the market was not intended to solve. "All the
markets can do is make matters worse," argued *The New Republic*,
"by punishing those companies that spend on what the Constitution
calls the general welfare."[9] William Ruckelshaus, who would soon
head BFI, was brought back temporarily to replace the disgraced
Anne Gorsuch Burford and to restore the credibility of the EPA, if
in no other eyes than those of its own employees.

The toxic garbage problem was escalating beyond control. The
United States alone annually produced nearly 60 million tons.
Every year Quebec, Ontario, Alberta and British Columbia contributed another 3 million tons. One often-quoted professor of occupa-
tional and environmental medicine scoffed at the $1.6 billion of
public monies already set aside to decontaminate the sickening
dumps. He reckoned it could cost $200 billion — an amount ap-
proaching the U.S. defence budget.[10]

Within private disposal economics there is embedded an irreduc-
ible trade-off between corporate profits (short run) and health costs
(long run). As a consequence even the most advanced corporate
landfills are politically vulnerable, and, not surprisingly, Chemical
Waste Management Incorporated (CWM), WMI's hazardous waste
arm, found itself in endless skirmishes with community groups.
One 1983 episode highlighted the clash of interests. During the
battle over CWM's Denver site, locals refused to believe their water
supplies would never be contaminated. A housewife who had
formed a group to protest the noxious landfill was chased through

the streets at high speeds and had a smoke bomb planted in her car.[11]

As always the stakes were high. The state-of-the-art facility near Denver was a regional monopoly serving both local industry and waste generators in five other states which lacked their own licensed depositories. Many Rocky Mountain industries faced skyrocketing costs if forced to use alternative sites in Oklahoma and Texas. But community pressure grew until Governor Richard Lamm accused the company of covering up a leaking evaporation pond.[12] After the state legislature awarded the county concerned control over landfill approvals, the Colorado Supreme Court was obliged to shut down the disputed dump until the local commissioners decided to reopen it. WMI was expected to lobby hard with state lawmakers for an exemption from the new regime of community control.[13]

Meanwhile, the tankers headed out of state carrying WMI's injured reputation with them. In response to an inquiry, Lamm informed his Texas counterpart: "It is the state's position that CWM's corporate management philosophy and attitude toward regulatory attempts have not been in the best interests of Colorado."[14] WMI, however, was hardly the sole villain of the piece. The horrors of chemical garbage were rooted in a longstanding aversion to public solutions for public problems.

Newspaper editorialists continued to look forward to some failsafe mix of regulation and market incentive, even as their reporters attacked the most blue-chip of private waste managers. In early 1983, for instance, *The New York Times* ran a front-page story about WMI's toxic empire, which sent company shares plunging (albeit temporarily). With material drawn from government documents, court records and the hostile commentary of former employees, the article piled accusation upon accusation. Seven states, it said, had charged the company with violating laws and regulations, had levied fines, or had taken other actions to force compliance or to halt company operations. The company admitted "a small grain of truth" to the charge that they had illegally dumped Canadian wastes in Ohio, but insisted all the others were "ludicrous" when seen in proper perspective.[15]

But even on its home turf where one might expect the most rigorous adherence to disposal regulations, there were troubling revelations. One rival toxic waste manager raised the old property rights spectre, drawing attention to the inherent conflict between acceptable disposal practices and competitive advantage. Its civil antitrust suit alleged WMI (which denied the charges) had used illegal hazardous dumping methods to acquire a monopoly in the Chicago area. In another local matter, WMI had supposedly dumped 400,000 gallons of toxic wastes without a permit. The Illinois attorney general, in reference to further charges of withholding information about toxic chemicals WMI was dumping, was quoted as saying that "this cover-up of illegal activities is a case of utter corporate irresponsibility," and his subordinate concluded that WMI's real motive was its pocketbook.[16]

Industry apologists downplayed this eruption of charges. In the aftermath of *The New York Times* exposure, giant brokerage houses were dispensing far different investment advice about WMI, but some Wall Street analysts saw in the allegations of anticompetitive practices little more than aggressive growth strategies "that are not uncommon among industry giants." At most they conceded that in growing so fast the major companies may have acquired some dumps with engineering problems. But if a firm could be, as WMI claimed, on the cutting edge of disposal technology, with investments in waste control facilities greater than combined investments of the states laying charges against it, and still be constantly at odds with lawmakers and citizens, the whole industry was being questioned. Could competing private waste managers ever be expected to satisfy community standards in handling industrial poisons?

While liquid waste remained at best an uncertain business, in the area of solid waste collection and disposal the situation of the majors was considerably more secure. By 1981 WMI estimated that it was serving ten million people worldwide. From his art-filled headquarters in Oak Brook a satisfied Chairman Buntrock commented on his company's number-one status by saying that "it is a position we have worked long and hard to attain and one we intend to keep." WMI's 175 municipal contracts were evidence that the monopoly practices lawsuits had not dissuaded city governments from dealing with the big contractors. In Phoenix, for instance, allegations that WMI had carved up the market didn't prevent the city from contracting-out to the company. It gave a WMI subsidiary more than 500 apartment complexes and the collection of loose yard debris, large appliances and other uncontained waste materials from 64,000 homes.

Some investment advisers already saw where the whole process was heading. Without the political will or imagination to invent new public agencies to manage wastes, municipalities would lay the basis for private utilities. And although the waste majors didn't like to think of themselves as utilities — a word that implied public regulation — they were already halfway there. "Their municipal waste business is almost like a utility," the knowledgeable analyst Roland Williams told *Chemical Week*. "They are well entrenched and there is virtually no possibility of someone taking their markets away."[17] As the waste managers came to resemble the local telephone or gas company in each urban market, the remaining trash-carting independents, who had dominated the industry only a little more than a decade earlier, were now a dying breed.

The Spectre of State Rights

The dynamic was changing so rapidly that in the next decade WMI would become a veritable mutual fund offering a broad spectrum of commercialized opportunities ranging from the parent firm itself to those in which it came to hold interests, such as the incineration company Wheelabrator, the asbestos removal company Brand, and prospectively, Waste Management International. The international arm operated in Europe as well as in Asia, where its alliances gave perfect expression to the catholicity of capitalism. In Hong Kong WMI had a partnership with communist China, while in Indonesia Dean Buntrock's firm had entered into a co-venture with a son of the murderously anti-communist President Suharto.

With every new round of environmental regulation, WMI looked forward to the accelerated withdrawal of lesser competitors as the company came to mirror aspects of the monolithic public service model it sought to replace. Increasingly, in its quest to dominate a globalized market, WMI would find itself inciting into existence an assembled opposition of citizens. Informal grass roots groups came together in places as distant as Kettleman City, California, Saint-Etienne-des-Gres, Quebec, and Forbach, France, to defend themselves from WMI's plans to include their communities in its globe-girdling waste treatment and disposal enterprise. This popular reaction promised to raise a whole range of constitutional issues involving the rights and duties of citizens and local governments in the defence of the environment.

Through the 1980s and into the 1990s, WMI, like BFI, would continue to earn its main profits from solid waste. But in terms of a larger strategy, management was — as one analyst tellingly stated it — "aggressively moving the company (principally through acquisition) into leadership positions in any developing area of global waste management where regulatory trends will support the superior growth and returns that the company long has enjoyed in its core North American solid waste operations. Politicians show a clear tendency to control this increasingly popular service via a thicket of regulations, dovetailing nicely with [the] company's proven ability to *shape ... the complex regulatory schemes that crimp most of the fragmented competition.*"[18]

This analyst went on to characterize WMI as "a happy combination of cash-flow machine and substantial opportunities to expand in its existing business."[19] At the centre of this happy combination was a many-tentacled legion of lobbyists, former regulators and public relations consultants working to shape the political environment so that every new regulation captured larger and larger waste (and cash) flows for the company.

From the industry's viewpoint, one of the crucial functions performed by regulators was the maintenance of the sanctity of the national and, where it suited its purposes, the international waste market. Any local attempts to defy an unbounded commerce in waste and elevate other values over those of free trade were met by determined corporate opposition.

In the U.S., where one southern state after another began reacting against being turned by "market" forces into one of America's dumping grounds, various legislative initiatives were proposed including import bans, differential taxes and even an eleven-state southern waste compact. From the perspective of firms like WMI, these trends, unless they could be controlled, foreshadowed the outbreak of a hazardous waste civil war.

North Carolina fired an early shot in this conflict when it challenged the power of the waste industry with Bill 114, a law to restrict what commercial hazardous waste facilities could dump into its rivers and streams. This bill had disrupted plans by Laidlaw's GSX Chemical Services to pour millions of dollars into a regional facility on the Lumber River. GSX quickly returned fire, joining with an industry trade association, the Hazardous Waste Treatment Council (HWTC), in petitioning Washington in 1987 to take away the state's authority to operate its hazardous waste regulatory program. They claimed the state was exceeding federal safety standards and thus illegally usurping federal authority. The ensuing round of salvos momentarily illuminated the hot pursuit by industry executives and lobbyists, behind closed doors, of the perfect fit between an unfettered market and new regulation.

Environmentalists and even federal legislators were stunned by the vigour with which the EPA moved in support of the industry against North Carolina.[20] Reasoning that Bill 114 had no basis in health or environmental protection and thus amounted to a bar against the constitutionally guaranteed right to move goods (waste included) across state lines, the regulators opened hearings to determine whether the agency should withdraw North Carolina's authority to control hazardous-waste disposal.

According to Velma Smith of the Environmental Policy Institute, EPA staffers had confided to her that the federal action against North Carolina was meant to "send a message to other states."[21] But the political reaction was so severe that the EPA administrator had to give in to Congress and drop his case.

This was a positive act from the viewpoint of the grass roots movement, for the EPA action would have placed all states at the mercy of the bottom lines of corporate head offices. However, for WMI and the rest of an industry which relied "heavily on EPA authority to overcome the community opposition it encounters when siting a waste treatment plant," the North Carolina precedent spelled trouble, and was regarded as a grave threat.[22]

One Greenpeace activist gained new insight into just how irksome a states'-rights approach was to private waste managers at an April 1989 EPA-sponsored conference. The meeting was attended almost exclusively by the waste disposal and generating industries and regulatory officials. As he later reported to colleagues, "these trends have WMI climbing the walls — they call it the 'Balkanization' of hazardous waste policy among the states."[23] Furthermore, senior industry executives wanted the EPA "to crack down — and fast" on all talk of regional waste authorities.[24]

The previous month, unknown to the Greenpeace toxics campaigner, Buntrock and other WMI executives had had what soon was to become a controversial meeting with William Reilly, the new EPA administrator who had been recommended to President Bush for the job by BFI's Bill Ruckelshaus. The president of the National Wildlife Federation (on whose board Buntrock sat), who acted as intermediary, arranged a March 1989 breakfast between his friend Reilly and WMI to discuss the implications of the latest affront to a sovereign national waste market. This time the offending party was not North but South Carolina. The Palmetto State had just banned the dumping inside its borders of the hazardous wastes of thirty-two states.

Though the U.S.'s foremost environmental regulator later offered varying explanations of the purpose of his breakfast with the managers of the world's foremost waste disposal company, no one disputes that at the time of the meeting the industry considered that Reilly's predecessor had — as the HWTC's general counsel put it — "cracked under pressure from our opponents."[25] In early 1989, GSX and the HWTC had filed suit a second time against the EPA to do something about North Carolina. A WMI briefing paper that was handed to Reilly at the breakfast described North Carolina as "the first visible domino" in a "full-tilt stampede of states disallowing facility development and resisting interstate waste transport."[26]

The paper portrayed South Carolina's ban as the next domino and predicted Alabama (site of WMI's Emelle facility which received 17 per cent of all the commercially landfilled hazardous wastes in the U.S.) would "probably approve" similar bans on the import of wastes. "Proponents of these measures (in the Alabama legislature) are citing EPA's apparent acquiesence in the North and South Carolina situations," the WMI memorandum stated. "There is only one solution here: EPA must break its silence immediately. If EPA emphatically restates its opposition to these State actions ... cooler heads in the state legislatures will have something to rely upon."[27]

Three weeks later, Reilly reversed an important national environmental policy and ordered resumption of the hearings into North Carolina's waste management authority under federal hazardous waste law. Almost immediately, two well-known EPA whistleblowers, Hugh Kaufman and William Sanjour, lodged a formal in-house complaint against their boss, arguing that "Waste Management and Browning-Ferris ... have a strong and abiding vested interest in overthrowing the North Carolina statute. They are weary of dealing with local citizens and they want to send a message to other States which have passed or are contemplating passing similar legislation, which may retard the growth of their industry, that they cannot beat 'city hall' or the hazardous waste management industry."[28]

The whistle-blowers went on to charge Reilly with having violated EPA ethics by arbitrarily and capriciously having overthrown "a laboriously crafted EPA policy" as a result of WMI's special pleadings.[29] Three months later, the EPA inspector general's office cleared Reilly of any misconduct.[30] But the matter did not rest. In October 1989, another whistle-blower, this time a special assistant to the EPA's assistant inspector general, fired off a memo to U.S. congressman John Dingell complaining that the ethics investigation appeared to have violated professional and EPA standards.

J. Richard Wagner, a federal criminal investigator for more than sixteen years, charged Reilly with staging his own investigation. Reilly had been quoted in the *Winston-Salem Journal* as saying he indeed had been lobbied at the breakfast but that assertion seemed in conflict with his subsequent claim to EPA investigators that the meeting was purely "social in nature." Wagner asked in his twenty-four-page letter: "Given that Reilly is the head of EPA (apparently using official time for the meeting), and that WMI is the largest waste management firm in the world, how could the meeting be social in nature? If Administrator Reilly is to be believed, it would seem that everyone except himself had an agenda for the March 16, 1989 meeting."[31]

Dean Buntrock told in-house EPA investigators that WMI "has no business interests in North Carolina and it would not be a matter that he or his staff would want to discuss."[32] Reilly later did admit to *The Amicus Journal* of the Natural Resources Defense Council that North Carolina had come up at the breakfast but that his real motive in re-opening hearings into the state's right to manage wastes under federal law was a desire for "an educational instrument, a way to generate more information on an issue that is rising all across the country."[33]

"In plain terms, it smells of cover-up," concluded Dr. Peter Montague of the indispensable grass roots newsletter *Rachel's Hazardous Waste News*. Montague went on to add the "American people deserve an independent inquiry by a special prosecutor."[34]

For WMI, however, the focus soon shifted to Alabama where its interests were much more immediately affected. Hazardous waste shipments to WMI's Chemwaste (CWM) facility at Emelle had risen from about two hundred million pounds in 1978 to more than one billion pounds by 1988. By the following year, of the 40,000 truckloads of wastes transported to Emelle, an estimated 35,000 originated outside the borders of Alabama.

Based on its survey of customer reports filed by CWM in 1987, *The Birmingham News* identified the twelve most dangerous chemicals being buried in the five-square-mile sand and gravel layered trenches of Selma chalk. This chemical catalogue was like an X-ray of the invisible toxic life of our economy. It included a lethal brew of electroplating cyanides, insecticides, larvacides as well as carbon disulfide (used to make rayon and cellophane) and arsenic acid (used to make glass and defoliants and to treat wood).

The wastes were created by a who's who of American industry: General Motors, Ford, Exxon, IBM, Mobil, General Electric, Chrysler, Texaco, Du Pont, Phillip Morris. Thirty-one of the U.S.'s largest forty companies, along with twenty-five Air Force bases, twenty-two Coast guard stations, twenty-two Army forts or ammunition plants, six Veterans' Hospitals and other assorted customers, answered the roll call of patrons of Emelle.[35]

Grass roots activists seeking legislation to limit waste being imported from out of state were forced to confront the growing linkage of the waste issue with economic and demographic conditions of the host community. Dumps not only meant jobs for poor, underclass communities in waste company towns such as Emelle and Kettleman Hills, California (a San Joaquin Valley community of Latino farm workers where WMI's Chemwaste wanted to build a major incinerator), but with the "New Federalism" of the Reagan and Mulroney era, more and more financial responsibility for protecting the health and well-being of citizens was devolving on local government.[36]

More than ever, the issue of control over waste flows became bound up with the question of control over the revenues (often what economists call monopoly rents) which derived from disposing of them. Reacting to a threatened Texas "solution" which would export 40,000 tons of PCBs from a toxic-waste site near Houston to Emelle, the state of Alabama obtained an injunction which a federal judge then overturned. But state legislators persisted, creating a blacklist prohibiting twenty-two states without their own toxic waste facilities from using Emelle. Finally, in April 1990, they passed, and Governor Guy Hunt signed, a landmark piece of legislation intended to wrest absolute control out of the hands of WMI.

Act No. 90-326 did three things. It imposed discriminatory tipping fees: a $25 per ton base fee on all wastes; and a $72 per ton additional fee on all imported wastes. As well, it included a "cap" provision making the amount of waste commercially dumped in 1990 the permanent ceiling for subsequent years. According to *Waste Tech News*, the state levy "halved the flow of hazardous waste to CWM's facility in Emelle, Ala., while raising operating costs by $34 million."[37]

Faced with a potential annual loss of millions of dollars, CWM challenged the Act's constitutionality. The governor filed a counterclaim. On 28 February 1991, a trial judge held the base fee and cap provisions to be valid but declared the additional fee a violation of the Commerce Clause of the U.S. Constitution. CWM appealed the former finding and Alabama, doing likewise for the latter, argued it had not been needlessly obstructing interstate commerce. Such were the scientific and technological uncertainties of this magnitude of landfilling that any miscalculation could result in a public health or environmental disaster. In the view of the state, Emelle was "a huge technological experiment. Alabama and its citizens are the guinea pigs."[38] Post-closure costs to be picked up by Alabama's tax-payers (and to which out-of-state generators would contribute through the proposed additional fee) were projected possibly to add up to a billion dollars — or more.[39]

The Alabama Supreme Court, in working out its position, recognized that local concerns about the permeability of the Selma Group Chalk Formation and potential leachate leakage were "important on a human time scale as opposed to a geological time scale." There always would be uncertainty about the chalk's faults and fractures and periodic checks on monitoring wells would be required — forever. In dealing with the perpetual surveillance aspects of the CWM facility, the court, without saying so, was underscoring the similarity between the long-term financial liability of hazardous and nuclear waste facilities. "Although it will be necessary to monitor, regulate, maintain (including the pumping, collection, storage, transportation and disposal of leachate from the trenches), and secure the facility forever, CWM has made no provision for the payment of such costs beyond a period of thirty years after closure."[40] According to the court, CWM's own expert estimates of annual costs of monitoring Emelle ranged from a low of $100,000 to a high of $1.5 million.[41]

The high state court took the position that landfilling is a perpetually threatening policy and disagreed with CWM's allegation that Alabama's benchmark limitations on future dumping levels were in conflict with three federal statutes. In terms of the Resource Conservation and Recovery Act (RCRA), the U.S.'s primary federal law regulating hazardous wastes by means of a cradle-to-grave regulatory program, the court argued that the cap provision actually conformed to the spirit of federal law. For by limiting future in-flows into Emelle, the state was providing an indispensable mecha-nism to stimulate the search by waste generators for alternatives other than landfilling "and this is exactly what Congress empha-sized in RCRA."[42]

Furthermore, in taking on the constitutional issue, the Alabama justices raised a crucial point. "The Supreme Court of the United States has not said that hazardous waste is an article of commerce," observed Justice Shore in upholding the lower court on all but its additional fee ruling.[43] Judge Shore held that the state's differential dumping charge "was merely asking the states that are using Ala-bama as a dumping ground for hazardous wastes to bear some of the costs for the increased risk they bring to the environment and the health and safety of the people of Alabama."[44]

The philosophical quality which the conflict had begun to take on was reflected in the tone of the concurring opinion of Justice Houston. "If the United States Supreme Court holds that waste containing poisonous chemicals that can cause cancer, birth defects, genetic damage, blindness, crippling, and death is an article of commerce protected by the Commerce Clause of the Constitution, then I am bound by that ruling under the Supremacy Clause of Article VI of the United States Constitution. Alabama lost that battle over 125 years ago; however, I do not believe that such waste is an article of commerce protected by the Commerce Clause, and I do not believe that the Alabama Supreme Court is bound by the decision of any *other* federal court on this issue."[45]

Because other states, including Ohio and Louisiana, were also on deck, considering similar bans, the U.S. Supreme Court agreed to hear a petition challenging Alabama and its high court by CWM (and numerous trade groups representing much of industrial Amer-ica) in April 1992. This hearing before the highest court would be made against the backdrop of political gridlock in Congress where activists (often without the sympathy of national environmental organizations) were pressing federal legislators to grant local gov-ernments the right to say no to waste imports. By early 1992 at least three dozen bills that would give states such authority were making the rounds in the U.S. Congress. In the Senate, many of them had been sponsored by conservative Republicans, while in the House of Representatives, populist Democrats were advancing the most important bills.[46]

Will Collette, a leading grass roots organizer, had predicted prospects for passage of right-to-say-no legislation governing municipal solid wastes were good. "All signs are that we have the votes, given this alliance of conservatives and populists," reported *Just Say No*, a publication of Dakota Rural Action, in acknowledging that overcoming opposition from liberal urban Democrats in the largest waste-producing states was going to be the key to achieving a degree of local control.[47] However, dealing with municipal trash was expected to be so daunting a task for Congress that no progress was expected in providing states similar powers to protect themselves from the bottom line of the hazardous waste business. In fact, business groups were expressing fears that without immediate intervention by the U.S. Supreme Court in various flow control cases, involving not only Alabama but also Michigan and New York, the engine of industrial America would back up and seize.[48]

WMI's critical position in the maintenance of the industrial status quo was demonstrated in the role played by Washington in the company's dispute with Alabama. In the late 1970s, Jimmy Carter's justice department had sided against waste haulers in their solid waste flow control conflict with Akron, Ohio. Now George Bush's solicitor general would ally the federal government against Alabama and, by extension, any other state conspiring to interfere with the free flow of waste.

"The United States Environmental Protection Agency has a vital interest in maintenance of the national market in hazardous waste treatment, storage and disposal," argued the Department of Justice in its *amicus curiae* brief to the Supreme Court in support of Chemwaste.[49] "Arbitrarily dividing waste management along state lines would inhibit the selection of the most environmentally sound and least costly treatment and disposal option for each particular type of such waste. And Balkanizing waste treatment and disposal would force the replication of facilities already existing in other States, at best resulting in unnecessary duplicative investments in waste facilities and at worst threatening the economic viability of both the existing and the new facilities."[50] Resisting Alabama's demotion of hazardous waste to a deadly sub-species well below the level of commodity, the Bush administration went on to state: "There is nothing unique about hazardous waste that places it outside the stream of commerce."[51]

In early June 1992, share prices of WMI and other major waste firms were given a fillip with news that the Supreme Court, in an eight to one decision, had ruled in favour of the primacy of the interstate commerce clause and free trade. The Rehnquist Court forbade the imposition by Alabama of its special fee on imported hazardous waste.

Whether or not the dominos now would ever fall, and in so doing fragment the waste market as WMI's executives had warned during their breakfast with William Reilly, was now an issue that would be thrown into the political arena, where it had belonged in the first place. Regardless of whether or not the authors of the two-hundred-year-old American Constitution (and, for that matter, the Canadian Constitution Act) had intended to distinguish between what one appeal court had called "goods" and "bads" as articles of trade, late-twentieth-century legislators ultimately would have to decide for themselves.

The justice department's position had been that in constitutional law desirable objects of trade were no different than undesirable ones. And when all was said and done, WMI and its rival waste enterprises had been built on such a premise. To challenge such a view now more than ever was a matter of politics.

Chapter 5

SCA: The Price of Scandal

*As long as the property rights concept is there, somebody has to
decide who has the property rights.*
Harold Kaufman, FBI undercover agent,
House of Representatives Hearings, 1980

Of all the new waste managers, the Service Corporation of America
(renamed SCA Services, Incorporated in 1971) most clearly bore
the stamp of its origins in the old rough-and-ready era of the garbage
trade that preceded the entry of the waste majors. Not coincidentally,
while in its early years SCA did manage to keep pace with BFI and
WMI, by the late 1970s it was clearly the struggler of the American
Big Three. And by the end of 1984, its main competitors were
scrapping over the spoils of SCA while seeking the means to avoid
provoking a hostile reaction from the antitrust authorities.

Unlike its rivals, the Boston-based firm did not set out to become
solely a waste manager. Founder Berton Steir wanted to build a
diversified company providing building maintenance, vending,
food, travel and waste disposal services. SCA started rather inaus-
piciously in March 1970 with seven vending companies. Then in
September it picked up another vending service, a building maintenance company and its first garbage company. When SCA went
public in 1971, however, it abandoned the diversification idea.
Garbage was where future profits lay. Over the next two years, it
used its newly issued stock certificates to buy itself a place on the
roster of waste management majors. The pitch was always the
same. Contractors were persuaded to sell their companies for SCA
shares, which were certain to go through the roof. During that initial
period of rapid growth, eighty-seven firms were merged into the
growing major waste contractor.

The Rise of Tom Viola

SCA was the first of the majors to enter the tough New Jersey market, thus making the Garden State a laboratory to test the major corporate waste disposers' ability to supplant criminal influences in the business. The experiment met with less than total success, for this market was light-years from SCA's head offices in cosmopolitan Boston. Independent contractors comported themselves like semi-civilized barbarians. Acts of violence, including murder, were carried out to control who carted what solid (and, later, toxic) wastes.

In 1972 SCA began fishing for independents in these dangerous waters. Their first catch — Tom Viola — was a big one. With Viola they not only got an important contractor in the thick of things, but also attracted his cronies who were among the major family-owned independents. Viola was made an SCA vice president, and by the time BFI showed its face in 1974, SCA had secured the services of some of the state's leading garbage barons. It had also cornered the top end of the municipal refuse cartage business.

Another SCA acquisition in these early years was the Utica, New York, garbage business of underworld associate Anthony Bentro. Like most other independent contractors bought out by agglomerates, Bentro remained with the merged operation. The new member of the SCA team was close to Anthony Provenzano, a Teamster potentate whose name was linked with plots to assassinate Fidel Castro, John F. Kennedy and Jimmy Hoffa. In late 1975, some months after Hoffa's disappearance, Provenzano, Bentro and Jimmy Fiorillo, owner of one of New York City's biggest garbage firms, were indicted for their role in planning a $2.3 million pension fund loan involving a $300,000 kickback to mobsters and Teamster officials. (Only Provenzano and Bentro, described as "a man who made millions shuttling between meetings with Mafiosi and top corporate executives," were convicted.)[1]

By early 1975 SCA's sales were within $88 million of BFI's, and only $9 million behind WMI's. Its operations stretched from its native Boston, where it had a large share of residential collection, to California.[2] But with its visible connections to the likes of Provenzano and associates, SCA never seemed quite prepared to meet the minimum norms of accountability required of U.S. public companies. When held up to close public scrutiny, SCA was put on the defensive, and its the other continental waste companies pulled even farther ahead. The company itself was already too well established to be scuppered by scandal, but the same could not be said for its crew. An anonymous SCA employee, calling the Boston regional office of the Securities and Exchange Commission (SEC) in March 1975, alleged that the company was being "ripped off' by its officers. An SEC probe was set in motion, and as disclosures of internal looting surfaced, senior management was seriously compromised. The revelations set the stage for a boardroom struggle for control. Berton Steir and three other inside directors resigned, and Tom Viola of New Jersey took over at the helm.

As a result of the disclosures in the SEC probe, SCA management filed suit against Steir, claiming that he had bought 100 acres of land near the company's major Boston-area dump in Amesbury, Massachusetts, for $150,000 and then had sold the property to SCA through a financial scheme for ten times the purchase price. This and other landfill deals also attracted the attention of the SEC investigators. In addition, the agency determined that deposed president Christopher Recklitis, aided by Anthony Bentro, had diverted nearly $4 million in company funds into a motel chain. Charges were brought against Recklitis in 1977, and the former president was jailed and fined. In return for his testimony against Recklitis, Steir received a one-year suspended sentence and a fine for his role in the deal. Bentro was never indicted, but he did agree to a federal court order enjoining him from working for SCA for two years.

With a new group of outside directors, the company appeared to be joining the respectable mainstream of American business. In fact, it was. Among the directors sharing a boardroom table with Tom Viola were a former chairman of the New York Stock Exchange, an editor of the *Harvard Business Review* and a director of IBM. Nothing was fundamentally wrong with the course that had been set. As BFI and WMI were proving, the future belonged to these national garbage chains. A 1976 photograph in *Waste Age* exuded a sense of self-satisfaction. The leading garbage contractors had assembled under the magazine's auspices for a roundtable discussion. Tom Viola explained the upbeat atmosphere this way:

> I just added up the sales of companies represented here, and there are $660,000,000 in sales represented at this table. That's a nice big number yet we only represent the tip of the iceberg in this business. There's the huge, vast municipal

market to be tapped yet. Of course, the private sector does roughly 90 per cent of the industrial-commercial business. But in the municipal end of the business, here again, in certain areas of the country, most of those cities are collecting their own refuse. There's a vast market right there waiting to be tapped.[3]

By 1977 SCA had a fleet of 1,800 trucks hauling wastes in 90 cities and operated 39 landfills. It had 100 municipal contracts, some 110,000 commercial accounts, and more than 100,000 steel dumpsters. At the same time, however, its market value had been depressed by scandal. Management's attention was diverted by investigations and impending litigation. Both rich and vulnerable, SCA was a natural target for a takeover attempt by one of its big sisters. In November 1977, just four months after the SEC laid its charges against Recklitis, WMI made its offer to buy the embattled company. The deal involved a share exchange for SCA and its 148 subsidiaries, representing a premium of more than $35 million over the market value of the outstanding SCA shares. But the company's investment counsellor advised that the offer was inadequate, and less than three weeks after the offer was made SCA rejected it.

A disgruntled shareholder launched a class action, suing the Viola team for damages on the grounds that the rejection of the WMI offer had been a reckless and self-interested act. Owning only 2.3 per cent of all the issued shares, the officers and directors had decided to weather the storm and disregard the best interests of the shareholders as a group. The company came back with a counter-claim, arguing that management's decision reflected an astute appraisal of the company's real potential. For despite the notoriety earned by the shenanigans at head office, 1977 sales were up 13 per cent while pre-tax profits had bounded ahead by 68 per cent. In 1978 SCA was again running free. A group headed by Prudential Insurance indicated that the garbage hauler was in safe enough hands by lending it $57 million, and the company set about developing its strong position in the Massachusetts, New Jersey, Ohio and California markets along with other segments of its geographically diversified chain.[4]

Although solid wastes accounted for more than 90 per cent of its revenues throughout the 1970s, SCA was also busy assembling a dominant position in liquid and hazardous waste disposal. It owned sites in Massachusetts, New York, New Jersey, South Carolina and Illinois, and its facility just north of Niagara Falls, N.Y., was among the country's most important. At one time government and industry had buried hazardous materials with blind abandon in more than 100 local dumps in this fertile fruit belt (revelations of the noxious effects of one of these dumps eventually drew attention to these practices and made the Love Canal a continent-wide symbol of environmental devastation). Then SCA and a single competitor, CECOS International, emerged, in this most contaminated area of North America, as the sole disposal operators. Giant lagoons on SCA's 630-acre site could hold nearly 100 million gallons.[5]

One report on SCA's internal affairs touched upon the acquisition that had established the company in the Niagara region. Referring to the early 1970s, the report's authors asserted: "We have confirmed that the company was innovative and technologically sound. However, we were also told that the company was at that time an 'environmental nightmare.'" One highway official testified to witnessing a 1976 fire on the SCA site in which flames leaped eighty feet and exploding drums flew into the air.[6] The Recklitis affair did nothing to reassure the local community. Citizens' groups on both the Canadian and American side of the Niagara River objected to an SCA plan to discharge treated industrial wastes from a treatment plant in Porter, N.Y., through a five-and-a-half-mile pipeline into the already highly contaminated river. The pipeline, which empties into the river just two-and-a-half miles upstream of the water intake for the town of Niagara-on-the-Lake, Ontario, stood unused while lengthy public hearings ran their course. In addition to the arguments at the hearings, action against the SCA plan took the form of dropping bowling balls and cement in the pipeline. Eventually an agreement was reached, calling for testing of the pipeline's contents and the effects of the discharges before any commercial dumping could take place. The tests were to be paid for by the company and supervised by municipal representatives and environmentalists from both sides of the border. Perhaps stung by its experiences in the Niagara region, SCA would show more prescience than its rivals in its approach to managing liquid hazardous wastes, staking millions on the need for incineration technology while BFI and WMI stuck with landfill burial.

Congress and the Ex-Con

Developments in the toxic waste field led indirectly to SCA once again becoming embroiled in scandal. New toxic waste regulations were proving too great a boon for many prospective haulers to resist. The less care a hauler showed for proper disposal, the better the cash flows and the more extraordinary the profit margins. Everybody wanted to get in on the act. A leading New York crime family, already in plain garbage, knew a bonanza when it saw one and elbowed its way in along with many seemingly legitimate businessmen. No real auditing or monitoring systems existed. Inspectors were few and far between. As ordinary unwanted industrial liquids such as printer's ink became classified as toxic materials, the disposal charges multiplied.

Contractors with larcenous dispositions branched out. But without secure landfills or incinerators of their own, they were pathetically unprepared compared to the Big Three. The service they offered was an illusion backed by the substantial "toxic" fees they charged. A liquid waste generator would get different bids from haulers, all of them in the same price range. The company would pick one without knowing that it was impossible for the contractor to dump legally at that price. Leading corporations such as Exxon reportedly signed manifests that recorded the transfer of wastes to a Delaware company that didn't exist.[7] Drums of chemicals were abandoned in warehouses, set on fire, or mixed with household garbage. Midnight-dumpers poured cancer agents and mutagens into rivers and down sewers, or offered them to unwitting municipal managers for oiling dusty roads. In December 1980, one month after important new federal hazardous waste regulations came into effect, a U.S. congressional subcommittee decided to examine the legislation's unintended side effects.

For Harold Kaufman the news of impending hearings to investigate criminal infiltration of the toxic disposal business was of more than academic interest. Kaufman was an ex-convict who knew the garbage industry; he had spent six years working for the Teamsters and contract firms in New York and New Jersey. At the time the hearings were announced, Kaufman was living under an assumed identity and awaiting market conspiracy trials in New Jersey in which he was the state's key witness.

It appeared that the New Jersey garbage industry still operated on the basis of "property rights," despite earlier investigations, new legislation introduced in 1970 to regulate the business, and the entry of the big contractors a few years later. State antitrust officials were curious about the acquisition patterns of SCA and BFI and about what lay behind some truck bombings, two murders, and the limited turnover in contracts since the previous investigations. The state probe which led to indictments was divided into two parts, one focusing on possible collusion among holders of municipal residential contracts — the area in which SCA's New Jersey interests were concentrated — and the other dealing with the commercial and industrial or "private" market.

Oil executives created their cartels in the splendid isolation of a Scottish castle or a private boardroom. Garbage contractors, by contrast, congregated in more plebeian and accessible settings. In southern New Jersey they met at a restaurant called Snuffy's II. After a luncheon of red snapper, bluefish and veal parmigiana, their trade group, the New Jersey Trade Waste Association, discussed industry affairs. According to one 1980 indictment, the association also had some highly illegitimate purposes. Evidence indicated that Snuffy's II was the scene of private meetings at which a handful of designated contractors arbitrated "property" disputes. The indictment asserted that "weekly meetings provided an opportunity for garbage collectors to resolve disputes, known as 'grievances', involving conflicting claims to particular customer accounts." ("Grievances" arise from an industry concept of "property rights" that are adopted and enforced by the conspirators.)

One "grievance" session cited allegations involving a cemetery served by BFI of Elizabeth, New Jersey, Inc. When the BFI firm raised its prices, the cemetery hired Statewide, another hauler. But as the state argued in a case which ended in a mistrial when the jury failed to reach a unanimous verdict, at the trial BFI claimed that its local rival had violated its "property rights." At Snuffy's, the interloper was ordered to hand back the contract. Unknown to anyone at the meeting, Statewide's representative, Harold Kaufman, was an FBI informer reporting to the antitrust task force. Kaufman, who was in a federal witness protection program, later contacted a congressman and volunteered to testify before the Congressional Subcommittee on Oversight and Investigation looking into the toxic waste industry.

The ex-convict spent a few days in advance of his testimony briefing such subcommittee members as Tennessee Democrat Albert Gore, Jr., a leading light in matters of environmental concern.

Then on 16 December 1980, flanked by guards and shielded from cameras, Kaufman appeared in the Rayburn Office Building. He began by describing how the concept of property rights works, making the point that "everybody picks up garbage the same way. There is no great technology in picking up garbage. So how are you going to protect it? You are protected by property rights." What if another company comes along and tries to sign a contract with a customer, offering to charge less money? That did not happen very often, Kaufman said. "When it does, they try to correct it by economic punishment. Secondly, by fear and intimidation. He knows there is a punishment coming because organized crime controls it. There have been beatings and killings in New York just as in New Jersey."

Gore asked, "Do you personally know of any murders which happened because of the encroachment of one company on the property rights of another company?" Kaufman referred to the deaths in New Jersey of Alfred Dinardi in 1976 and Gabriel San Felice in 1978: "At the time in Jersey [Dinardi] was taking towns. He took about ten towns from SCA. After he was killed, that is when the association came to New Jersey. After that all these towns reverted back to SCA."

The Tennessee congressman and future vice president wanted to make sure he had understood correctly: "After both these murders, the properties in dispute reverted to SCA?"

"Custom Cartage had 'stole' these. That is the term used in the sanitation industry. If you take a stop from somebody you are considered an outlaw; you are not a member of the crew. [Dinardi] had taken these stops and commercial stops from other people too, but primarily SCA."

"This is one of the largest waste disposal companies in the United States, and it is traded on the stock exchange?" Gore continued. "Yes," Kaufman replied. Gore said he was particularly concerned about these revelations because SCA was planning a disposal facility in his home state, and asked Kaufman to talk about the "genesis of this company, SCA." The FBI informer obliged: "The way they operate, they buy companies and they give the president of the company stock in the company and a job for five years. You have the same people into organized crime." Later in his testimony, Kaufman was even more explicit: "SCA is putting up facilities all over the country. Tom Viola is the president of SCA, he buys a company ... They give the same president of that company a five-year contract. They have some of the toughest organized crime figures in the world through the Viola family ... Here is a company that was born on the property rights concept."[8]

Of course, so was the entire industry born on that concept. But such bad publicity was the price a major waste company had to pay for storming the traditional bailiwicks of eastern crime families. These markets were far more formidable than the civilized territories of boss scavengers. Kaufman's statements reverberated in SCA's boardroom. The company vigorously denied Kaufman's charges, but decided to cut its losses anyway. The company was reportedly trying to sell its New Jersey subsidiaries back to their original owners. Tom Viola described Kaufman's allegations as ludicrous, but his days at the heights of corporate power were numbered. After a lengthy directors' meeting in June 1981, Viola resigned. He was replaced by Henry Russell, at the time a senior executive with the Boston Safe Deposit and Trust Company, a venerable Massachusetts financial institution.

Once again SCA was vulnerable to a takeover attempt. The allegations of organized crime connections and the management change were not the only factors. SCA had followed a different path from BFI and WMI in the area of hazardous waste management, taking signals from the ecology movement seriously and investing heavily in alternative incineration technology. This long-term, capital-intensive approach was based on the assumption that there would be increasing government regulation. It appeared to be paying off in 1980, when the Environmental Protection Agency, under the Carter administration, banned the wanton dumping of liquid wastes in landfills and open lagoons. But under Ronald Reagan, the EPA reversed its position and scrapped the ban in early 1982 as part of the administration's attempt to de-govern America. SCA found that its foresight had been transformed into a competitive disadvantage, as short-term market forces were allowed to resume their previous sovereignty. As a result, the Boston company joined ranks with the Environmental Defense Fund in a lawsuit to force reimposition of the ban. SCA's maverick approach to liquid waste disposal created tensions between it and its major competitors, and it also broke with the National Solid Wastes Management Association over policy differences on how the industry should react to the EPA's lifting of the landfill ban. By swallowing SCA whole, BFI or WMI could eliminate these tensions.

This time it was BFI, eager to re-establish its former position as the leading waste manager, that made the move. In March 1982, fresh from its victory over WMI in Riyadh, BFI put a proposal on the table to merge SCA and its 147 subsidiaries into the Houston-based chain. The terms of the offer involved an exchange of one BFI share for every two of SCA. But just as the Viola team had rejected WMI's offer in 1977, the new SCA management rejected what would have amounted to a $210 million deal.

Sinking Toxins in South Carolina

In re-making its Neanderthal image, SCA entered territory where many a less desperate player feared to tread. The company's strategy was to stake a place for itself in the high risk realms of toxic waste management. What better way after all to distract investors and critics from past delinquencies than to establish your credibility within rather than beyond the precincts of government regulation?

In April 1978, at the very time SCA was embroiled in New Jersey's bloody waste wars, the company established itself as WMI's only rival in hazardous waste disposal for the Southeastern United States. The company quietly slipped into rural South Carolina and paid a geologist $1.5 million dollars for his mining operation. A gray band of clay (known as "fuller's earth") runs below the surface in Sumter County near the town of Pinewood, and the geologist had taken advantage of the clay's absorptive qualities to make kitty litter. But Tom Viola recognized in the remoteness of Sumter County something far more lucrative than kitty litter.

Fewer than forty secure chemical landfills in the United States were permitted to accept hazardous waste from outside generators. All of them were operating under interim permits and faced increasingly stringent engineering and management requirements to obtain permanent permits. Clearly, as Jim Tharpe of the *Greenville News* put it in a series on South Carolina's emergence as a toxic waste burial ground, "the few licensed commercial hazardous waste landfills already doing business would likely be the ones developed, pumping big bucks into the pockets of companies like SCA."[9] In fact, except for WMI's Alabama facility, no other new hazardous waste landfill was permitted east of the Mississippi.

Neither public announcements nor hearings heralded the new SCA facility and, as a state senator later observed, "they slipped it under the door."[10] Not even local environmental regulators, with the possible exception of those whom SCA hired, were informed of the company's plan to turn Pinewood into a major out-of-state waste repository.[11] SCA began burying vast quantities of solvents, pesticide residues, metal sludges and other hazardous chemicals. The noxious industrial effluvium was placed on a liner three-sixteenths of an inch thick which sat atop a fifteen-foot bed of natural and packed clay. Below lay the Black Creek and Tuscaloosa aquifers, an underground water source for the state's Coastal Plain.

Soon tractor-trailer rigs were roaring down Sumter County's dusty roads bearing the hazardous wastes of twenty-three states to Pinewood, as well as those of Puerto Rico and the Virgin Islands. Besides Pinewood, where annually 100,000 tons of toxics now were being buried in the ancient clay beds, SCA built a huge incinerator in Chicago. By 1983 these high-risk practices, in addition to a total lack of waste management expertise in the upper echelons of SCA, began to cause the industry's Wall Street boosters concern.

That year, a past president of the Environmental Control Analysts of New York rated SCA as a suitable investment only for "risk-oriented clients."[12] While nobody was challenging the probity of Tom Viola's successors, misgivings surfaced at the analysts' roundtable. Were things perhaps a mite out of control and SCA's novice senior executives sticking their necks out too far? One of the industry watchers noted sourly that "just because [SCA's] now run by Boston Brahmins doesn't mean SCA's got its act together." He went on to predict that "they're getting ready to sell out."[13]

Dividing the Spoils

The Boston Brahmins indeed did plan to sell. Laidlaw's Mike DeGroote was offered the company but he remained leery of managing hazardous wastes. Besides the evident risks, the Canadian trucking magnate found the asking price too high. WMI, however, still coveted SCA if only it could work out some quite obvious antitrust problems.

Notwithstanding its full-scale retreat from antitrust and environmental prosecution, President Reagan's Department of Justice could hardly let pass unnoticed the take-over of a highly controversial company with 123 divisions in at least 28 states. Besides, such a WMI/SCA combination would intensify corporate concentration in every one of the industry's various markets.

Merging SCA into WMI would affect the degree of competition in the collection of residential and of commercial and industrial solid waste in at least nineteen major cities including Atlanta, Boston, Dallas, Fort Worth, Detroit, Los Angeles and Washington, D.C.; in the disposal of solid waste in Louisville, Kentucky, and Fort Worth, Texas, and of hazardous waste in the entire southeastern United States and portions of the Midwest; and in the national market for large municipal contracts.[14]

Rather than a multiplicity of local markets, the municipal market actually constituted only one market, at least in the eyes of the Department of Justice, by virtue of the fact that only a few highly capitalized companies (seldom exceeding six) met the performance standards required by big cities. Furthermore, the nationals and transnationals often bid for large municipal contracts before actually having established themselves on the scene. Once in hand such cash-rich contracts provided a base from which to expand locally. Both WMI and SCA were known to pursue such a strategy.

So it is hardly surprising that in targeting SCA again, WMI would devise in advance an agreement for divesting whatever SCA assets might cause objection to the take-over on antitrust grounds. A deal was struck by WMI with Genstar Corporation, which only had a minor waste management presence in the western United States but had access to major resources. Genstar, a Canadian construction materials and financial company worth $1.5 billion, had as its largest shareholder Societé Générale de Belgique, Belgium's most important multi-national.

Genstar agreed in July 1984 to put up 40 per cent to WMI's 60 per cent of the actual cash needed to buy SCA. Once acquired in late September, SCA became a wholly owned subsidiary of WMI. In attempting to anticipate the Department of Justice's reaction, an initial division of SCA's assets was made between WMI and Genstar's new waste management arm, GSX. Furthermore, WMI retained the right to divest to Genstar whatever else the trustbusters might require. In the first carve-up, WMI kept all of SCA's hazardous waste operations.

The Hazardous Waste Consultant, noting the obvious, observed that either "Genstar did not wish to be involved in the hazardous waste management business, or ... WMI wanted all of SCA's hazardous waste operations."[15] However, Washington was not satisfied with the arrangement, particularly insofar as hazardous waste disposal was concerned. By allowing WMI to control both the Alabama and North Carolina facilities, the government would be sanctioning a virtual private monopoly in the hazardous waste business of the southeastern United States.

Accordingly, between July and September of 1984, WMI divested more of SCA to Genstar as it worked towards settlement of a government injunction then in the works. The Department of Justice's assent was eventually secured and the deal became a *fait accompli* when Genstar assumed control of SCA's Pinewood site, as well as of twenty-six SCA solid waste collection operations and five existing and two proposed solid waste landfills. About 60 per cent of SCA thus ended up in the hands of WMI.

An assistant attorney general assured the public that these divestitures would suffice to "resolve the antitrust concerns that would otherwise be raised by Waste Management's acquisition of certain of SCA's operations in the same geographic areas served by Waste Management."[16] But his statement proved to be wishful thinking. The industry continued to demonstrate its penchant for honouring antitrust law in the breach as well as in the observance.

The court provisions which carried the government's seal of approval of the take-over paid particular attention to the spinning off of SCA's California assets (including System Disposal) to GSX in such a way as to guarantee competition. Yet much of the commercial and industrial waste business would continue to be run, well beyond the 1984 signing of the judgement, like a typical cartel. The basic *modus vivendi* of the business seemed to outlast its changing cast of owners.

Cartels Continue in Los Angeles County

The evidence for this came the following year when a small hauler realized his trucks were being followed by an agent for GSX. The tail was scouting his rival's customers with the intention later of "blitzing" (offering below market prices) and luring them away. The hauler contacted Los Angeles District Attorney Ira Reiner's office which put an investigator on the case. But given that the D.A. had already looked into the clannish business some years previously and failed to penetrate it, expectations were not high.

However, the investigator got lucky. He found someone who once had been a sales manager at System Disposal, the new GSX subsidiary, and prevailed on him to provide a rare glimpse into the secret workings of a waste haulers' cartel. Based on detailed information about GSX's alleged involvement in a property rights scheme, the D.A. raided its offices and seized boxes of internal memos and expense vouchers. What they found far exceeded what they had anticipated. Once decoded, the cryptic notes were to become the key to the largest criminal antitrust case in California's history.

"It's rare to find the smoking gun," was how one of the D.A.'s staff described the fruits of the raid. "The challenge of these cases usually is having to prove a conspiracy when agreements are mostly verbal."[17] What the seized material revealed was a familiar litany of tactics by which waste companies conspire to give their industry the public mask of typically competitive business enterprise, and meanwhile treat commercial and industrial customers as private property, which is to say, hostages.

Whenever a customer wished to change haulers, the current and prospective contractor arranged for that customer to be offered a "high-ball" price. If the customer switched, the haulers would divide the windfall profit, often with payoffs as high as ten thousand dollars. Should the customer decide not to change, he ended up being stung with a series of stiff annual price hikes. "The standing rule," reported an Assistant D.A., "was non-competition."[18]

Faced with the wealth of information in the government's hands and given that a significant amount of the misconduct had occurred before the take-over, GSX approached the D.A. in late 1985 with an offer to help "clean up" the industry by providing company officials who would "essentially bare their souls." In early 1987, by which time Genstar had been taken over itself and, in the reshuffling of corporate assets its subsidiary GSX had changed hands, local officers of GSX's System Disposal were freely naming names of co-conspirators to a grand jury.[19] Among the names named were none other than Waste Management Inc. and Western Waste, an important regional operator. "You just never know where a conspiracy will lead," a prosecutor told the *Los Angeles Times*.[20]

System Disposal and its parent GSX paid $236,000 to settle outstanding civil charges and two years later, in 1989, the company (now controlled by Laidlaw) was tagged a further half million dollars as a result of the coming to light of yet another cartel arrangement. The Department of Justice, which had gone to particular lengths to ensure competition in Orange County outside Los Angeles in its 1984 consent to the SCA takeover, was to end up charging the GSX subsidiary in Orange County with being party to a commercial and industrial market conspiracy lasting from April 1985 at least until March 1986.[21]

As for the world's leading waste manager, the baring of souls to the authorities exposed the fact that their California subsidiary had (according to charges levelled by the D.A.'s office) participated in a cartel as it jockeyed with other haulers to rationalize, expand and re-rationalize its operations. Having blitzed GSX accounts in Beverly Hills, Long Beach, Vernon and elsewhere in Los Angeles County to retaliate against GSX for having taken away commercial business, WMI sales personnel were then said to have been directed to limit their sales efforts so as to put into effect what the state charged was a "horizontal market division scheme." This included use of a variety of implements from the property rights tool box including limiting sales efforts to new businesses which did not already have accounts with other disposal firms, discussing with rivals the allocation of customer accounts, methods of account compensation or restitution, and communication of customer price information to fix and stabilize prices.[22]

The exposure of the L.A. cartel in a market that annually yielded hundreds of millions of dollars in business had its ritualistic conclusion in early 1989. WMI pleaded no contest and a cheque was written out on its behalf for the maximum $1 million fine under California's antitrust law. Similarly, Western Waste so pleaded and paid $900,000.

However, by the time those cheques had been cashed and the smoke cleared from view, WMI and Western had moved on to conquer new markets and Laidlaw's Mike DeGroote had become North America's third largest solid and second largest hazardous waste company by buying, in his largest acquisition ever, the whole of GSX.

The Waste Management Shuffle

The GSX sale was the byproduct of a deal which had nothing to do with toxic trash and everything to do with the desire of Imasco, Canada's largest tobacco company, to gain control of the country's seventh largest financial institution, the Canada Trustco Mortgage Company. As Genstar owned Canada Trustco, Imasco assumed considerable debt buying Genstar to get its hands on the trust company. But the image problems of the cigarette business were severe enough without compounding them with those of waste management, so Imasco helped finance its take-over by unburdening itself of the entire GSX operation to DeGroote for the sum of $500 million.[23] That price (perhaps ominously, given growing concerns about hazardous waste disposal practices) was less than the asking price two years earlier when DeGroote was first offered SCA.[24]

In early 1989, the veteran Kosti Shirvanian, chairman of the board of the closely held Western Waste, made a move which signalled his own professed belief that there would be less room than ever in the industry. He expanded his board of directors to make room for Tom Fatjo. The BFI founder had recently suffered his worst career setback with the collapse of his national chain of fitness centres. In taking on Fatjo, who was to assist in targeting acquisitions for Western, Shirvanian explained to the *Houston Business Journal*, "we're the smallest of the five giants in the industry and I think we're ready to move ahead, and I can use Tom's expertise. I decided if we don't become a national company we'll be wiped out."[25]

Not too long afterwards, with Shirvanian and Fatjo having fallen out in a dispute over control of a small Houston trash company, Mike DeGroote met WMI founder Wayne Huizinga for lunch in Fort Lauderdale. DeGroote had just sold his controlling interest in Laidlaw and moved to the tax haven of Bermuda, where retirement was proving irksome. Huizenga told the Canadian that Fatjo was trying to work his old price-earnings magic again with a newly acquired oil and gas company and DeGroote agreed to meet the Texan at the Hamilton Princess Hotel in Bermuda. At that 1991 meeting, Fatjo explained he needed money to close a California landfill deal and succeeded in talking DeGroote into lending him $10 million — but not before the wily DeGroote received as quid pro quo what soon would amount to one third of the shares of Fatjo's current garbage enterprise, Republic Waste.

As the waste business entered the 1990s and took on its new public character, and various companies scurried to be the last to join the ranks of the few who would dominate the entire disposal industry, control of the established transnationals was passing out of the hands of the original entrepreneurs who created them. The dazzling success they had all enjoyed, in building an industry that capitalized on opportunities inherent in the first wave of green legislation, now seemed less and less relevant to finding solutions to what ordinary citizens everywhere and in increasing numbers were coming to see as a profound and intractable social crisis.

Chapter 6

Laidlaw: The Canadian Player

A landfill is like an oil well in reverse.
Michael G. DeGroote, Chairman, Laidlaw Industries Inc.

It is arguable no one on earth ever is likely to make as much money from the privatization of waste management as has Michael De-Groote. Through two decades, the Canadian trucker gave life to a financial colossus, ingesting, as he went along, hundreds of waste companies. The more he swallowed, the larger the next bite had to be to sustain that growth, so that investors would buy stock and make possible the next mouthful.

Yet, while market analysts were forever marvelling at the magical aura surrounding DeGroote as he built his empire of empires, issuing stock at twenty times earnings to buy companies at ten times earnings, arguably the ultimate expression of his money-making genius was his knowing when to get out. In fact, such was the apprehension the day news hit the Toronto Stock Exchange in the spring of 1988 that DeGroote was considering a private sale of his controlling interest in Laidlaw, that the TSE transportation index took the second worst decline in the history of the exchange.

Like the other major waste corporations, Laidlaw had found itself propelled out of the arena of rough-and-ready entrepreneurship into a different league. This change required a new brand of management relying less on high risk gamblers and more on PR, political connections and environmental savvy.

Mike DeGroote began his working life in a tobacco field. Born in the West Flanders region of Belgium, the young DeGroote immigrated with his family to southwestern Ontario. After a spell of farm labour, at the age of eighteen he began hauling manure from dairy to tobacco farms around Tillsonburg and Delhi. DeGroote's two-ton army surplus truck eventually multiplied into a vast fleet because of his single-minded entrepreneurship. Early in his career he bought Laidlaw Motorways, an operation consisting of twenty-one tractor-trailers, and this was to be his vehicle for building a major freight transport and garbage-hauling conglomerate. He also built up a large contracting business in the uranium boom town of Elliot Lake. Though it made him a millionaire on paper, he went bankrupt when the United States dropped its uranium purchase options and the boom turned to bust. DeGroote recovered from the bankruptcy and continued his climb to success.

DeGroote was one of the journeymen acquisitors who helped define the postwar period of Canadian economic life. Unlike some of the others, he managed to do his work in relative anonymity. Our guide to Canada's business establishment, Peter C. Newman, took note of him only as an entry in a list of acquisitors and their $35 billion worth of corporate booty. And yet the trappings of his life are the stuff of a Newman description — the head office on the waterfront next to the Royal Hamilton Yacht Club, where he often dined in the early 1970s; the nineteenth-century handcut stone house on the secluded estate; the yacht in Florida; the skiing at St. Moritz. In what Newman called "the greatest wave of cannibalism in Canadian business history," DeGroote was an active participant. As a writer in *Canadian Business* put it, "DeGroote's real love — and talent — is buying more companies."

The Acquisition Drive

Like the American Big Three, Laidlaw relied from the very beginning on stock market financing for the growth of its garbage collection chain. The company went public in April 1969, and four months later DeGroote became the major garbage hauler in Canada's most affluent province when he bought Superior Sanitation Services Limited of Kitchener, Ontario. From the time the city of Kitchener first farmed out municipal garbage collection in 1961, Superior Sanitation had held the contract. By the time of the Laidlaw takeover, Superior Sanitation was hauling trash from the residences of 10 per cent of the province's population. From its home base it had branched out into Galt, Sarnia, Windsor, Brampton, Burlington and surrounding townships. Manned by a non-unionized staff, the company's 100 packers collected the refuse of 750,000 people.

New buy-outs of assets and markets soon established Laidlaw in Hamilton, and then in the metropolis where it was to become the chief rival of the American majors. Laidlaw was a darling of a buoyant stock market, and although it was still primarily a freight transporter, analysts attributed the high price/earnings multiples at which Laidlaw shares were trading to the great expectations speculators held for the conglomerate as a waste manager. Stock prices reflected the hope that Superior Sanitation might capture all or part of Toronto's residential garbage, although a Toronto *Globe and Mail* financial reporter cautioned that "waste collection in the city is handled by unionized municipal employees and it is probable that Laidlaw would have to acquire this business gradually by contracting individually with boroughs in the metropolitan area."

Meanwhile, DeGroote began laying down his refuse collection base in western Canada, which was to be one of his major areas of concentration over the next few years. In 1972 he bought 60 per cent of Grey Goose Corporation, which operated 90 per cent of all intercity bus service in Manitoba, and picked up refuse in Winnipeg, Edmonton and Red Deer. The former owners, Abram Thiessen and his sons of Winnipeg, remained as managers. By 1973, the year all the waste majors hit an initial peak, Laidlaw shares had risen to ten times their original value. On the road DeGroote's drivers spoke with awe of their chief executive officer's rise from personal bankruptcy to become the country's largest non-Teamster transporter. According to the DeGroote legend as recounted in trucking barns and roadside cafés, his seemingly limitless supplies of capital came from the coffers of the King of Belgium.

Now that he was Ontario's largest hauler of steel and garbage, much of DeGroote's attention in the mid-1970s focused on picking up more garbage companies in western Canada and trying to develop a position in liquid waste management in Ontario. First, however, he picked up a trust company and the Hamilton Tiger-Cats football team, causing some confusion on Bay Street about just what the acquisition hunter had in mind.[1] Hamilton Trust and Savings Corporation provided a range of real estate and deposit services through six branches in the Hamilton-Wentworth area and one in Toronto, and administered $120 million in accounts. As *The Financial Post* commented, the Hamilton Trust takeover did "lead some to wonder what this basically transportation and waste management company was up to."[2] Whatever else the deal accomplished, it increased DeGroote's control over Laidlaw itself, for the

21 per cent of Hamilton Trust picked up by Laidlaw was purchased from a holding company controlled by none other than DeGroote. In exchange, 173,110 Laidlaw treasury shares were turned over to the holding company, and the young acquisitor now owned 39 per cent of the merged enterprise.

The onset of the recession in 1974 did not throw DeGroote off his stride. In that year Laidlaw entered the Lower Mainland of British Columbia, buying two-thirds of Haul-Away Disposal, a hauler serving suburban Surrey, and at the same time bringing in a motorized cavalcade of Superior Sanitation trucks. Haul-Away had been owned by Len Remple, a veteran contractor who had come to Vancouver after the Winnipeg outfit he owned with his brother-in-law was bought out by BFI. Like the Thiessens, Remple stayed on to manage his former company. During the economic downturn, DeGroote credited Laidlaw's expanded garbage interests with buoying up the entire conglomerate. "The most significant profit increases," he informed his stockholders, "were derived from our waste management operations now conducted in four provinces of Canada where efficiency controls proved most successful." In future planning, this relative immunity of refuse markets to economic cycles was not to be lost on the company.

Laidlaw's position in the Vancouver area markets was not won without a struggle. Vancouver's garbage baron, Ascher Smith, felt caught in a pincer movement. Both Laidlaw and BFI, poised to attack from bases in Calgary and Victoria, threatened his dominance of the local market (see Chapter 3). As Haul-Away proceeded to take stops away from his Smithrite Disposals Limited, Smith raised a ruckus. He cried foul play in the local press and had his lawyer fire off a complaint to Ottawa's anticombines branch charging that his rival's price-slashing tactics were a breach of the Combines Investigation Act. The independent contractor alleged that:

> Haul-Away Disposal Ltd. is apparently offering to provide the service provided by Smithrite Disposal Ltd. at a price $5 less per container per month than the lowest price offered by Smithrite ... Based upon its knowledge of the cost of providing this service, it is Smithrite's feeling that Haul-Away is operating at a loss in providing this service and that because Haul-Away's price is framed with reference to Smithrite's lowest price, the intent is to lessen competition or eliminate a competitor.[3]

No legal action was ever taken against Haul-Away and, for the time being, Smithrite survived. But according to the union that organized its workers, the company never recovered its original position. An arrangement emerged which left each firm serving a different area of the Lower Mainland, with the Fraser River as the dividing line. By 1977 Haul-Away was serving 180,000 residents in Surrey and Delta. The smaller operators, meanwhile, had been pushed into the less dense areas, and Laidlaw's target now shifted from the independents to the public sector.

The pursuit of municipal contracts was carried on in a highly politicized environment, forcing contractors unaccustomed to such activities to engage in ideological debates. Requesting a contract was a political act, and in Vancouver one's approach to garbage collection became an expression of one's social convictions. Beginning in July 1980, Remple made several attempts to convince Vancouver City Council to farm out half of its domestic trash collection to Haul-Away. Invoking the spirit of California's Proposition 13, he recommended the introduction of free enterprise to improve productivity, even though the city had already achieved comparatively low collection costs. He also proposed building an incinerator if city hall guaranteed him the necessary garbage stream. The city's municipal employees submitted a brief containing a litany of counter-arguments. The union argued that selling off the municipal equipment and privatizing residential pickup would not only increase the city's fixed overhead costs per ton but also require special billing arrangements and make transfer to disposal sites less efficient. It also feared that privatization would lead to the introduction of Remple's system of subcontracting to independent owner-operators, which it argued might create a heavier health and safety toll in an industry already characterized by an excessively high frequency of disabling injuries.[4] For the moment at least, the municipal employees prevailed.

But the debate seemed endless and polarized, and was exacerbated by a long and difficult municipal employees' strike in 1981. After the strike Remple found a new ally in a right-wing tax revolt group called Human Action to Limit Taxation (HALT). Made up of economic fundamentalists for whom the sine qua non of freedom is greatly reduced government power to tax its citizens, HALT asked the mayor to conduct an immediate investigation of the possibility of contracting out garbage pickup. Another ally was a retired provincial court judge who wrote to the *Vancouver Sun* commending the "quiet, Grenadier Guards-mustached Surrey businessman by name of Len Remple." Judge Les Bewley portrayed Vancouver as wallowing in filth, confrontations and rates while Surrey and Delta "wallowed in the fiscal and sanitary benefits of a little free enterprise."

While Len Remple fought Laidlaw's battles in British Columbia, in Manitoba Abram Thiessen was proving a suitable ally for a garbage contractor covetously eyeing municipal markets and government contracts. In 1974 Thiessen resigned as director of the Manitoba Development Corporation over the issue of public sector management of the bus-manufacturing plant he had sold to the province's New Democratic Party government. He went on record as saying that government couldn't run such a specialized industry — a similar claim to the one private waste managers were making as they descended on towns and cities all over the continent. At the same time William Thiessen was party to an agreement with fellow contractors in the greater Winnipeg market that sought to bring excessive competition, with its unfortunate effect on profits, under control. It was here that federal anticombines enforcers made their stand against the new waste managers. (The agreement and the ensuing court case are the subject of Chapter 8.)

The Rival Tricil

By the time the Winnipeg case was finally concluded (it was thrown out of court), Laidlaw not only had expanded its operation in the Manitoba capital and moved into Thompson, but had also set up shop in Calgary where it took over the local solid waste assets of Tricil Limited, a joint venture of Canadian Industries Limited (CIL) and a Calgary firm called Trimac Limited which entertained ambitions not too different from Laidlaw's own. The two expansion-minded companies encountered each other on a number of occasions; one notable meeting involved liquid waste disposal in Ontario where Tricil came out on top. However, even though Calgary was the home territory of one of Tricil's parents, its interests in the city's solid waste market were bought out by the eastern-based firm.

The growth of Trimac from a humble enterprise, which first did business the year Wall Street crashed, to a significant transportation and waste management company and one of the world's major drilling rig operators is another of Canada's postwar entrepreneurial sagas. In 1929 Jack McCaig began hauling coal in a horse-drawn wagon through the streets of Moose Jaw, Saskatchewan. The McCaigs prospered, and eventually moved into oil-hauling. In 1960 their trucking outfit, now known as Trimac, bought out a Calgary trucker, and McCaig and his three sons migrated to Alberta. The brothers soon diversified from over-the-road freight to transporting sulphur in bulk by rail. Later they moved into resource exploration and, in 1971, into garbage collection.

Trimac's garbage business began in Edmonton, but the next year the Albertans moved into the Ontario garbage markets alongside BFI, WMI and Laidlaw. With its purchase of Lohner Canada Limited (renamed Dominion Waste Management), Trimac became the province's fourth largest solid waste hauler with municipal contracts in Ottawa, St. Catharines and some smaller communities. In the next few years Trimac — by then a co-venturer with CIL in Tricil Limited — expanded its Ontario business considerably, although it lost its Ottawa contract to a firm owned by construction entrepreneurs Louis and Silvio Bot (in spite of a local controversy inspired by Silvio Bot's admission that his company hired a Mafia "soldier" to protect the company's interests on the James Bay hydroelectric site).[5] Tricil gained a contract in Kingston where it took advantage of the exhaustion of the municipal dump by offering a site it had bought from a farmer fifteen miles north of town. In addition, it picked up commercial and industrial contracts in Ottawa, Belleville and Sarnia, hauled more liquid waste in Ontario by 1978 than either Laidlaw or BFI, and had its own liquid waste treatment plants in Mississauga and Sarnia in Ontario and Ville Mercier in Quebec.

Market Forces and Toxic Wastes — Upper Ottawa Street

In the 1970s Ontario made attempts of a sort to introduce more up-to-date methods into the handling of the vast quantities of liquid wastes generated within the province. This was an opportunity both Laidlaw and Tricil were eager to seize.

As the decade began no Canadian government had any real idea where toxic garbage was dumped. In 1971 a director of the Waste

Management Branch of Ontario's Ministry of the Environment organized a meeting of about 200 government and industry representatives to discuss the problems posed by industrial refuse; at that time it was assumed that about half the province's annual output of fifty million gallons ended up in landfills.

The 1971 Ontario Environmental Protection Act did prohibit landfill dumping of certain materials such as oil-laden aqueous wastes. There was no other alternative. Hamilton and the Niagara Peninsula alone produced an estimated eight million tons of oil-laden wastes each year. Every industry from Dofasco to a small machine shop with oil-cooled cutting equipment was producing some, and most of it was finding its way into rivers, lakes, streams and Hamilton Bay. In rushed Laidlaw with its own plans for the region. By the summer of 1972 its new Interflow systems division was set up with a liquid waste destruction plant in Hamilton that could handle the whole eight million tons. The facility's beginning, however, was not an auspicious one. After attending its opening day at the bayfront site, a retired senior ministry official commented: "The thing was as primitive as could be. It was only supposed to burn oil residues but, as the circumstances would have it, they fed everything into it."

It seemed likely that natural market forces would turn future generations into walking mutants before they ever justified huge investments of the kind Laidlaw had made in Hamilton. Government enforcement was the key to ensuring that wastes flowed towards the Laidlaw incinerator. As DeGroote described it to a financial reporter, "The Ontario government, we hope, will be our biggest sales force." Provincial authorities, however, did not live up to Laidlaw's expectations. Three years later, in its 1975 annual report, Laidlaw complained that Interflow had "suffered a substantial loss to date due to lack of business caused by non-enforcement of provincial environmental standards." Laidlaw's entire venture in liquid waste management ran its course without much improvement in the provincial monitoring and enforcement program. Its waybill system, for instance, was still inadequate in the early 1980s. Through this system, the ministry was supposed to account for what was dumped where, but the system covered only liquid wastes hauled on public roads, and even wastes that fell into that category were often disposed of without the required two copies of the waybill (one submitted by the waste generator and one by the disposal site operator) ever reaching the ministry.

In addition to the Interflow operation, Laidlaw began solidifying industrial liquid refuse at Hamilton-Wentworth's Upper Ottawa Street landfill, a desolate eighty-foot mountain of garbage and earth cover, a surreal setting appropriate for a convention of alchemists. Eventually this landfill created local unrest; leachate poured from the site at a rate of forty gallons per minute, and stinking, brown, polluted fluids ran into nearby sewers and a passing creek. Despite government assurances that there were no health hazards, people living near the dump believed otherwise, and studies revealed abnormal numbers of sore throats, earaches and kidney and bladder problems. To stem the political controversy, dumping of industrial liquids generated outside the Hamilton-Wentworth region at the Upper Ottawa Street landfill — including the K-D facility — was prohibited.

In December 1976 a well-known independent tank truck operator alleged that the Interflow facility was being used as a front for wastes coming from all over Ontario, Quebec and the United States. The independent claimed that what went into the Interflow plant and what went out were the same, that the liquid was untreated in any way. Whenever the provincial Liberal Party brought the improper dealings at Upper Ottawa Street to the attention of the Ministry of the Environment, it was assured that the ministry was right on top of things and that there was no cause for alarm.

The controversy simmered, until the Liberal Party eventually took up the cause. Its researchers descended on the Steel City to learn for themselves how toxic garbage was handled in the real world rather than in the sheltered, air-conditioned universe of policy-makers. One of their guides, Alderman Henry Merling, gave them a tour of a number of sites where he suspected wastes had been dumped illegally, but he warned them not to sleuth around any further on their own. Merling, the chairman of Hamilton's pollution control committee, told the researchers that he would not rule out Mafia involvement, and pointed out a Murray Street sports club as a place where he believed ruffians connected with one particular garbage contractor congregated. The researchers returned to Queen's Park with images of the dark side of the toxic garbage business — truckers with their own keys sneaking onto the site to midnight-dump, empty tank trucks pulling out in the early morning as security guards arrived for the day's work, tip-offs to haulers when inspectors were expected, doctored test samples, students hired by the regional authority to spy on a suspected gatekeeper, stolen waybills, menacing goons on the docks warning two small independent contractors against accepting liquid-waste-hauling business.

In late 1978, Liberal leader Stuart Smith, for whom environmental issues were a special concern, demanded an investigation into the possibility that Interflow was transferring unspecified out-of-region liquid wastes from its bayfront site to Upper Ottawa Street. A special three-month waybill audit by the ministry revealed that the Laidlaw subsidiary could not account for 540,000 gallons, half of the amount carried during the period. Only 1 per cent of the wastes received by Interflow during September 1978 was generated within the borders of the municipal region. In that month the company provided 24.7 per cent of the liquid wastes used in the solidification process at the landfill.

The Liberals pressed on. Smith, who was now in contact with a strange assortment of characters privy to the secrets of Hamilton's contractors, demanded a full judicial inquiry into the local liquid industrial waste disposal business. The opposition leader said to a television interviewer that "we have to know what has happened to all the money involved — millions of gallons at even half a dollar a gallon, and people pay that sometimes to get rid of liquid waste, that's a lot of money that's going into somebody's pocket and only a judge would have the power to look into this properly." The environment minister declined the invitation.

In effect, Smith asked the government to expose the whole chaotic waste management system — from the waste generators themselves who didn't really know the final destination of their PCBs and cyanides through the virtually unregulated (not only environmentally but also economically) disposal industry to a government that washed its hands of the matter by relying on the private sector to solve the problem of toxic garbage. Had the government accepted Smith's call, it could not have avoided implicating itself, for if a waste industry was necessarily the child of government regulation it must surely also be the child of non-regulation. As one waste disposer told the Toronto *Globe and Mail,* "everyone is playing a game of sham, because everyone has to play to stay alive. The [Ontario] Ministry invites you to."[6]

However, some sign was necessary to satisfy the public that its government was vigilant. The Ministry of the Environment had to make an example of the "smugglers." Laidlaw, its Interflow division, a company manager and one driver were charged with the relatively minor misdeed of falsifying waybills and were convicted and fined $13,000. The fired Interflow manager, who had a profit-sharing stake in the disposal operation, claimed that he had simply been in the wrong place at the wrong time. Questions of personal morality aside, it was with some justification that he could regard himself as a scapegoat in a political battle over waste disposal and wonder why others with equal or greater responsibility for the mess were not touched.

The chief beneficiary of Laidlaw's problems in Hamilton was Tricil. The Upper Ottawa Street site was closed forever and was replaced by a mass incinerator, the Solid Waste Recovery Unit (SWARU). Tricil signed a ten-year contract with the regional authority to process annually at least 150,000 tonnes of municipal waste in SWARU. In addition, it ran three transfer stations and a landfill site in the nearby township of Glanbrooke. SWARU was a harbinger of garbage's future role as an energy source. Plans were made to produce electricity for sale to Ontario Hydro. In 1981 Tricil also signed deals to operate the contentious Recycle Energy System in Akron, Ohio, and another energy-from-waste plant on Prince Edward Island.

Meanwhile, with Upper Ottawa Street closed and the proposed BFI/Ministry of the Environment plant near Chatham coming apart on the rocks of rural outrage (see Chapter 3), Ontario was suffering a serious shortage of liquid waste disposal sites. This meant trouble for all of the province's liquid waste haulers. Without sites to haul to, independents could not survive except by becoming midnight dumpers. Without guaranteed liquid waste volumes, prospective disposers would not put up expensive facilities. As in the case of solid refuse, the interests of the haulers and those of the waste managers clashed. The totally integrated disposer needed control of upstream waste flows just as a hydroelectric utility needed the rivers that turn its turbines.

An example of this conflict surfaced one Friday morning in April 1979 at a meeting of liquid waste haulers in a west-end Toronto suburb. Four representatives of a newly formed Laidlaw division, Frontenac Chemical Waste Services Limited, showed up with a proposal that unsettled the independents. Acknowledging that the Interflow situation was bad and that Laidlaw was looking at other sites in Ontario and the United States, the Frontenac spokesmen offered the haulers a disposal service. They assured everyone of their desire to stay out of the hauling business. How the wastes got to the new sites would be the independents' problem. Frontenac proposed taking responsibility only after the wastes were delivered. In order to enter into disposal contracts, however, Frontenac needed lists of the truckers' customers. This request sent a chill through the room. The haulers did not have to be particularly paranoid to see the proposal as a gambit to steal their clients away. Their businesses were natural takeover targets for a giant garbage contractor in the process of rationalizing its financial structures.

According to Rusty Drew, a seasoned contractor who attended the Rexdale meeting, the Frontenac proposal "fell flat on the floor." Drew, one of Ontario's more trustworthy haulers, observed that "you could hear it. We knew the individuals ... that they would not be satisfied until they had all the business in their pocket. We knew they were going to take over our customers."

But obstinate tank-truck operators, unwilling to kowtow to forces altering the face of their industry, were not the only obstacle Laidlaw had to contend with. Ontario's twenty-four toxic burial sites had dwindled to seven city dumps and the Tricil incinerator and landfill near Sarnia. Even these were not without their problems. In 1978 farmers near the Tricil facility began complaining about smoke and smells from the incinerator and chemical wastes running off from open lagoons into neighbouring fields, in one case killing a farmer's corn crop. The provincial government had to issue a control order to get the situation changed. With a disposal crisis looming and the atrocious environmental track record of the private sector making joint ventures politically indefensible, the government was forced to change the rules of the game and become an active player. It mandated a provincially owned company, the Ontario Waste Management Corporation (OWMC), to establish a province-wide network of toxic facilities. The speed with which the new institution moved to distance itself from both the private sector and the Ministry of the Environment was a telling comment on the effectiveness and reputation of the existing system. In announcing that it was hiring consultants to do a study of waste quantities, the OWMC noted that it could not be sure of the reliability of the ministry's data. The private sector, meanwhile, still entertained the hope of spin-off contracts, but its future role in toxic waste management was in doubt.[7]

South of the Border

In general the expansion potential in Canada for a growing private waste manager seemed constrained by a political climate less hostile to public forms of enterprise. The views of public-sector unions were echoed in 1980 by Eugene Forsey, an authority on constitutional law and Canada's labour movement, who described "privatization" as "just a fancy name for the biggest international romp ever mounted by the rich for skinning the poor."[8]

Few Canadian cities had not witnessed campaigns by organized municipal (or, for that matter, provincial and federal) employees against wholesale dismantling of in-house government production facilities. The battle to "make" rather than "buy" was fought over every conceivable form of labour associated with a civilized society. The experience of BFI in Canada is interesting in this regard. Although the Texas-based firm hauled commercial and industrial wastes in markets stretching from British Columbia to Nova Scotia, after eight years in Canada it had succeeded in landing only two small residential contracts, in Winnipeg and Halifax. American municipal markets, however, were proving more congenial to the garbage majors. The tax revolt set in motion by California's Proposition 13 and the market-oriented values of the Reagan era provided the political climate for large-scale contracting-out of government economic activity. Garbage corporations stood to flourish wherever it was taken as an article of economic faith that the private corporation was better suited to deliver almost any service other than the armed forces and the town lock-up.

So Mike DeGroote, acquisitor extraordinaire, increasingly looked south of the border for future expansion. He already had pickup operations in Utah, Maryland and Florida in 1980 when he decided to buy out Theta Systems, the sixth-ranking U.S. garbage collection firm. This takeover moved Laidlaw up behind the Big Three to become America's fourth largest. Theta, based just outside Chicago, brought the company new markets in Illinois, Indiana, Michigan and Ohio. Acquisition begat acquisition. Through Laidlaw's Grey Goose division, which had followed opportunity by moving its head office from Winnipeg to Edmonton, more U.S. trash outfits were added to the spreading network. The Denver market came on stream, as did those of Corpus Christi and Dallas. The laissez-faire politics of privatization yielded Laidlaw thirty municipal contracts in seven states. Indicative of the company's new orientation was its decision to move its waste headquarters from Kitchener, Ontario, to the Chicago suburb of Hinsdale, Illinois. The competition enforcers in the antitrust division of the Illinois attorney general's office, with their longstanding interest in the garbage industry, took note of the new arrival.

It was also in the United States that Laidlaw made its next attempt to establish for itself a position in toxic waste. The company invested $1.2 million in design and engineering costs for a treatment plant in New York State. In this field public clamour was fairly universal but was particularly intense in a state that had been subjected to the abominations of Occidental Petroleum's Hooker Chemicals at Love Canal and at its Hyde Park landfill.[9]

When objections to a projected Laidlaw plant that would dump treated wastes into the Niagara River emerged, DeGroote finally threw in the towel. Even though his company's annual revenues had just doubled to $200 million in its most ambitious acquisition program ever, he conceded in early 1982 that Laidlaw had not made any headway where toxic waste management was concerned. He told the *Globe and Mail* that "we are now out of the liquid waste business. We don't need the aggravation. We are staying with what we do best and that is the disposal of solid waste."[10]

DeGroote's foresight in building up a strong position in solid waste management was now clear. As the economy once more headed towards heavy seas, it was again Laidlaw's garbage operations that kept the entire array of general commodity carriers, intercity bus lines, packaged bus tours, taxis, school bus services and a Calgary oil company afloat. In the trucking industry, general economic woes were compounded by deregulation in the United States, a legislative anti-union act that a Teamster bribe plot was unable to kill. Deregulation turned the U.S. trucking business into a hornets' nest in which existing outfits struggled to survive in the face of a swarm of 10,000 newly chartered operators paying 20 to 30 per cent less than union wages. In this climate DeGroote sold off a newly acquired, Teamster-organized American trucking subsidiary, BossLinco Incorporated of Buffalo. But Laidlaw's garbage firms and contracts spared it from the debacle of the other golden boy of eastern Canadian trucking, Maislin, which was threatening to come apart in the competitive storms. By late 1982 Laidlaw shares were trading in the record range of $13 to $15. On this course the company looked forward to revenues of $250 million in 1984

— more than half of which would be generated by garbage contracts.

DeGroote was offered SCA in 1984 and at that time he found the asking price for the company unenticing, particularly when combined with what euphemistically was referred to as the firm's "management problems." However, as we saw in Chapter 5, as a result of the Imasco spin off of GSX in 1986, Laidlaw ended up with about 40 per cent of what had been SCA and with it the hazards of chemical waste. Given that DeGroote had foresworn that aspect of the business in early 1982, his return suggested that when it came to disposing of waste once you were in for a penny you might as well be in for a pound.

By pooling GSX's income with its own, Laidlaw pushed towards the billion-dollar revenue mark and fulfillment of Wall Street's expectation that the company was a heavyweight in the making. Once BFI's Bill Ruckelshaus jettisoned CECOS and the Last Chance, Colorado, landfill (the only hazardous waste facility to succeed in being permitted in the U.S. since 1980), the Canadian firm emerged as North America's second most important in the disposal of toxics.

Ten Downing Street

What had attracted DeGroote to America also was to attract Attwoods PLC, a British waste disposer which soon would find itself financially interlocked with Laidlaw. Both foreign firms were drawn by a market made immense not only by the sheer volume of waste but by a unique combination of additional factors. First, there was the American tradition of civic activism which drove legislators to write laws protecting the air, water and ground. Then, once the laws were on the books, the highly commercial personality of the U.S. took over, sanctioning a process which took toxic waste to be a commodity like any other, and thus a legitimate object of trade and source of private profit.

In the United Kingdom, on the other hand, where Thatcherism was uprooting traditions of municipal socialism and privatizing public service, what was missing for would-be commercial waste managers was sufficiently widespread environmental protest to drive public servants into washing their hands and letting the market and private waste disposers cope with the crisis. For when all was said and done, waste magnates owed their unearthly salaries, mansions, limousines and corporate jets to unceasing grass roots activism against pollution.

In *America's Future in Toxic Waste Management,* Bruce Piasecki and Gary Davis contrast the tumultuous U.S. process with the "profound lack of citizen activity" in the U.K. They illustrate this difference by observing that in a 1981 hazardous waste report prepared by the House of Lords' Select Committee on Science and Technology only 6 out of 641 pages of written and oral evidence had been submitted by environmental groups and none by citizen activists.[11] Under such circumstances, it was not surprising that an aspiring waste manager might look covetously across the Atlantic.

Attwoods was the brainchild of a rich used car salesman named Wickens who in 1983 convinced family friend Denis Thatcher, the husband of Prime Minister Thatcher, to join his board. With that cachet, the firm set about to conquer the impressionable New World. However, by the early 1980s, the carcass of North America's old waste industry had been picked fairly clean and (as the SCA-buying public had found out) whatever still remained threatened to be tainted by past associations. So, in negotiating to buy the Florida-based Industrial Waste Service (IWS), Attwoods risked blackening its own nose.

The presence of Attwoods' new deputy chairman Denis Thatcher in the American waste business soon attracted attention. His annual business tour of the company's U.S. operations was local news in Florida. And, in the course of inquiring into a scheme to trans-ship American toxic wastes via Europe to Benin in Africa, a few London-based television producers became intrigued by the protests of some Pennsylvanians about IWS's pursuit of a dumping permit. What worried the protestors — besides imported wastes befouling pristine streams and forests in a wilderness area in the centre of their state — were the possibly disturbing connections between IWS and the underworld.

IWS had been founded in the early 1970s by members of two families, the Casagrandes and Veloccis, long associated with waste carting in Long Island, New York. In buying IWS in 1984, the year after Thatcher came on board, Attwoods not only ingested a much larger operation than its own, thus instantly tripling in size, but also became the second largest waste hauler — after WMI — in Florida.

According to Penn State criminologist Alan Block, who was retained by the British TV producers, Box Productions' interest in the IWS-Attwoods connection was at least twofold: "First, they wanted everything and anything rotten about IWS over the years, and second they wished to know what Attwoods and in particular Denis Thatcher knew about IWS and when. They rightly felt that if there was sufficient evidence of IWS criminality, especially links to organized crime, and that Attwoods and Thatcher had known of this and nevertheless proceeded with the take-over, then this was indeed a very important story."[12]

The focus of the subsequent Box Productions investigation was on Jack R. Casagrande and Ralph Velocci, who as IWS's key executives now ran Attwoods's fast growing U.S. operation. As such they sat cheek-by-jowl on the Attwoods board with the husband of a political leader whose privatization crusade was soon to assume world-wide dimensions with the collapse of Eastern European communism. With their Italian names and their hailing from Long Island, the stigma of Casagrande's and Velocci's origins raised the old issue about the presence of the Mafia in the waste business. For much of the cartage industry of New York and New Jersey had remained — for complex historic reasons — largely immune from takeover by big business culture.

Box's exposé, "A Special Relationship" (presented by *Financial Times* reporter John Plender and telecast across the U.K. by Channel 4 in the summer of 1989), claimed that two companies IWS bought in 1978 were acquired from Joseph Laratro, "an identified member of New York's Lucchese family." The Luccheses were a major crime family who were involved in operating a property rights cartel in Long Island. A counterclaim made to the producers by an Attwoods solicitor that "there is absolutely no evidence from anyone that Jack Casagrande knew or had any contact with Joseph Laratro" is contradicted by other material facts revealed by the program.[13]

Denis Thatcher felt assured by Attwoods' own investigation of IWS. He is reported to have asserted in 1986 that he was "completely satisfied [IWS] was above board. The firm was so clean it wasn't true. We have no concerns of any mafia connections."[14] However, while the Channel 4 program was careful to stress that neither American IWS director nor any members of their families "are or ever have been members of organized crime," it did go on to observe the more noteworthy fact that even as Attwoods was coming to a decision to buy IWS the British directors were aware of (but apparently undeterred by) a grand jury investigation of IWS and the entire South Florida waste industry.[15]

On the heels of the Attwoods takeover, charges of a criminal conspiracy reaching back to the early 1970s to illegally regulate the waste market of populous Dade and Broward counties were brought against IWS, as were subsequent ones under the Sherman Antitrust Act which fingered WMI for having been party to a customer allocation scheme involving IWS and said to have lasted at least five years. WMI was accused of having met with the likes of IWS and others to "even things out" in South Florida.[16]

This alleged meeting of minds between IWS and the world's largest publicly held garbage firm was hardly market regulation by underworld fiat. Sir Denis was right: the important IWS connection here was not with the Mafia. It was with big — and getting bigger all the time — business.

IWS pleaded no contest in 1986 and, in mitigation, its lawyer tried a bit of name dropping before the judge passed out the fines. Not only did he try to assure the court that Attwoods had taken steps to curb monopolistic practices but added that IWS now was associated with some very prominent people, the most prominent of whom shared quarters with the occupant of 10 Downing Street. For its alleged part in secretly regulating a market which by 1984 allowed waste contractors to share annual revenues exceeding $45 million, WMI pleaded no contest and paid out the maximum $1 million fine. Two of its officers were convicted and fined. One was briefly confined.[17]

The Ocala Garbage Converter

However important the nuances which differentiate under and upper world business practice for the purposes of public policy-making may be, they collapse into irrelevance when the pollution control industry in any of its various guises is endangering human prospects for a healthy and safe future. So for Jack Casagrande and his colleagues, the controversy surrounding a disposal scheme in the farming and horse breeding country of central Florida raised perhaps the most serious questions of all.

In the mid-1970s, some promoters got behind the idea of a pyrolytic converter which was supposed to convert garbage into commercial grade fuel. The scheme was the brainchild of Rocco

Velocci and Salvatore Avellino, a close associate of the notorious Luchese family. Also involved were Pericles Constantinou, a convicted securities swindler and former associate of fugitive financier Robert Vesco, and Mel Cooper, a New York waste industry financier, now serving thirty years for racketeering and extortion.[18]

The waste-to-energy scheme bore all the trappings of a Hollywood farce. The promoters exploited technology said to originate with a Santa Ana, California, engineering company backed by movie star John Wayne. A marketing firm set up by the promoters and an affiliate, Urban Waste Disposal, granted the right to sell and operate the system. According to court and official documents, as reported in "A Special Relationship," Jack Casagrande and Ralph Velocci's brother Rocco sat on the board of Urban Waste from 1982 until 1987. Casagrande's lawyer told the producers of the documentary exposé that "Casagrande's name only appeared as a result of a clerical error."[19]

But even as Casagrande began reaching for the social and political heights in England, his reputation was to be entangled by the continuing ties of IWS to the lower depths of the commercial world. According to the Channel 4 program, the civic fathers of Ocala, Marion County, Florida, fell under the spell of the promoters in 1982, and signed on for a fifty-ton-per-day version of the garbage convertor. In return for the promised delivery of the wonder machine which was supposed to produce one barrel of marketable oil per ton of solid waste and "pipeline-grade" gas, Urban Disposal got control of a coveted local landfill — the key to the multiple-pronged tax break and stock promotion — whose daily operation was then contracted out to an IWS subsidiary.[20]

Not too surprisingly, given the provenance of the promoters, Ocala never laid eyes on pipeline-grade anything. What they got, however, was a landfill operation which allowed "numerous people on a daily basis to come upon the landfill with thousands of gallons of raw, stinking, untreated sewage from septic tanks, much of which contains human feces, urine and other deleterious substances and to dump the same openly on the ground."[21]

By 1987, believing their groundwater to be suffering, and still no pyrolysis machine in sight, the authorities of Marion County cried fraud and launched legal action to have the Attwoods subsidiary removed from the landfill. But before these charges were settled, IWS was to find itself allied with even more powerful waste managers than Sir Denis's Attwoods.

In 1988, Michael DeGroote, asserting that the time had come to turn his mind to planning his personal estate, declared that he wanted to sell his controlling interest in Laidlaw. At the time of his announcement, DeGroote was only 55 and Laidlaw still was riding the crest of investor confidence with share profit growing annually at 50 per cent. But in wanting out, DeGroote was possibly acknowledging, to himself at least, that the industry's entrepreneurial phase was ending. Actually managing what he had wrought was going to make far more complex demands than simply deal-making and operating the business like so many oil wells in reverse (as once he had claimed it was): the more you pumped into the ground, the more profits you pumped out.[22]

Canadian Pacific

At a press conference on 30 March 1988, DeGroote explained that the "zeros behind the numbers are getting so big, the company should not belong to one person. It's a big machine and it's rolling pretty fast."[23] He added that whatever offer was made must include a bid not only for his control block but also for non-voting shares held by the public. Major investment houses began ringing to learn the ground rules for the sale of the $4-billion firm: there were questions such as whether DeGroote's wanting a Canadian buyer was a condition or merely a preference.

Swallowing Laidlaw whole meant paying an enormous price for goodwill, or the money value of the company's intangible assets and reputation. As Cecil Foster reported in the *Globe and Mail*, 28 major investment bankers, six banks and several accounting firms met with the company to try securing a deal. All came to nought, foundering on the issue of goodwill, that accounting confection which DeGroote was prepared to pass on like a mystical aura. The asking price for goodwill was at least three times the book value of the company's tangible assets.[24] Speculators drove up share prices, anticipating that a buyer for such a prize cash flow machine would surely be found.

In May 1988, having had no serious offer for the voting and non-voting shares, DeGroote ended up selling his personal stake in the company to one of the bluest of Canada's blue chip corporations. For a reported $220 million in cash plus shares in the purchaser, Canadian Pacific Limited of Montreal (CP), DeGroote turned over control of Laidlaw and in the process ended up being the largest individual shareholder in the transportation and resources conglomerate.[25] Left high and dry to watch their non-voting shares nose downwards to record lows were the minority shareholders whom DeGroote had proved unable to protect. His aura proved not to be readily transferable and, as a result, the only shareholder to profit massively from the sale turned out to be DeGroote himself.

The merging of the railway and waste businesses was further evidence of the continental evolution of the waste trade with the consequent transfer of control further and further from the local level. The previous year, Union Pacific Corporation of New York, which owns Union Pacific Railroad, paid $415 million for a small Oklahoma waste firm, evidently convinced that, as one analyst put it, "the hazardous and waste management industry is good to get into. It provides synergies for the railroads and there is more money in transporting the waste than in moving some commodities."[26]

DeGroote's final year at Laidlaw was marked by the issuance of millions of new non-voting shares and major acquisitions that were not unlike the culminating bursts of a fireworks extravaganza. But for many, including Laidlaw shareholders, the grand finale was less than impressive.

Canadians in Britain

First of all there was the matter of ADT Incorporated, whose chairman, British businessman Michael Ashcroft, had been one of Laidlaw's prospective suitors. CP beat out ADT, but DeGroote and Ashcroft, who was also on the board of Attwoods, reportedly hit it off, and joined each other's boards. By 1989 DeGroote had bought what amounted to 52 million shares in ADT, a major stake in the rising British firm, whose business combined such ostensibly recession-proof activities as security systems and, through its 5 per cent holdings in Christie's, art auctioning.

Business reporter Diane Francis found this marriage of waste, security and fine art a dandy one. She informed readers of her *Financial Post* column that "ADT is the world's biggest electronic surveillance company, with 90% of its sales in the crime-ridden U.S. There, paranoia means profit and ADT is twice the size of its biggest rival."[27] To top it all, Laidlaw had also bought Ashcroft's 29% share in Attwoods.

But this billion-dollar buying spree almost instantly began to provoke misgivings. Under an August 1989 *Globe and Mail* headline announcing "a nice ride, but time to leave the Laidlaw bus," analyst Peter von Orden was quoted as saying the "bloom is off the [Laidlaw] rose."[28]

In June 1990, DeGroote nimbly bowed out from Laidlaw. Just as he was getting caught up trying to buy Perot's Island, one of Bermuda's grandest estates, from a wealthy heiress, a bitter power struggle between Laidlaw and ADT spilled into the courts.

Matters cannot have been helped by press reports (denied vigorously by ADT) of speculation arising in the British parliament about an alleged investigation of ADT's Michael Ashcroft by the British Serious Fraud Office.[29] As reported by the *Toronto Star*, Laidlaw, having become increasingly dissatisfied with how ADT was managed by a tightly knit group of executives around Ashcroft, was seeking representation on ADT's board proportional to its stake in the company.[30] The Canadians ended up getting what they wanted in a 1991 agreement which saw all litigation withdrawn.

Ashcroft was to step down in a 1991 reshuffling of the Attwoods board, to be replaced by Laidlaw's top three officers. The stolid blue-chip Canadians, whose company owned almost 30 per cent of Attwoods, were to take their places beside other Attwoods directors as such as Chairman Ken Foreman, Sir Denis Thatcher, and Jack Casagrande and Ralph Velocci of IWS.

This then was the cast of characters which now turned its collective mind to bringing the benefits of privatization to the benighted regions of the former Soviet Eastern bloc. "Reunification has opened up a captive market in eastern Germany," trumpeted the 1991 Attwoods annual report, "providing established companies in Germany with unique potential for expansion." But the prospect of capturing East Germany did not divert investors from trouble at home.

Lost Trust

Laidlaw fought diligently for several years to control Tricil (Canada's largest hazardous waste company) and, according to environmental writer Jeffrey Smith, the jewel in that corporate crown was the country's highest volume incinerator, treatment plant and landfill facility at Sarnia, Ontario. But the discovery of hidden PCB containers on the Mercier, Quebec, site which was part and parcel of Laidlaw's 1989 acquisition of Tricil contained "all sorts of unpleasant surprises for investors."[31] The reckoning for a decade's fevered deal-making was now at hand.

Laidlaw's antiquated GSX treatment facility in Cleveland, Ohio, had to be written off following public demonstrations and threatened court action. And no sooner had Laidlaw's new CEO, Don Jackson, assured analysts that the Cleveland facility was his only problem site than the *Globe and Mail* ran reporter Zuhair Kashmeri's catalogue of on-going controversy about the health and environmental impact of hazardous waste facilities which the company had inherited in Pinewood and Roebuck, South Carolina, and in Columbus, Ohio.[32]

Then, the following month, came more unsettling news. In Operation Lost Trust, a Federal Bureau of Investigation exposure of vote-selling in South Carolina, more than a dozen state senators, a circuit judge, a governor's aide and six lobbyists were eventually entrapped. The State House sting also led indirectly to the indictment of Rep. John I. "Jack" Rogers III on charges that involved the Laidlaw GSX subsidiary there.

While on most issues, Rogers, the speaker *pro tempore* and the state's second most powerful legislator, had been regarded as politically progressive, in the area of waste management environmentalists saw him as a representative of Laidlaw's interests. "On hazardous waste he had a zero rating," claims Bill MacIntosh of Citizens Local Environmental Action (CLEAN). "Jack Rogers was Laidlaw's floor leader. Period." Rogers's ultimate fall resulted when his close relationship with a GSX lobbyist went mysteriously awry.

The GSX/Laidlaw lobbyist, Ken Kinard, was never named in the criminal charges but sources did identify him to the local press as the person who gave Rogers $13,500 of his salary in return for his votes.[33] Charges included accusations that Rogers had corruptly accepted gifts and gratuities "under an implied agreement and understanding with a representative of GSX (Laidlaw) that the defendant's vote ... would be given ... on a particular side of a question, cause and proceeding involving the handling of hazardous waste in South Carolina."[34]

Laidlaw denied any involvement in the pay-off and claimed Kinard was the only one who knew what his activities were.[35] Rogers eventually pleaded guilty to racketeering and was sentenced to forty-six months in prison. Kinard was portrayed by his lawyer as Rogers's involuntary victim and neither he nor his employer, Laidlaw, were ever charged with wrong-doing.

All the controversy — coming after DeGroote's retirement to his Bermuda tax haven — so depressed Laidlaw's stock that soon it was trading at about half what CP had paid DeGroote for his. Fifteen months after the founder's departure, one American analyst told *The Financial Post* that "there are a lot of people who are still pissed off with DeGroote, because when he left, the stock plummeted."[36]

Scapegoating the once venerated DeGroote continued into Laidlaw's December 1991 annual general meeting, which grass roots activist Rhonda Hustler was attending for the third time. Hustler, a modern literature professor and the Warwick Watford Landfill Committee chair, and her activist colleagues (part of an Ontario network of citizens' groups at Laidlaw landfills) were attending the Royal York Hotel gathering in downtown Toronto to attempt a bit of consciousness raising. They handed shareholders pamphlets apprising them of what they took to be evidence of the company's environmental crimes and misdemeanors, and of its irresponsibility in relying on landfilling and incineration as sound means of managing wastes.

What struck Hustler was how — in contrast to previous Laidlaw AGMs — attitudes were changing. Shareholders made a point of seeking out the activists and expressing support. Profit-addicted analysts muttered (as they had when Ruckelshaus replaced Harry Phillips at BFI) about DeGroote's departure having cut off the company at the knees. But senior executives like Don Jackson, the University of Western Ontario-trained MBA who took over from DeGroote, admitted that waste management in the 1990s was going to be different than it had been in the 1980s.

Negative reaction to the changing of the guard illustrated how uneasily the pure and simple profit motive sat with socially responsible waste management. Cecil Foster provided evidence for this in a March 1991 article in *The Financial Post* where he noted that "analysts were describing Jackson as a mere manager — a conservative strategist concerned with maintaining what was already on the balance sheet — not the kind of risk-taking entrepreneur some investors felt should be the natural heir to DeGroote."[37]

Recognizing that the Rhonda Hustlers of the world were here to stay, corporate language was beginning to be refashioned. In response to Hustler's claim that "there was no more political space for landfills," Jackson tried to assure shareholders that Laidlaw was going to seek dialogue and common cause with citizens.

One germane example of fast-closing political space came far from the Toronto gathering. It was the lawsuit which had — like an overturned stone — exposed the pyrolysis promoters. Edwin Cluster, the lawyer representing Marion County, was amazed by how much interest his seemingly backwater Florida case had provoked. Not only was he to be hounded by the British documentary producers but he also found himself fielding telephone inquiries from as far away as Germany and the Persian Gulf.

The makers of "A Special Relationship" reported that IWS had been prepared to pay up to $15 million to clean their mess in Ocala, build new cells and further develop the landfill.[38] But according to Cluster, who negotiated with Attwoods' Ken Foreman and Ralph Velocci, his clients would have none of it. They insisted on straight cash and IWS out. "I wanted them to pay me with a cashier's cheque," reported Cluster — which is what he got from Attwoods in February 1991. For $2 million and a further contribution to Florida's law enforcement agencies for its costs, the case was dismissed.

The Channel 4 inquiry ended on a woolly note. The program gave the Attwoods board the benefit of the doubt, assuming that but for a more rigorous inquiry into IWS's background, "Denis Thatcher might not have subsequently professed such a lack of concern" about the associations of their future American business partners. For his part, an Attwoods spokesperson sought to assure Britons that the company's Miami lawyer had produced a thick antitrust compliance manual and gone so far as to appoint an attorney whose sole job was to make sure that every individual complied.[39]

The audience was left, in effect, to draw its own conclusions about the state of affairs at Attwoods. "There must be some prospect," concluded John Plender, "that the whole business will spill over into the political realm."[40] Indeed, the entire waste management business was spilling over into the political realm.

On the other side of the Atlantic, in New York City, an emeritus Columbia School of Journalism professor and distinguished broadcaster was advising students on the look out for career-making subject matter to turn their minds to the yet unexplored matter of garbage and what happened to it.

Yet to expose to public view the actual character of the waste business today, these fledgling reporters would have to look beyond the myth of the omnipresent Mafia and the industry's ancestral face. The dominant companies — the ones said to be evolving into a "shadow government" — were becoming corporate entities quite unlike anything yet seen. Exactly what kind of institutions they were becoming is the important question to which we next turn.

Chapter 7

Derelict Conduct? Captive Markets and Class Action

Reasonable minds can only conclude that the activity which generated the antitrust violations, law suits, and fines, was not solely the acts of BFI's employee, David M. Yeager.

J. Ronald Bowman, Judge, April 1991

The Coach

In the past few years, serious allegations have been made of the existence of an entente between WMI and BFI that reached far beyond local "property rights" cartels into the upper reaches of the corporations' national headquarters. In the recent history of the waste industry few attempts to expose this alleged national entente have been more determined than that of David Yeager.

Yeager seems an unlikely candidate for the role of whistle-blower; he was neither an environmental activist nor was he fighting to keep his backyard free of a mega-dump or billion-dollar incinerator. He was a second-generation garbageman, and his obsession with exposing corporate misconduct was more a matter of circumstance and character rather than of conscious design.

Significantly, at St. Mary's High School, Yeager played fullback and, according to one of his lawyers, had a reputation for loving to run over rather than around people. He began hauling refuse midway between Columbus and Toledo, Ohio, in the early 1960s when, at twenty-three, he took over part of his father's refuse business with both men sharing one truck. He was the first local hauler to get into containerized pickup and thereafter his E-Z Pack rear loaders were a familiar sight around the resort town of Sandusky on Lake Erie. Yeager served as a city commissioner and on the board of health, captained the United Fund Drive, and belonged to the Chamber of Commerce, the Knights of Columbus, the Jaycees, the Eagles, the Kiwanis Club and, of course, the National Solid Wastes Management Association.

One year, at an Erie County Fair, he demonstrated a drive-through refuse disposal station. Then, later on, he got himself arrested repeatedly by defying a ban on private pickup in Sandusky until he succeeded in having the ordinance overturned. In 1972, during BFI's first round of acquisitions, Yeager sold his firm to Tom Fatjo's group and stayed on to manage the new subsidiary. He and BFI's local operations manager invented a tabletop compactor to measure the pressure required to crush various types of industrial waste and, for their efforts, ended up with a patent number as a testament to their inventiveness. Thus, by 1976, when BFI brought the Sandusky native into its Toledo office as vice president and general manager of BFI of Ohio and Michigan, it is fair to say he was a self-starter and a man who knew a thing or two about making a living in the waste trade.

At first, Yeager's streak of all-American entrepreneurialism flourished inside BFI. In 1976, BFI and WMI were Toledo's key waste haulers. But the former was not making the profits required by head office, and quickly, by means of his aggressive efforts, Yeager increased BFI's market share at WMI's expense.

By setting high goals for his staff, encouraging team work, holding pep rallies and even introducing a trophy room with a Most Improved Player and Toledo Superbowl Award, Yeager became known as the "Coach." Colourfully decorated blue and white company trucks entered parades and a BFI radio jingle was set to the "William Tell Overture." A September 1977 congratulatory letter signed with best wishes and kindest personal regards by BFI president Harry Phillips commended the new man for his spectacular performance. Copies were sent to such senior executives as John Drury and Tom Fatjo and as well to Yeager's immediate superior, regional vice president Bruce Ranck. By the following March, Phillips was telling Yeager, in a letter cc'd to Drury and Ranck, that BFI might suggest a Yeager Cloning Program in the interest of long-term personnel planning. CEO John Drury later wrote Yeager too. His note of appreciation lauded the local vice president for having turned around a hopeless situation.

Clearly, Yeager had arrived. But the "Coach" was not cut out for falling into line in a regimented corporation. He began to find being a team player had its limits, particularly when it came to pricing strategies which had been mandated on high. Mysteriously, he found that these strategies seemed to lack the competitive drive that was Yeager's forte.

A senior BFI executive was to assert that "all pricing of BFI's waste collection services is done *strictly* on a local level." Yet Yeager and the plaintiffs in a class action later filed in Philadelphia against BFI and WMI on behalf of all consumers of containerized waste collection (a lawsuit spearheaded by the firm of Kohn, Savett, Klein & Graf and heavily reliant on the say-so of Yeager) were to dispute this claim. "Discovery has confirmed that, far from being an aggregation of autonomous regions and districts, defendants' operations are highly centralized, with senior executives from corporate headquarters monitoring, controlling, dictating and enforcing pricing and marketing strategies, and virtually every important aspect of field operations." [1]

Compared to WMI, where everything of importance was said to be decided in Oak Brook, BFI's approach was reputedly far looser. Harry Phillips's penchant for overseeing the company from his Memphis home seemed to confirm this hands-off attitude.[2] However, much legal effort was to be expended attempting to debunk this myth of BFI's laid-back decentralism. The counter-reality saw the firm as a highly centralized hierarchy whose senior officers extended their control by serving as directors and officers of operating subsidiaries.

"The magic I'm talking about is the results we'll achieve by management getting personally involved in the details of the business," John Drury reportedly told his regional vice presidents. "We also need to get personally involved in the productivity and sales programs. While I'm on this subject, we've been hearing too many excuses for too long a time as to why so and so program hasn't been done in my district, etc., etc. There is no excuse for the programs not being done, each and every program in each and every district. These programs are mandatory and anyone that isn't doing them properly should be looking for a job."[3]

Kohn, Savett's investigation indicated the company had devised internal accounting mechanisms allowing headquarters to "actually dictate the pricing and profit margin formulae."[4] Districts were linked by computer terminals to what Oberlin College economist Jim Zinsor (hired as an expert in subsequent predatory practices lawsuits) describes as "awesome" programs allowing Houston and

Oak Brook systematically to identify "successful" and "unsuccessful" local operations.

In fact, notwithstanding his having been retained by opponents of the Big Two to find damning evidence of conspiracy in company-generated data, Zinsor marvels at their accounting systems and attributes much of the firms' success to their skilled use of them. As they move from operating subsidiary through the regional to the head office level, monthly operating records (or MORs, as they are called) consolidate financial and operating data so as to provide management with the most minute operating data, from the waste volumes being generated by a particular pizza parlour or mall to how many yards of waste per hour are being hauled by an individual packer on the streets of any one of hundreds of towns and cities. Most crucially, the MORs inform local managers about the pricing structure necessary to achieve profitability levels mandated by senior officers.

Pricing tools were said to be set, controlled and monitored in Houston. These directives were seen as a serious matter. The founder's son, W.C. Fatjo, Jr., is quoted as stating that BFI had spent years and hundreds of thousands of dollars "developing the methods and computer programs which determine BFI's costs and prices for each type and category of service that BFI provides."[5] Houston's banking role further tightened control. Not only were "all monies received by the district ... extracted from the local bank accounts and pooled into two 'national office bank accounts'" but all bills including local payrolls were said to be forwarded to Houston. "At most, $1,000 may be left each night in a district's operating account."[6]

"Coach" Yeager's results were highlighted in BFI's 1979 annual report, which quoted him as saying "we have now created an image of being a winning company, and everybody likes to deal with a winner. It makes the customer feel like a winner, just by association." That summer, Yeager wrote John Drury in Houston to say that WMI had thrown everything possible at him, including low prices and five changes in management but he had prevailed. He asked for enough resources to ensure BFI's absolute dominance. Then, that December, he wrote Bruce Ranck in Baltimore explaining his theory (in words that later must have struck him as fantastically naïve) that winning was simply a question of picking up waste better and cheaper than the competition. He acknowledged to Ranck that he was aware of considerable corporate pressure at the regional level but implored his immediate boss to have the conviction and confidence to take exception to some of the mandated programs — and let him loose.

Claiming his success made his district the exception and BFI's other 155 line companies the rule, Yeager asked Ranck for a free hand to give new meaning to BFI's slogan about being a company building an industry. BFI's general sales manager was sent to Toledo in early 1980 for hands-on experience, and Yeager was thanked effusively by Houston for his efforts. But in spite of Yeager's growing reputation (Toledo revenues up 300 per cent and dramatically increased profits), Ranck evidently was tiring of his rambunctious subordinate's reluctance to submit to compulsory procedures. He admonished Yeager, explaining that he would approve any request and explain it to John Drury so long as he first got a purchase order. By 1980, purchase orders were not the half of it. Yeager's grandstand act, as he later was to allege, was beginning to disquiet his superiors.

According to a subsequent court memorandum, BFI's vice president for labour relations raised the matter of the on-going local war against WMI with Yeager during a meeting about labour problems.[7] When later asked under oath, "And what did Mr. Mooney say to you on the subject of your competition with Waste Management?" Yeager testified: "The specific instance that is clear in my mind is, he said words to the effect, Dave, the only one that wins in a price war is a customer, why don't you get together with Waste Management and work something out."[8]

Yeager was to make further claims (all denied vehemently by BFI) implicating his superiors in an illicit scheme to conclude a peace. He alleged that BFI's outside national labour counsel added his suggestion that Yeager arrive at a *modus vivendi* by getting together with WMI under the pretense of wanting to dump in their landfill "and see what you could work out."[9] Still, he refused to act.

The following year at a regional BFI meeting in Baltimore, Ranck called him aside and, according to later testimony, allegedly said, "Dave we have more to lose than we have to gain. Waste Management simply will not tolerate further embarrassment or loss of market share."[10] Yeager claimed he resisted, thinking the sacrifice of some short-term profit would ultimately see BFI displace WMI and emerge as the only national company in greater Toledo. But eventually, fatefully for himself and his employer, the Coach had a change, if not of heart, certainly of mind.

Believing his refusal to go along with a fix might jeopardize his career, and that the message to him had added authority by virtue of what he took to be the close relationship between Ranck and John Drury, Yeager claimed that he threw in the towel after — again according to his testimony — Ranck said "he had a contact at Waste Management that he worked with in other areas that could be trusted. He told me he had been in contact with that individual, that individual's willing to meet with me and to work something out in Toledo to end the price war ..." [11]

The contact, Richard Evenhouse, worked for BFI in the mid-1970s and had reported to Ranck. In 1980, he held a position similar to Ranck's with WMI in Detroit where the subsequent class action alleged the two waste executives met in late January 1981. Evenhouse denied he ever discussed Toledo with Ranck but, as the Yeager scenario had it, on Sunday, February 1, Ranck phoned him at home and instructed him "that Evenhouse would be calling the following day and that they should arrange a meeting for the purpose of ending the price war." [12]

Yeager, who claimed to have been instructed by a senior BFI executive to tape his calls, recorded the one he did receive the next day from Evenhouse and agreed to meet two days hence in Monroe, Michigan. At that meeting a deal supposedly was struck to conform with what eventually would be portrayed by the class action as a larger master plan between the Big Two to even out market share nationally. Aggressive competition between the majors ended soon afterward in Toledo, leaving BFI to turn its attention to other pressing matters, such as a $300-million lawsuit filed against it that year in the free-enterprise city of Houston.

In Houston, a firm called Conservation Management was alleging that BFI had attempted to put a lock on the solid waste market in its home turf and surrounding Harris County. But a few days into the trial, the case was disposed of by means of a settlement. The multi-national purchased Conservation for millions of dollars and succeeded through the sealing of all court material in burying from further scrutiny details of the case (which involved a controversial $25,000 payment to a Texas state senator). [13]

While the alleged understanding in Toledo was typical of ones with which the reader by now is familiar, what was not typical was how it continued to haunt the lives of waste executives. The Toledo entente became part of the foundation on which were raised various private lawsuits which, for the first time, began to reveal evidence suggesting the possibility that cartelization was not (as the firms repeatedly liked to claim) a matter of unconnected and unsanctioned "local" conspiracies. It might be nearer to the truth to portray it as a matter of conscious design.

Controversy surrounds Yeager's departure from BFI. One reason he had been brought to Toledo in the first place was to handle the Teamsters. A source close to Yeager claimed that the outlaw union gave BFI a choice. Either Yeager went or BFI didn't get labour peace. Yeager did leave at the end of 1982, later asserting he quit because he could not stomach the anti-competitive ethos. But whatever the cause, the private accord to regulate greater metropolitan Toledo's waste market apparently continued without him. Evidence was to emerge later in a government lawsuit of illicit off-premises meetings after Yeager's departure. Local officers of the Big Two allegedly met to co-ordinate price increases and rig bids. Then to cover their tracks, records were falsified to hide the true nature of these private sessions to regulate the market.

"Evergreen"

In August 1983, Yeager bounced back as an independent, painting jungle scenes on his trucks and running under the name Community Disposal Service. His publicity campaigns attracted customers, some of whom had been served by BFI and WMI. But those who decided to switch to CDS found themselves boxed in.

The majors had introduced nearly identical service agreements, whose finely printed clauses and complicated cancellation terms gave legal gloss to an underlying reality. By signing them, customers for disposal services found themselves being corralled onto the domains of one or the other of the continental waste overlords.

Yeager complained to Ohio officials and later was to allege that these agreements were "part of BFI and WMI's attempt to create a permanent consumer franchise in accordance with their national master plan."[14] The companies, in enforcing them, were alleged by Yeager to be sewing up much of his potential market with legal threats to customers who wished to switch to CDS. WMI's counsel had warned Yeager not to solicit its customers and BFI, asserting that Yeager was in breach of an undertaking not to compete with it, sued him. At the time, Ohio was unprepared to look at these agreements, called "evergreen" because they never expired. But when Laidlaw sought to introduce evergreen agreements elsewhere, the Canadian company was to discover that in other jurisdictions they were viewed less benignly.

Laidlaw had mailed agreements to commercial and industrial customers in San Diego County and throughout California, and, like Yeager, the customers raised a stink. The documents had removable stickers indicating the forms were required for insurance purposes or as pledges that customers (20,000 reportedly were involved) were disposing only non-hazardous wastes. However, according to California's attorney general who laid fraud charges under the Business and Professions Code, once the signed forms were returned, the stickers were peeled off and filed as binding contracts.[15]

Furthermore, the company (as was alleged in *California* v. *Laidlaw*) gave short shrift to customers claiming to have been gulled, refused to remove its dumpsters, threatened lawsuits, demanded a six-month service charge as a cancellation fee, threatened other waste firms who were invited in by their former customers, and, for good measure, threatened employees impudent enough to protest such behaviour.

Without admitting liability, Laidlaw settled the California lawsuit for $3 million only to have similar cries of outrage arise from disaffected customers and competitors clustered along Highway Nos. 1 and 19 on the eastern side of Vancouver Island. These protests caught the attention of the Canadian anti-combines authorities who brought the matter to the Competition Tribunal.

Laidlaw had entered the Cowichan Valley, Nanaimo and Campbell River areas in the late 1980s and moved aggressively to buy out local competition. Evidence presented before the Tribunal revealed that the industry's primitive pre–Wall Street culture lived on in its supposedly more evolved stage of development. One small operator was warned that if he did not sell his company "Laidlaw would see it put out of business by causing [it] extensive and expensive litigation costs." Another was told Laidlaw would use its market power "to ensure that it was put out of the market by way of price competition." Yet another message had it that "Laidlaw had other methods of achieving what it wanted."[16]

Once Laidlaw was in control of what the Tribunal estimated to be 87 per cent of the markets in question, the firm did what Dave Yeager had been complaining had been done to prevent the likes of CDS from competing in the Ohio market. The firm threw up a barrier in front of would-be independent poachers using the "ever-green" roll-over contracts.

The Tribunal raised a collective eyebrow upon hearing how Laidlaw managed to get these contracts signed: "A disturbingly recurring theme through much of the evidence before the Tribunal was that signatures on many of these contracts had been obtained by representing to the customers that the documents they were being asked to sign were 'a mere formality', or because it was 'the national corporate practice which Laidlaw followed.'"[17]

As Yeager had asserted, customers only realized they had a written contract when they attempted to take their business elsewhere. Laidlaw quickly made its captive customer and prospective competitor aware that unless they desisted they would be in breach of contract, and the attendant legal costs would wipe out the customer's hoped-for savings. If the customer persisted, Laidlaw unleashed its local counsel. "I have personally handled several such actions," read one such lawyer's missive. "If Mr. Andrinopolos winds up paying Laidlaw damages for breach of contract, he will inevitably find that the expected short-term price of reduction will disappear." One local contractor opened his mail to find himself being apprised by a solicitor acting on behalf of the world's third largest waste disposal firm that "Laidlaw has pursued many such actions against its customers over the last few years and has not been unsuccessful to date."[18]

In seeking to convince the Tribunal that the contracts were not designed specifically to restrict competition in Vancouver Island, Laidlaw made a very revealing argument. It asserted that the contracts were necessary on the larger stage where it had to go up against its real rivals — BFI and WMI. The Tribunal was unimpressed by the argument of "we are doing it because they are doing it" and ultimately found (as Yeager originally had claimed) "there is no credible explanation for many of the provisions of these contracts other than to create barriers to entry for would-be competitors."[19]

"No one can read the evidence concerning the use Laidlaw made of litigation and the threat of litigation in this case without a sense of outrage," the presiding Tribunal members wrote, quoting with approval the reflections of the conservative American jurist R.H. Bork. "As a technique for predation, sham litigation is theoretically one of the most promising ... This mode of predation is particularly insidious because of its relatively low antitrust visibility."[20] The

Competition Tribunal went on to say that Laidlaw "used its vastly larger size and economic resources together with the threat of litigation to prevent customers from switching to competitors. It commenced spurious litigation and threatened litigation against its competitors to drive or attempt to drive them out of business by raising their costs of doing business. This is certainly predatory behaviour."[21]

The Tribunal ordered Laidlaw to modify its agreements in the minuscule markets at issue, but as for the question of the legitimacy of their on-going use throughout North America, this was a matter beyond the purview of the Tribunal and had to be left for another day and other jurisdictions.

Witness

Besides such service agreements, Yeager and CDS had faced other impediments as well. He was later to claim (in a lawsuit against WMI) that following an "across-the-board" price increase by WMI's Ohio Waste Systems in late 1982, BFI responded to an avalanche of calls from WMI's customers by coming up with two different price lists: a prohibitively high and unattractive one for WMI's customers; a low and enticing one for customers of independent haulers. Furthermore, these latter customers were promised a written guarantee of low rates for up to three years and an inducement to switch from the independents. That done, according to Yeager, "BFI then intends to recoup their initial investment by exercising their 'property rights.'"[22]

Though independents often can co-exist alongside dominant haulers, making good money under the umbrella of the oligopolistic pricing regimes, Yeager was unwilling to continue any longer. In April 1985, he once again sold out to BFI. Besides his trucks, radios, containers and customer lists, Yeager agreed to turn over undestroyed tape recordings and transcriptions of statements made by BFI officers or which concerned BFI. But what BFI had not yet bought was Yeager's silence. And not having that threatened to end up costing far more than whatever BFI had shelled out for a few packers and some tapes.

Eventually Ohio did take a closer look into the waste business and, when it did, it came to Yeager. He first invoked the Fifth Amendment to protect himself against self-incrimination for what he had done while at BFI. But by the next year, having secured immunity, he began to let his tale spill out. His story sought to incriminate high BFI officials and, after one year's investigation and the production of 80,000 pages of documents, it led Attorney General Anthony Celebrezze, Jr.'s staff to conclude "the regional divisions of the two largest waste companies in the world [had] conspired to fix prices and control the waste disposal business in the Northwestern Ohio and Southern Michigan areas."[23]

In May 1986, Celebrezze laid charges, accusing the majors (which controlled about 70 per cent of the greater Toledo market) of having operated a regional cartel in the Northwestern Ohio and Southern Michigan areas between 1981 and at least 1984 — two years after Yeager's leave-taking from BFI. The civil complaint named Bruce Ranck and John Taddino (who had replaced Yeager at BFI in Toledo and would be later promoted to head BFI's Italian division). The familiar catalogue of allegations included the charge that the accused had "developed separate price lists which were used for quoting inflated prices to their co-conspirator's established customers, and [had] disciplined sales representatives who quoted competitive prices to their co-conspirators established customers."[24] But before Ohio's charges could play themselves out, Yeager was caught in another investigation.

The year 1987 was to see a quickening of judicial examinations of the waste industry with a reported eleven grand juries looking into its business practices across the U.S. Federal Justice Department attorneys wanted the "Coach" to appear before a grand jury in Cleveland, but he was fearful. He did not envy facing his old team alone, becoming the only ex-BFI player to testify against his former employer. However, with another grant of immunity, Yeager was persuaded and by so doing, became a central force in a tidal wave of lawsuits to come.

BFI, for its part, succeeded in having Yeager added as a defendant in Celebrezze's lawsuit, a move the former fullback saw as a way to intimidate him from further co-operation not only as a key witness for Ohio but also in a pending national class action. By means of a Third Party Complaint, BFI was positioning itself on the legal chess board to pin any cartel conspiracy on Yeager and hold him personally liable for damages to the company arising out of the charges. Even though, by his own account, he was overcome by paranoia, Yeager became obsessed with wreaking vengeance for what he saw as BFI's betrayal. "I was afraid of being shot at or having my car bombed, and I would often suspect that I was being followed or placed under surveillance or that my telephone was being tapped. I had recurrent nightmares involving these sub-jects."[25] But, given his experience, Yeager surely must have known in his more lucid moments that Houston hardly needed to rely on physical violence. BFI could dislodge obstacles from its path far more licitly by means of the all-purpose solvent, money.

In September 1987, a federal antitrust attorney informed a BFI counsel that "your client, Bruce E. Ranck, is a target of a current grand jury investigation. The grand jury has substantial evidence linking your client to the commission of a crime and, in our judge-ment your client is a putative defendant. The Antitrust Division is seriously considering recommending to a grand jury that your client be indicted."[26] Just one month after the issuing of the target letter, BFI (and WMI) bargained their ways out of a corner, pleading guilty to a one-count felony charge up to November 1982. The date happened to coincide with Yeager's departure from BFI. Both companies wrote out $1-million cheques to the Clerk of the U.S. District Court for the Northern District of Ohio. And Houston issued a press release which laid the entire blame for the criminal conspiracy during a twenty-month period from February 1, 1981 until late 1982 at the feet of Yeager:

> Yeager's activities came to light after he had approached Ohio law enforcement authorities while he was a competitor, com-plained that BFI and other competitors' service contracts were anti-competitive. When authorities rebuffed him, he added the suggestion that he had conspired to fix prices during his period of employment with BFI. Yeager then sought to implicate others in exchange for immunity for himself. While Yeager received that immunity, no Browning-Ferris employees were indicted or charged.

> The upshot of all this is that a disgruntled former employee and competitor who left the company five years ago, received immunity from prosecution for his unlawful conduct, and his former employer was fined $1 million.

> Browning-Ferris does not tolerate violations of anti-trust stat-utes by its employees. The company has a strong affirmative action program in place to support its policies. The Toledo

affair occurred over five years ago in defiance of these policies, and solely as a result of Yeager's derelict conduct. While
this kind of unauthorized, spurious activity is impossible to
completely guard against, the company believes its system of
vigilance provides the necessary safeguards to prevent a re-
currence. We believe this case represents an isolated instance
where, as here, a supervisory employee abandons his responsibility and knowingly and maliciously ignores both explicit
laws as well as the company's own antitrust policies.

The next evening, Sally Yeager watched her husband throw away
his newspaper and storm out of their family room into the kitchen.
Hearing David swearing and slamming cupboard doors, she picked
up the paper and saw an article based on the BFI press release.
Close to that article was a picture of a business associate of
Yeager's being presented an award for his efforts as chairman of
the United Way fund drive.

   The BFI statement drove a humiliated Yeager to fits of brooding
and drink. He was galled that the release made no mention of Bruce
Ranck having been specifically named in the Ohio Attorney General's complaint against BFI and WMI. Why had other employees
not ever had to reimburse BFI for the sums paid out by Houston in
settlement of monopolization lawsuits?

Class Action

This picture of isolated responsibility offered by BFI was at odds
with one so painstakingly being put together in Philadelphia where
the Kohn, Savett-led legal force now was gathering momentum. It
had combined various pending lawsuits into one major one. Of the
seven plaintiffs involved, the most important was Cumberland
Farms Incorporated of Canton, Massachusetts, a convenience store
operator in twenty-one states. The undertaking arguably would
produce, in the form of a 1990 court submission summarizing its
entire case, one of the most significant primers on the waste management business. Never before had anyone outside the industry set
out with such a commitment of resources to analyse the role of
national and regional (rather than local) levels of the corporate
hierarchy in the pricing and marketing strategies of the major waste
firms.

At the time of its waste industry case, Kohn, Savett were already one of the U.S.'s leading practitioners of this type of lawsuit. They once had taken over an antitrust case against Honda and won a $7-million settlement. In Philadelphia, Kohn, Savett convinced the court to recognize its case as a class action potentially on behalf of all consumers of containerized waste collection services in the United States. Its complaint was that BFI and WMI had conspired at a national level to treat such consumers as a captive market. In place of BFI's "Yeager's derelict conduct" thesis, Kohn, Savett would propose another — and not implausible — way of making sense of the slew of price-fixing cases involving the majors.

Through 1988 (when Ohio accepted offers by the Big Two to settle the Toledo lawsuit, without admitting liability, for $350,000 each) until late 1990, Yeager and BFI sued and countersued each other as the Philadelphians worked to fit together more pieces of its case. Kohn, Savett's challenge — if it was to succeed in demonstrating that the most significant aspects of the Big Two's operations throughout the U.S. were controlled from their respective national headquarters — was to break through the corporate veil and tie senior officers to local activities.[27]

Besides the alleged Ohio-Michigan cartel which arguably provided the class action its most compelling evidence, and which they called their "paradigm," the plaintiffs were seeking other examples with which to illuminate the existence of a pattern of anti-competitive conduct "which cannot be sheer coincidence."[28] They sought evidence directly involving national and regional officers in previous cases against the Big Two in Vermont, Georgia, Missouri, Manitoba, Pennsylvania, New Jersey, Texas, Illinois, New York, Florida and California.

Their four-year investigation focused on the importance for the firms of their nationally mandated pricing minimums and the concern of senior executives with stabilizing markets so as to be able to improve total market pricing. They also discovered widespread use of differential charges (called "A B C" pricing) "as part of [BFI's] commitment to stay away from the customers of WMI."[29] One Kohn, Savett court exhibit had a former BFI employee, a Mr. John Thober, stating:

> My duties as a BFI sales representative included calling on existing customers and seeking new customers for BFI's waste removal services. Mr. Peckham [Thober's superior]

provided me price guidelines with three possible prices for each sized container and pick-up frequency. I considered A pricing to be top dollar, and B pricing to be a fair dollar for fair service. Mr. Peckham told me that C pricing was below cost. I generally had the discretion to get whatever price I could within that range. However, when a Waste Management of Toledo account was involved, I was instructed by Mr. Peckham to quote the potential customer at A pricing or higher.

In June or July of 1983, I picked up three or four former Waste Management customers who were acquaintances of mine. I wrote up each service contract at B pricing and noted that they had been serviced by Waste Management. Shortly thereafter, Jeff Peckham called me into his office and chewed me out. I remember him saying something like, "From here on out, friends or no friends, you will sell Waste Management accounts at A or above. Don't rock the boat."[30]

Various other examples were gathered from around the country of salespeople who had reacted against the strictures of "A B C" pricing and been caught in Yeager's conundrum. What represented a logical winning approach locally (price competition, more customers and more commissions) was not necessarily so when seen from the viewpoint of head office, where attention had to be paid to other realities. These included what Kohn, Savett was to describe as BFI's and WMI's alleged concern for "not disturbing the *entente* in other areas of the country."[31]

BFI was not prepared to concede an inch in the face of Kohn, Savett's audacious allegations. The plaintiffs' lawyers remarked on how, over time, testimony seemed to shift to synchronize with the majors' contention that pricing was carried out autonomously and not as directed from above. In 1985, for instance, Kohn, Savett quoted a former BFI regional vice president as testifying that "price lists are prepared at the regional level and given to the districts." Then years later, on being deposed by Kohn, Savett, the same person asserted that "pricing is a district function. And the specific lists are generated by the district manager, district accountant, district sales manager, and would be reviewed periodically at the regional level."[32]

As the whole matter inched towards a courtroom showdown, and BFI underwent its sea-change with Ruckelshaus taking command, the issue of responsibility still was being slugged out between BFI and Yeager.

The Toledo Row Drags On

BFI insisted that Yeager was wrong to assume that its out-of-court settlement of the Ohio/Michigan charges meant Yeager was not going to have to indemnify them for the damage his conspiracy had caused. For his part, Yeager (by now a Mack truck distributor) wanted to be compensated by BFI for his damaged health, peace of mind and reputation. After all, had not the evidence overwhelmingly revealed him to have been the servant of their will?

BFI showed the court unconventional business letters Yeager had sent his superiors, including a scatological one to Bruce Ranck imploring his boss to forget mandated programs so they might tear — as the author put it — the industry a new asshole. By trying to focus on Yeager's vulgarity, BFI sought to underscore its point that "by his own sworn testimony, [Yeager] is a profane man who uses hate as a motivator. By any reasonable standard, his attitudes, language and conduct are extreme and outrageous. It is inconceivable that a press conference and court pleadings referring to Yeager's admitted antitrust violations could either constitute extreme and outrageous behaviour or cause Yeager any, much less severe, emotional distress."[33]

Yet when all the jockeying for higher moral ground was done, one important question still remained. It had less to do with how emotionally devastated Yeager had been by what he considered to be the total falsehood of BFI's claims than with who, in fact, was telling the truth. Asked under oath about what kind of treatment he had had for his stress, Yeager responded by saying, "if you're going to call it treatment, I guess I treated myself, because I tried to deal with it myself."

"All right. And humiliation and embarrassment, did you have any treatment for that ?"

"I didn't have any treatment from a doctor or anything like that … I dealt with it through my attorneys in that particular regard, to try to get the truth out, I suppose, so I dealt with those kinds of things by trying to get the truth out."

In 1990, Yeager indeed had reached out to adversaries of the waste industry as a means to broadcast his insider's view. He contacted one of North America's most respected grass roots organizations, the Citizen's Clearing House for Hazardous Waste, the Virginia-based environmental centre founded by Lois Gibbs and other Love Canal veterans. CCHW is an important ally of ordinary citizens faced with defending themselves against the depredations of polluting industries, and works with more than 7,000 local grass roots groups. Beginning in June 1990, Yeager's information about such matters as the fate of other BFI's officials who had been named in price-fixing cases (they were promoted) began appearing in the CCHW's widely disseminated *Everyone's Backyard.*

"Chinese Wall"

By early 1990, Kohn, Savett had accumulated four million pages of documents and deposed eighty-three individuals. They had had to rent a separate building as a repository. But still they pressed on, seeking evidence to rebut the derelict local conduct defence and bolster the centralist theory at the heart of their claim.

Bruce Ranck, whom Kohn, Savett believed would probably be the single most important witness called at trial by any party, had until 1989 been responsible for BFI's operations in seven American states, the District of Columbia and several Canadian provinces. In its deposition of him, Kohn, Savett asked specifically about BFI's pricing in New Jersey — that state into which the waste majors tread at their great peril. When Ranck proved unable to recollect to their satisfaction, the plaintiffs tried going back in time, requesting a copy of Ranck's August 1984 testimony to a New Jersey grand jury.

BFI's counsel informed the court there was no transcript to discover "because [Ranck] did not testify before a grand jury."[34] As it turned out, Ranck had testified and eventually a copy turned up. A New Jersey lawyer who had represented Ranck sent it to Kohn, Savett on the mistaken impression that he had been ordered to by the court. But BFI's counsel claimed the production of the transcripts was inadvertent and succeeded in getting a ruling that a "Chinese Wall" be erected around those plaintiffs' lawyers who already had read it.

When finally the court did release six pages of Ranck's testimony, Kohn, Savett protested again, arguing this was insufficient. They claimed they were on the trail of — among other things — possible fraudulent concealment of anti-competitive conduct and the buying of potentially hostile witnesses.[35] But no matter how hard they pressed, a court-appointed Special Master (having read the transcript in camera) would not concede that any more of the unreleased portions were relevant to the matters currently at issue. The "Chinese Wall" stood.

As the trial date approached, the defendants asked the court to render a summary judgment and Kohn, Savett scrambled to marshal its argument and supporting evidence in opposition to the defendants' request. They needed to make it fully evident they had a credible chance of convincing a jury that key officers of the Big Two had seen the occasional modest fines meted out for violating antitrust laws as a reasonable price to pay for the immense profits to be reaped by conspiring to treat waste-generating customers across America as private property.

In July 1990, the plaintiff's memorandum in opposition to summary judgement was delivered to Judge Bechtle. On the face of it, the document seemed a stunning catalogue of misdeeds, the likes of which had never before been seen in the public domain. WMI, having reckoned the risks and benefits to it in continuing its defence, (the legal costs, the time, the publicity, the impact on market capitalization, the potential treble damages) broke ranks with BFI, becoming the first of the defendants to near an out-of-court agreement.

Oak Brook moved to block BFI's attempt to have the whole matter brought before the American Arbitration Association.[36] Then in September 1990, in return for being fully discharged from any and all claims against it "which were asserted, or could have been asserted in this action or in the related actions pending in federal and state court in Toledo, Ohio," WMI deposited $19.5 million in trust with the Philadelphia National Bank.

Being first to settle, WMI got off the Kohn, Savett hook at far less cost to it than did BFI. For later that year, with much of the world's attention on the build-up to the Gulf War, BFI, also admitting no wrongdoing, settled. It paid out into a specially created fund the record sum of $30.5 million to be rid of Cumberland Farms. Monies from the fund were to be distributed to all approved claims of customers of containerized solid waste removal services throughout the United States.

The allegations and denials would remain just that: allegations and denials. Dave Yeager never would repeat his story in a Philadelphia courtroom. Ranck (by now BFI's executive vice president in charge of all North American operations) and others would never be required to defend themselves against Kohn, Savett. The only remaining forum for Yeager's charges (and with it a fuller public exposure of the true character of the industry and some of its executives) was in Ohio, where BFI and its former employee continued to skirmish.

In the Court of Common Pleas of Lucas County, Ohio, shelves sighed under the weight of filings of charges and counter-charges. Yeager continued to maintain he had had nothing to gain by engaging in unlawful activities in Ohio and Michigan solely — as BFI had claimed — on his own. In fact, with a wife, five children, substantial mortgage and limited education outside his chosen profession, he had had everything to lose.

In Yeager's eyes, he had been a rising star in BFI. His boss, who was also working his way up the corporate ladder, had asked him to meet with a major competitor with whom he had already made arrangements. What was he to do? His response was to go along to get along. At least until he could afford to do otherwise.

In early May 1991, a judge, going to the nub of it all, took the whole matter a small step towards vindicating Yeager. "In the present case, although BFI contends that the antitrust violations were solely the activity of David Yeager, the evidence does not support that contention," Judge J. Ronald Bowman wrote in an opinion on a motion of Yeager's. "From the evidence before the Court, reasonable minds can only conclude that the activity which generated the antitrust violations, law suits, and fines, was not solely the acts of BFI's employee, David M. Yeager."[37]

Tumbling Down

On 4 September 1991, the day after BFI's financial problems were made public (see Chapter 3), Bruce Ranck reportedly left a board meeting in Houston "so his fellow directors could discuss, in essence, whether he is an honest man."[38] The directors were discussing a report of a special committee which they had commissioned to respond to threatened legal proceedings by Sally Yeager in her capacity as a shareholder. Mrs. Yeager was charging BFI directors and senior officers with having harmed the company by violating antitrust and other laws. She requested steps be taken to obtain compensation from them.[39]

The committee retained legal counsel, held thirteen meetings to review the evidence and delivered its findings to the BFI board in August. At the board's September meeting, the report was considered, and by the time Ranck had returned to the room, not only had Sally Yeager's invitation to pursue Ranck and others for mismanagement been rejected, but he found himself named to replace the departed John Drury as BFI's president and chief operating officer.[40] In choosing Ranck for BFI's number two post, Bill Ruckelshaus assured the *Wall Street Journal*'s Jeff Bailey that he had watched his rising employee very carefully. "Invariably, he made the right judgement," said the former FBI director, "I have no qualms about his integrity."[41]

The promotion of Ranck to president of BFI transformed Yeager into an even more determined nemesis. He talked of a new class action, this time on behalf of all of America's independent haulers and based on the service contracts which the Canadian Competition Tribunal had viewed with such a jaundiced eye. His wife became the named holder in the stockholders' lawsuit launched that October against BFI (see Chapter 3). The complaint painted the corporate culture prevailing at BFI in lurid colours, and honest employees of the company might have wondered why Mrs. Yeager had held on to her shares so long in the face of all the alleged wrongdoing.[42]

An unflattering piece written about the industry's antitrust woes by reporter Jeff Bailey the week following Ranck's elevation provoked an appeal from BFI's chairman to the *Wall Street Journal*. "Any antitrust violation is deplorable, and is a violation of company and societal standards. But our record hardly constitutes widespread or pervasive practices as your story strongly implies," wrote Bill Ruckelshaus. "[BFI's employees] deserve to have this company treated in a more balanced way by the country's leading daily business newspaper."[43]

Then, the next spring, what had appeared to be developing into a public (albeit judicial) inquiry into the inner workings of the industry turned out to have been a mirage, for suddenly the battle between Yeager and BFI was over. The hatchets were buried. The details of the settlement were secret. But what was fully evident was that the out-of-court resolution of the conflict was bought at the price of keeping David Yeager's mouth shut. There would be no more calls to the CCHW. He would say nothing more against BFI.

As part of the private deal, the parties agreed to a final court judgement which saw Judge Bowman vacate his 3 May 1991, "reasonable minds" order. By doing so, he left it an unanswered question as to what reasonable minds reasonably might make of the underlying reality of Yeager's charges and the business stratagems of a company like BFI.

Lawyers continued to deal with such outstanding issues as Sally Yeager's yet-to-be-resolved shareholders' suit and her husband's claims against WMI. Just what Yeager got out of his peace treaty with BFI remains a mystery. But given what we know about him, it seems unlikely his vow of silence came cheap.

PART III

Waste Wars — Private Profit and Public Resistance

Chapter 8

Winnipeg: The Quest for Urban Ore

Crown Attorney: "What would that [STSOOT] stand for?"
Former BFI Salesman: "Well, publicly, it was Stamp The Stuff-
ing Out Of Them, and privately, with all due respect to the ladies,
it was Stamp The Shit Out Of Them ..."
Crown Attorney: "This was referring to competition, I take it, it
wasn't stamp the shit out of the customers?"
                    Restrictive Trade Practices Commission Hearing, 1978

When the Texans of Browning-Ferris Industries first began pene-
trating Canadian garbage markets in 1971, the three contractors who
dominated commercial pickup in Winnipeg — William Sokol, Eric
Johnson and the Perfanick brothers — were feuding over market
shares. BFI took advantage of the chaotic situation. Through its
newly established subsidiary in Calgary, BFI bought them all out
and amalgamated the former rivals by juggling shares and assets in
November 1971. Eric Johnson (whose brother-in-law was Len Remple, the prominent Vancouver contractor) took charge of the local
operation for the men in Houston, and one of his employees, Bill
Omiucke, was given responsibility for fusing the various factions
into a going concern.

By so entirely displacing the competition, BFI created a vacuum.
A batch of new rivals rushed into the market to fill it and began
jostling with BFI for dominance over the half-million tons of refuse
discarded there every year and the not inconsiderable opportunity
for profits such a position offered. Prominent among them was the
Thiessen family of Winnipeg, whose Grey Goose Corporation operated one of the country's leading bus lines and the largest taxi
service in Edmonton, Calgary and Red Deer. Soon after they added
garbage to their portfolio of enterprises. In July 1972, the Thiessens

sold a controlling interest in Grey Goose to Mike DeGroote's Laid-law. Instead of remaining proprietors, they assumed a role more typical of Winnipeg's business establishment: they became managers of Grey Goose and its new trash-hauling arm, Acme Sanitation. Also joining the fray was a fast-rising trucking entrepreneur and condominium developer named Paul Albrechtsen, whose Haul-A-Way Services was soon giving senior BFI management some misgivings about its ability to control events in Winnipeg.

BFI, Acme and Haul-A-Way accounted for most of Winnipeg's commercial refuse hauling equipment, both front-end and roll-off. But the garbage business being what it was, the barriers were not sufficient to scare off other, smaller competitors. Even a firm with one or two vehicles on the road and a couple dozen dumpsters could prove irksome to the majors. With the yellow pages full of possible competitors, it became awkward for the local managers to respond effectively to orders from distant head offices demanding that truck routing be rationalized and prices adjusted upwards.

One of these new operators was Joe Kalika, a former army cook who had driven a bus for a line that was eventually bought out by the Thiessens. Given the way the winds were blowing, naming this new enterprise Breezeway Disposal was something of an act of defiance.

In the next two years, three of Breezeway's trucks burned, and it was only natural to suspect that they had been deliberately torched. Fires, started by hot ashes from incinerators picked up at factories or by oil-soaked cans, papers or rags, were always a hazard in the garbage business, but so intense was the jousting for market shares in Winnipeg that contractors suspected arson whenever a truck went up in flames. A later investigation of various burnings, however, did not satisfy the RCMP that arson had been resorted to in Winnipeg. Nevertheless the paranoia induced by the intense competition was a real part of working conditions in the city's garbage trade. Undeterred by the fires, Breezeway bought a few old junkers from the east and kept on going.

Raymond Richter was another small-timer who entered the market in 1972. His Monarch Disposal had been a marginal operation from the beginning. It started out with a single roll-off truck and some big refuse containers. Richter claimed that he had received threats in his early days in the business. "If I didn't conform they would put me into the dump and I'd never be found again," he was told on one occasion. On another he recalled being warned that he had better smarten up or "we'll send a hit man after ya." Richter later remembered laughing at the threat and replying: "You can't afford one." Another contractor was under the impression that Richter had had his life threatened to stop him from cutting prices to keep customers. Whether or not these were serious threats or the bluffs of underlings, they contributed to the prevailing atmosphere of menace.

Over at BFI a special bonus program was introduced to exhort the staff to greater efforts. As Bill Omiucke (who in a subsequent investigation provided a window on the industry) explained: "We were running under a battle cry if you will ... As a matter of fact, we had six foot letters in the back of our office in brilliant red that said, STSOOT." In the summer of 1973, an interoffice memo revealed that BFI was more than holding its own, although it was far from complacent about the state of affairs on the banks of the Red River: "It appears that our people in Winnipeg have fought the new competition to a standstill for the time-being. May would have been a break-even month for gains vs. losses if we had not lost Canada Packers to Sokol, one of the previous owners." Omiucke described the atmosphere at the time as "a fiercely intensive, competitive climate. We fought tooth and nail daily for new business, and to protect our old business." The company's hottest sales representative, Omiucke later had his performance recognized by a grateful management, which bestowed an all-expenses-paid Caribbean holiday. Practical family man that he was, he took the equivalent in cash.

In this competitive struggle, BFI possessed two singular advantages. One was its size, which gave it a much better position than even its two major rivals in a prolonged price war. The second was its access to the Fort Garry landfill site. No other contract hauler had its own dumping grounds. Since its arrival on the local scene in 1971, the company had held an operating permit to the Fort Garry landfill and had hauled there day and night from long distances to take advantage of the free dumping. This second advantage was in some jeopardy. According to a senior municipal administrator, R. J. McRae, management of the site left something to be desired. He described the problem as "intolerable operating conditions." BFI executives were chagrined to learn that the city might not automatically extend the company's permit.

In January 1973, when BFI's local service and operations manager wrote to the Winnipeg Board of Commissioners to make his firm's case for continuing at Fort Garry, the American company was the biggest garbage hauler in Manitoba next to the city of Winnipeg itself. "If the City is our competitor and not required to make a profit," the letter stated, "an increase in dumping charges would greatly accelerate the swing to a city pickup. We are sure that this is not the City's long range intent." Pulling out all the stops, the BFI officer portrayed his corporation as standing at the farthest reaches of waste management technology. He claimed that BFI was doing a great amount of research in both Canada and the United States regarding recycling of refuse. "We plan on having the results of this research being exhibited to all interested bodies in Canada at an early date in 1973. This recycling, coupled with the disposal field operation, could be of great interest to industry and government as a permanent answer to disposal field operation ... The information and 'know how' that our company now have could mean a complete change in the present concept of handling refuse. This is one of the prime reasons we have requested a contract extension."

BFI's arguments fell on deaf ears. The request for an extension of the rights to operate Fort Garry was denied, and as of 1 June 1973 the dump was taken over by the city, which faced the expense of final cleanup. The city now controlled all available dumps and intended to establish a uniform tipping fee of $3 per ton for eight projected sites. This disposal charge would increase BFI's costs by $15,000 per month. Eric Johnson, the local BFI manager, mounted a campaign to pressure the authorities into lowering the fee. He tried to get some support from the business community. In a letter soliciting his customers' backing, Johnson included a mimeographed form which was headed "HELP!" The text asserted that the "actual" costs of disposal should not exceed $1 per ton, and the city was in effect imposing a 200 per cent "garbage disposal tax." It objected to this "tax" and asked that the dumping charges be dropped to $1. Recipients were asked to sign the enclosure and mail it to the city clerk. Since Johnson gave no evidence for his statements and the environmental standards had not even been identified, the origin of his figures was something of a mystery.

Johnson intended to appear before Winnipeg City Council with an offer to do all of the city's disposal work at $1.50 per ton. When Tom Webster, a senior BFI executive, learned of this impending offer, he panicked. Realizing that Johnson's figure had all the substance of cotton candy, Webster told the local manager that "the city might just know enough about the costs of running eight proper sanitary landfills to let us have it all for $1.50 per ton and make us operate all eight of them under good standards." He instructed Johnson to get full approval from Houston and from the vice president for BFI's Arrowhead region, Ed Drury, in Minneapolis before approaching the city council.

The city refused to budge on the tipping fee. Facing increased costs on the one hand and waging a price war on the other, BFI managers asked themselves what advantage Acme and Haul-A-Way might gain if BFI unilaterally increased prices to match the new disposal fees. Webster doubted that they could take away enough business fast enough "to hurt us over the long haul," but for the time being he was not certain that the "competition won't try to take advantage of us fairly severely. Neither am I sure that [Acme and Haul-A-Way] know enough about what they are doing to realize what the increased dump fees will do to them if they don't raise their prices accordingly. They each apparently have enough capital to operate quite awhile at loss."

Webster was right. As summer turned into fall, the other haulers made big inroads. BFI was recording losses not only to Acme and especially to Haul-A-Way but even to an also-ran such as Joe Kalika's Breezeway. Acme and Haul-A-Way seemed capable of waging an extended price war, and as late as the spring of 1974 BFI still didn't feel that it could move its prices upwards without further losses. In an internal communication dated 30 April 1974, BFI executive Bill Johnson, a former line manager in Kansas City (where a minor price war had led the major competitors to strike a "property rights" type of accord), described how the Winnipeg operation continued to be "faced with the severe competition problem. The competition situation has been more severe than normal because of the amount of business that these two new companies have taken from us and at the price that they have taken it." But there did appear to be some light at the end of the tunnel. Anticipating some respite from the intense fight for market shares, Bill Johnson looked forward to the local affiliate again becoming profitable: "We feel this situation will taper off to the point that we can accomplish the scheduling of customers plus hopefully by July 1 we can initiate a 10-15% across the board increase on all existing customers."

The Airport Accords

As it turned out, an imminent end to the price war was more than just a possibility. As the week of 13 May 1974 began, it was clear that changes were afoot. On Monday Eric Johnson advised Bill Omiucke that a new rate structure was in effect. Omiucke later recalled the instructions Johnson gave him: "The prices that we were to charge at that time were established on the rate sheet which [Johnson] gave to us and those were the only prices we were to charge, and we would not make any lower prices without permission from Mr. Johnson." The new price list significantly raised collection charges. And the STSOOT program was finished. Omiucke, who already felt that the takeover by the Houstonians was insidious, wasn't happy to learn that head office had terminated the bonus program. In the diary where he kept a record of his business experiences, the sales representative wrote: "This is the day of final insult. American owners have decreed less money for sales men."

Two days later representatives of Winnipeg's leading garbage contractors — Eric Johnson of BFI, Bill Thiessen of Acme and Dave Tuckwell, part-owner and manager of Haul-A-Way — met at the Airport Motor Hotel. At the top of the agenda was the havoc they were wreaking on each other. Terry Penton, an insurance underwriter from Brandon and an acquaintance of Tuckwell's, joined the gathering to serve as secretary. Penton recorded what the participants said and what conclusions they arrived at, and three days later he mailed Tuckwell his summary of the meeting. In a covering letter containing an accounting of his expenses, Penton observed that he had "enjoyed the session very much, and hoped that some semblance of order can come out of the chaotic situation which has existed in the past." These words suggested the possibility of some unlawful connivance, and Penton's letter and summary would come back to haunt the garbage contractors.

The discussion boiled down to two issues: minimum rates for the various services the companies provided, and operating guidelines for the companies to follow. Although there would be great debate over the extent (if any) to which all three were parties to an agreement and their success (if any) in imposing their understanding on the marginals, the memorandum Penton submitted suggested very strongly that the contractors had crossed over the boundaries of pure competition into the realm of collective private planning.

Minimum charges laid down in the Penton memorandum dealt with front-end containers, loose and compacted roll-off collection, service station pickup, apartment pickup, rear-end packer pickup, a service described as "special" front-end pickup, and large non-tendered accounts. The seven guidelines dealt with existing accounts, accounts held by the city, new accounts and unprotected accounts. The "property rights" nature of the agreement came out clearly in the first guideline which covered existing accounts:

> *Any rate that is being charged can be retained, and the operator is free to change the rate to any point he wishes. However, if the customer does not accept an increased rate and decides to tender the job, the operator, at that point, is free to cut his rate if he wishes in an attempt to keep the account from being tendered. If however, in spite of the cut, it still goes to tender, the operator cannot cut his rate on his tendered quote further than his last quote. All the other operators who quote will, of course, quote tariff rates.*

To make as many inroads into public-sector territory as possible, the contractors were prepared to lower their minimum charges. The Airport accords contained the provision that "if it is possible to get an account away from the city, but customers will not agree to pay tariff rates, then, providing the three parties agree, a reduced rate may be quoted. If all three parties are not available for discussion, and two of the three agree, a deal can then be made." In addition, some accounts were identified as "open" accounts that could be quoted less than the agreed-upon "tariff rates." For whatever reasons, these "open" accounts included such substantial customers as Canadian National, Canadian Pacific, Manitoba Hydro, the Canadian Forces bases, Winnipeg General Hospital and all government buildings. With these exceptions, all new accounts were to be quoted tariff rates.

While the agreement changed the working environment of the Winnipeg garbage industry, it evidently did not change the contractors' image of themselves as active competitors. Penton concluded his memorandum with the statement that "these guidelines are not intended to restrict competition between the operators but rather to encourage it," although he added that "in any question, the majority should govern the procedure to be followed, and frequent meetings between the parties should be held to change, delete or add to these rates and guidelines. The effect desired can be obtained only to the extent that the parties sincerely co-operate with each other." A little over a year later in a brief requesting that the city further limit its involvement in waste removal, the contractors assured the Committee on Works and Operations that they "actively compete with one another for all of the business accounts available, with the result that prices are maintained at a reasonable economic level and the standard of service is high."

Less than a month after the Airport meeting, however, there was some evidence that a common minimum price structure was being respected. At least that was the impression of someone as close to the events as Bill Omiucke. In early June, Haul-A-Way put in a quote to Mr. Goldman at Northwest Bakery, a BFI account. Omiucke learned by phone that this quote was lower than BFI's, and this confused the salesman because "I had understood that the rates would be the same no matter who quoted them, so I asked Mr. Johnson what was happening." Omiucke recalled his boss phoning to find out what was going on at Haul-A-Way. As it turned out there had been a misunderstanding. The rival contractor was not undercutting but was instead quoting tariff rates for a smaller container, a four-yarder in this case. BFI's quote had been for a six-yarder. Omiucke was assured that Haul-A-Way was "charging tariff rates" and was instructed to "call Goldman back and tell him that we will do the four-yarder, but at the four-yard rate." Omiucke also later testified (during the preliminary stages of a price-fixing trial) that according to his boss the initiative for the price agreement had come from BFI's Ed Drury in Minneapolis.[1]

Other evidence indicated that BFI, Acme and Haul-A-Way tried to impose their agreement on their smaller competitors. A month after the Airport meeting, Johnson, Thiessen and Tuckwell met with Raymond Richter of Monarch Disposal and Joe Kalika of Breezeway in the offices of Haul-A-Way. According to an affidavit Richter signed later, during the meeting he and Kalika were handed copies of a minimum-rates schedule and set of regulations that were actually photocopies of the Penton memorandum. Richter went on to claim that Thiessen feared the document, which included the names of the three major haulers at the top of a sheet outlining the new prices, might be incriminating. In the wrong hands, it could be evidence of a combine. Thiessen suggested removing the top of the sheet, and the names of the Airport trio were cut off. The affidavit stated that the major contractors asked Richter and Kalika "to abide by the terms set forth in the rates and the guidelines." Richter also alleged that in subsequent meetings discussions focused on pickup charges, the division of accounts and bids on upcoming tenders, and indicated that there had been attempts to rig bids on the CNR and Gulf service station accounts.

In January 1975 BFI, Acme and Haul-A-Way put virtually identical new price lists into effect, with price increases from previous schedules. Johnson and Tuckwell supplied Kalika with this new list, which they asked him to follow. And in early September BFI circulated price lists dated 15 September 1975, leading Acme and Haul-A-Way to issue virtually identical price lists dated 22 September 1975.

Whether it originated in conspiracy, conscious parallelism or pure coincidence, the new pricing dispensation proved a great boon for BFI. For the six-month period ending March 1974 — that is, the period immediately preceding the Airport meeting — the Winnipeg subsidiary recorded a $12,000 loss on revenues of $677,000. For the same period one year later, BFI earned a $305,000 profit on revenues of $938,000. The company "was virtually printing money at its Oak Point Highway offices. Among the seven cities reporting as profit centres to BFI's Arrowhead regional office in Minneapolis, the highest profit rate was achieved in Winnipeg — 33 per cent. Its closest competitor was Thunder Bay with a net income of $75,000 on revenues of $280,000 for a profit rate of 27 per cent, followed by Minneapolis with a 25 per cent and so on down to a 3 per cent rate in Denver.

Omiucke and the Trustbusters

Bill Omiucke left his job with BFI in late 1974. Having refused to sign a non-competition clause in a long-term employment contract, the salesman was soon hauling garbage himself. He drove around with a suit in the cab of his one truck, and when he finished making a pickup he would do a quick change and try to make a sale in the vicinity. "Actually we had two trucks but somebody burned one," Omiucke later said, echoing the prevailing paranoia. Undeterred, the former BFI employee also began acting as an agent arranging for customers for roll-off haulers such as William Sokol of Ace Disposal and tried to defend himself against raids on his accounts by his larger competitors. "When they started zeroing in on me," he recalled, "I went after their customers on a selective basis." One evening in the summer of 1976, Omiucke was home with his children while his wife was playing Bingo. There was a knock at the front door, and Omiucke opened it to find himself face-to-face with a Mountie and a federal anti-combines investigator. He invited the night visitors to join him in a bottle of scotch.

The Department of Consumer and Corporate Affairs began investigating Canada's garbage industry in May 1976. Federal investigators started looking into the affairs of contractors in many metropolitan areas, including Winnipeg. In late May the offices of BFI, Acme and Haul-A-Way were raided and documents seized. Price lists found on the different premises were sent to the RCMP's Crime Detection Laboratory in Ottawa to determine whether they had their origins in the minimum-rate structure contained in the Penton memorandum.

When the investigators confronted Bill Omiucke, they found him quite willing to talk openly about the garbage business. Omiucke brought out the little black books that contained his business diary. He started the diary, he later explained, because "I was made aware by a sales manager of mine that the memory is not infallible, but the written word has the ability to remind you of events, and you have a better record than the mind does." Though written in tiny strokes with a broad-nibbed pen and practically indecipherable, the diary contained a record going back to 1971, the year BFI entered the local scene. Already somewhat familiar with how things had unfolded in Winnipeg's garbage industry, the investigators listened eagerly as Omiucke began recreating events from the entries he had made. He allowed the little black books to be taken back to Ottawa where they were photographed and blown up to more legible proportions. "They were nothing more than corroboration of what everybody else was saying," their author observed.

The investigators' interest in the Winnipeg market increased with the appearance of Richter's affidavit in June 1977. A year later, before a member of the Restrictive Trade Practices Commission, some evidence emerged from the contractors to imply that the atmosphere at the Airport meeting had been tense and the agreement had been stillborn. The trustbusters, however, were more inclined to believe the unequivocal statement in the Penton memorandum that minimum rates had been agreed upon. A lawsuit was prepared, and charges were laid on 2 April 1979. The three firms were accused of having combined to "prevent or unduly lessen" competition under the Combines Investigation Act in the rental or supply of disposal containers. The period of the alleged conspiracy was from 1 January 1974 to 31 December 1975.

The Impossible Search

During his first term as minister of consumer and corporate affairs (before his public questioning of the sanity of a judge in a monopoly practices case led to his temporary withdrawal from the cabinet), André Ouellet quoted with approval the statement by a former U.S. attorney general that "price fixers should go to prison ... they are no better than the car thief or the burglar or the robber."[2] However, the instrument Ouellet's department had at its disposal to pursue price fixers and other market conspirators was a notoriously imperfect one. "The present Combines Investigation Act is a joke," wrote Geoffrey Stevens of the *Globe and Mail*. "The government has been searching for a way to preserve competition in the marketplace without offending businessmen whose interests are not necessarily served at all by open competition. It's an impossible search."[3]

The Combines Investigation Act only prohibited "undue" interference with the marketplace. Entering into an agreement to prevent or lessen competition was not itself an offence, unless — as the lawyer for the merged Acme/Haul-A-Way (Laidlaw) reminded the court in the garbage trial — "the intended lessening or prevention is undue. ..." Thus to obtain a conviction in a market conspiracy case, prosecutors had to prove not only that the accused had engaged in anti-competitive behaviour but also that this behaviour had resulted in a significant degree of market control. This raised the contentious question of how market shares should be defined, and in the garbage industry, both the relevant geographic market and the relevant product market could be matters of disagreement. These issues would later be argued in American courtrooms in the context of the federal government's attempt to block WMI's takeover of EM Waste Resources on the grounds that it would substantially lessen competition in the Texas markets.[4] In the Winnipeg case, the trustbusters argued in terms of commercial and industrial pickup alone, while defence lawyers lumped this segment of the industry in with residential collection — where municipal forces were still a factor — in an effort to depict their clients as less formidable players with less consequential market shares.

A second limitation of the act touched even more directly on the garbage industry. Until the act was amended in July 1976, it was still legal for a service industry to set minimum prices. The Airport accords set out not only minimum service charges but also rental charges for garbage containers. To win its case against the waste haulers, the Department of Justice adopted the attitude that these containers and the garbage they held were articles of trade, and hence subject to competition law. This was why the charge referred only to the rental or supply of disposal containers and not to other aspects of the trash hauling business. Lawyers for BFI and Acme/Haul-A-Way contended that the "rental" — which in their view should more properly be called an "on-site charge" — was actually incidental to providing collection service, and their clients were therefore exempt from the conspiracy provisions of the Combines Investigation Act. As one Consumer and Corporate Affairs investigator put it, "their lawyers argued what they did might not have been ethical and moral but was legal. We say it was unethical and immoral and criminal." It remained to be seen, however, whether a judge would see things in the same light.

A third obstacle to enforcing competitive behaviour through legislation arose as a result of the growth of multi-national corporations. Government agents had no central vantage point from which to share the companies' unbroken view of the entire picture. There was no good reason for giant firms to limit their carve-ups to individual markets. If the world was their oyster, they could divide territory on a regional or even an international basis. Trade-offs between markets in one continent and those in another would be impossible to identify. In the waste industry, the growth of the major waste firms added a potentially new dimension to "property rights." One of the participants in the Winnipeg agreement was international in scope, and another had continental ambitions. Was there any reason to suppose that their strategic thinking was confined to one middle-sized Canadian city?

The Trial

But despite all these limitations to the legislation and the investigative process, the garbage case went to preliminary hearing and eventually to trial. Raymond Richter and Bill Omiucke were the major witnesses for the Crown, and Terry Penton was called to determine whether his memorandum was an accurate reflection of what went on at the Airport Motel meeting. Because of an outstanding judgement in the Manitoba courts as to whether an executive could be compelled to testify against his own company, Eric Johnson, Bill Thiessen and Dave Tuckwell were never called to the stand. The issues the court had to deal with included the extent to which the three accused dominated the local market, the legitimacy of the Crown's action in attempting to isolate container rental from the rest of the garbage business, and the reliability of Raymond Richter's memory. Penton testified that the participants in the Airport meeting never agreed to weaken competition. Richter described the bizarre paper-cutting ceremony during the meeting at the Haul-A-Way office.

The courts heard a variety of estimates of the three accused companies' market share. Omiucke and Richter estimated their share of the commercial garbage business at about 90 per cent. The federal investigators calculated that they dumped about 76 per cent of all commercial solid wastes carried by private contractors in 1975; operated 85 to 89 per cent of the front-end loading trucks from 1973 to 1976; owned 92 per cent of the front-end containers in use in 1976; operated 75 to 80 per cent of the roll-off trucks in use from 1973 to 1976; and operated 79 per cent of the roll-off containers in use in 1976. However, defence lawyers imaginatively widened the definition of the market until the three companies shared less than 21 per cent of the city's waste flows.

In sending the accused to trial, the judge at the preliminary hearing accepted the Crown's argument that the contractors could be considered to be in the business of renting container boxes even though the rental charges were an insignificant part of refuse disposal prices. He also assented to the notion that the operations of the accused had a major impact on the market and observed that, despite Penton's testimony in court, "his evidence to me is only words endeavouring to minimize the evident words in the agreement that carry the intent that the parties to the agreement should fix prices and conditions of contract for the purposes of minimizing competition. Encroachment was forbidden."

The Crown's arguments were less convincing to the trial judge, John Hunt, who acquitted the accused on 1 December 1980. Hunt ruled that the supply of the dumpsters was a service, and consequently the accused were not subject to the act at the time of the charges. It was, in fact, BFI's competitive excesses in the pre-Airport era that the judge found most reprehensible: "I do not wish to appear to approve of the procedures of the accused, or at least some of them. The use of a record by Browning-Ferris, designated as 'S.T.S.OOT' does not receive my commendation, nor does their treatment of Richter." However, he found little room for criticism in the behaviour of the accused during the period of the alleged conspiracy. Even if the companies had been subject to the law, Hunt would have thrown the government's case out of his court:

> There is no evidence that there was a prevention or lessening of competition, and, therefore, no evidence that whatever agreements may have been entered into were "undue" ... It is not incumbent on the Crown to prove a monopoly, but it certainly appears from the evidence that this was not, nor was it intended to be, a monopoly. Nor was it intended to achieve control of the market. The companies concerned did not control the market but, in fact, only serviced less than one-half.

Although the judgement contained no method to explain how he had arrived at such a measure of the accused's market share, Hunt (unlike a judge in the subsequent Waste Management/Waste Resources case in New York City) appeared to accept the definition of the market proposed by the defence — as all solid waste collected by the city, by contractors for the city, under direct contract with the commercial garbage industry, and by refuse generators themselves. Because the court did not make a distinction between commercial and industrial collection, in which the three companies loomed large, and residential collection, dominated by the city of Winnipeg, Richter and Omiucke were disappointed. "I still say BFI and Acme have 90 per cent of the established commercial market," Omiucke declared. "I think the judge figures the city was a commercial contractor. I find that difficult to accept because they never did it to make a profit." Wearing his patriotism on his sleeve, Omiucke grumbled that he didn't like being dominated by foreign multi-nationals and thought American senior executives had pressured their Winnipeg affiliate into trying to reach an understanding with Acme and Haul-A-Way. In a fit of pique, he sent off a $6,000 bill for consulting fees to Consumer and Corporate Affairs in Ottawa.

The industry had not been marking time since 1974. Mike De-Groote increased Laidlaw's control over Grey Goose to 82.6 per cent and expanded throughout Manitoba. Laidlaw also acquired Haul-A-Way for $1.1 million in 1976 and merged it with Acme. In late 1980 the volume of wastes flowing to private contractors was increased when the City of Winnipeg withdrew even further from refuse collection. Underscoring Bill Omiucke's point about city collection not being part of the garbage market, the city decided that it would no longer collect any refuse whatsoever from businesses that exceeded a limit of two cubic yards. Previously, municipal forces had removed up to two cubic yards twice weekly from commercial establishments, with the waste generator taking responsibility for the excess. Now, however, the business community would be a captive market of the commercial garbage industry. The Woolworth's store on Selkirk Avenue, for instance, was informed that as of 14 October 1980 it would have "to arrange with a private firm for the removal of all refuse generated by your business."

The irony of the situation was that some of the smaller operators had also done well. By 1980 Richter had three roll-off trucks and thirty containers. Omiucke had also survived. A marginal operator such as Richter had more to lose from the endless competitive strife than did the giants, and the price war had ceased before he had been eliminated. As one government official close to the garbage investigation put it, "the little guy can operate on the fringe under cover of monopoly rents and make all sorts of money."

However, as the 1980s got underway, the small operators still felt threatened. Not only did they have the waste majors to contend with, but the increasingly onerous requirements for obtaining the obligatory performance bond were making it impossible even to place bids. "The performance bond is killing the little guy," said Abe Allarie, a former Acme foreman. "The bonding office in Winnipeg wouldn't look at me. Said if I had $100,000 in the bank they'd consider it." Allarie had just lost his dead-animal pickup contract to Laidlaw, which undercut his bid. He thought that they would leave him alone then, and when they didn't he said angrily, "If I'd known what they were going to do to me I'd have gone to testify before the trial." The Kalikas considered themselves lucky in 1980. Unexpectedly, they were able to secure a bond from a local source and underbid Laidlaw on a 12,000-residence contract in suburban St. Vital. "It was $150,000 lower than Acme for the three-year period and Acme was already doing St. Vital," explained Bob Kalika. "Eric Johnson and Bill Thiessen just walked out shocked when the tenders were opened. They didn't think my father was bondable. That's the problem. The city only wants to deal with the big guy. In three years we could be eliminated."

Whatever the legal issues, competition in the waste business was more than ever a contest amongst unequals. BFI and Laidlaw had roots in the soil of modern corporate life while the likes of Monarch and Breezeway did not. They existed at the sufferance of larger forces, not the least of which were the waste majors.

Little Guy

Ray Richter soon got out of the business, ceding Monarch Disposal to Bill Sokol of Ace Disposal. Some years later however, the whistle-blower on the local refuse collectors' entente got another taste of the waste wars. This time it was a Washington, D.C., lawyer who sought him out. The visitor represented Chambers which, as we saw in Chapter 3, was clashing with BFI in a high-profile legal battle. The attorney was anxious to find Bill Curtis, the ex-Winnipeger whom BFI had sent to run their Pittsburgh operation and who had left town before he could be served a copy of Chambers's lurid complaint. Curtis had gone to high school in Winnipeg, been a BFI salesman and owned horses with another local refuse carter. But that day when Richter made the rounds with the American lawyer, checking out the Concord Hotel and making lots of calls around town, nobody knew what had become of the waste executive since his flight from Pennsylvania.

As for Bill Sokol, his strategy consisted in steering clear of the transnational waste-hauling juggernaut. His survival — right into the 1990s — depended on securing a niche unlikely to be begrudged him. In Ace's case this turned out to be hauling refuse from the packing houses and chicken manure from poultry producers.

Bill Omiucke, who would run unsuccessfully for Parliament as a Progressive Conservative, had set his sights somewhat higher than the leavings of the waste majors. Luckily for him, he possessed a contract coveted both by BFI and Laidlaw and used it to make his escape from marginality. Given Omiucke's brand of economic nationalism, he may have taken satisfaction in eluding the grasp of the Houstonians by selling his company in 1984 to Mike DeGroote. Omiucke stayed on as a Laidlaw sales manager until 1989, by which time the Winnipeg market had become a more complete reflection of the continental reality. BFI gobbled up Breezeway, and Waste Management Inc. made its appearance on the scene, albeit — for the time — in an offstage role.

BFI lobbied to gain more market share for the contractors. Its local helmsman, Eric Johnson, claimed that by allowing the private sector to pick up a full 80 per cent of residential refuse the city would save $1 million in 1987. A confidential report commissioned following these solicitations went part way to paving the way for city hall to increase the level of privatized collection.

When Council voted to contract out one of the city's six districts, the successful bidder was neither of the two resident multi-national waste managers, but a numbered company with no track record. It had nary a truck, a law office on Main Street was its business address and its owner was the resident of another province. Yet one local councillor, in supporting the award of the contract, told the *Winnipeg Herald* that he was happy to see it had been won by a "little guy."[5] The little guy began operation in May 1988 as Canadian Waste Disposal and Management Limited. Then, the firm (whose owner had previously worked for Laidlaw) metamorphosed almost overnight. In June of that same year, Canadian Waste entered into a joint venture called Winnipeg Waste Disposal Limited. Its partner was Waste Management Incorporated, the biggest guy in the world.

Typically, the waste majors regarded residential contracts as beachheads on unconquered turf and often held out a franchise or partnership arrangement to independents who secured them. The deal usually went as follows: for about 17 per cent of gross revenues the established partner provided the local owner with invoicing, technical back-up, performance bonds and equipment. As well, after a certain period, say ten years, the senior partner could step forward and buy out the franchisee. In 1989, as an example, WMI acquired the interests and equipment of sixteen such partners.

So, in proclaiming the triumph of the little guy, the city father had misread the script. By the summer of 1988, the Big Three dominated the local waste trade here as they did elsewhere. And each new market linked to their centralized computer data banks signalled the twilight of local control. What works commissioner, politician or concerned citizen could match the accumulating knowledge of the multi-national waste managers? In privatizing continental waste flows, they were also privatizing knowledge of the waste economy.

Graceland

Dumping grounds were filling up and closing, and every closing left in the balance the question of who would develop future options: local elected authorities or private waste managers. The latter were facing the prospect of only one public site from 1994 onwards and the consequent public control over pricing and windfall revenues, as well as many other aspects of policy including recycling and composting projects, public education, sponsorship of waste minimization technology and waste reduction staffing programs. Consequently, BFI began to hunt for its own facility. But its hush-hush wooing of rural politicians ended up exposed in the harsh headlines of the Winnipeg papers.

The firm targeted a potential site (one with a capacity to handle half of Winnipeg's annual garbage output) in West St. Paul, a scattering of houses and a stretch of farms on the north edge of town. In 1987, West St. Paul's population numbered 3,000, and its annual spending about equalled the cheque BFI wrote out that year to settle its federal and state price-fixing cases in Ohio. If a local editorial writer is to be believed, its methods of municipal administration were "naive and unsophisticated. A small-scale land developer with a goose farm is more than they can readily handle."[6]

In 1987, BFI invited the civic eminences of West St. Paul on a tour of a landfill it ran near Minneapolis. Local municipal staff were ordered not to ask questions, and money for the trip was paid without a motion of council. Then, unknown to most local ratepayers, there was another such trip. A BFI landfill proposal was discussed at in-camera meetings. But in early 1990, a tip-off to the *Winnipeg Free Press* scotched the attempted detour around public opinion and control.

An anonymous caller phoned reporter Don Campbell claiming four West St. Paul councillors could be found in Memphis, Tennessee, on a BFI-financed junket. Campbell figured it was too perfect. What better place to have chosen to discuss a dump with music-loving Manitobans than the vicinity of Graceland, Elvis's home? It was as if in order to beguile some Muslim municipal worthies one had flown them gratis to a dump on the outskirts of Mecca.

Campbell phoned the Peabody Hotel in Memphis where he discovered that not only was the delegation from West St. Paul there but so was Eric Johnson, whose 1974 Airport Motor Hotel meeting with other waste contractors had produced the Penton memorandum and the unsuccessful federal anti-combines lawsuit. (In 1992, BFI promoted Johnson to its Canadian head office in Etobicoke, Ontario, where he was to preside over the entire eight-province Canada-wide operation.)

A stunned councillor would not tell Campbell why he was in Memphis, who had paid for the trip or how many previous ones he had accepted. He demanded to know "how did you find out where we were?"[7] Two other councillors also refused comment. A few days later an editorial in the *Winnipeg Free Press* denounced the trip, dubbing BFI a "garbage monster" and calling on the provincial urban affairs minister to "establish orderly and democratic public control."

"Browning-Ferris Industries can buy itself a few rural municipality councillors as easily as it can buy a piece of farmland and get a zoning change for it," charged the editorialist. "Before you can say regional waste facility, the matter has been taken out of the hands of the accountable officials and settled in a cozy chat between some part-time councillors from West St. Paul and some extremely nice, polite, sympathetic and well-informed executives from BFI. If the West St. Paul folks play their cards right, they might get to meet Mr. Ruckelshaus."[8]

Soon thereafter, angry West St. Paul residents crammed into their town's council chambers to hear what the returning junketeers had to say about the news reports. Someone presented a brief charging that "because municipal money was taken for the trips (later to be reimbursed by BFI) without a resolution from council, that the members had misused public funds."[9] After admitting the expenses for his trip were to be paid back by the waste company, one councillor, trying to calm the angry crowd, promised "I'm going to go with whatever the people want."[10]

The political space for dumps was narrowing everywhere and in early 1992, in an overture to changing times, BFI tried another tack. The firm retained consultants to assist it with a series of public meetings north of Winnipeg. A company that often behaved as if its part had been written by the authors of "Dallas" now was sounding like a public outreach program. Its flyers invited citizens of West and East St. Paul as well as those of Brokenhead and Rockwood, St. Andrews and Rosser to talk. In place of yesterday's tactics, BFI now sought what it described as a long-term partnership with a community to site, construct and operate "an environmentally-secure regional landfill capable of incorporating recycling programs."

But even this overt approach alarmed the likes of the new Chair of the Works and Operations Committee of the Winnipeg City Council. Generally considered to be a green politician, novice councillor Terry Duguid had been appointed by the mayor in November 1990 to head the committee and had worked hard to see that he had reasonably progressive allies working alongside him inside the highly polarized hothouse of Winnipeg politics.

Duguid's concern over privatized dumping arose out of the fact that Works and Operations had been delegated authority over a newly created Waste Minimization Fund. The $1-million fund depended for its existence on charges paid the city to dump commercial waste in its publicly controlled Beare Road facility. "BFI's proposal will in my view undermine our waste management system here in Winnipeg," declared Duguid. "We receive most of our recycling and waste minimization funds from tipping fees and a private waste disposal facility near the city limits will divert waste and money from that fund."

By the early 1990s, the effect of increasing hostility to burying refuse was shifting the focus from disposal to recycling and reuse. BFI acquired Winnipeg Paper, a long-established processor, in anticipation of local calls for recycling programs. It was against the possibility of this sort of resource grab that in March 1992 various members of Terry Duguid's Works and Operations committee opposed another omnibus proposal by BFI to collect, process and ship old newspapers to International Paper Industries Limited (IPI) in British Columbia. (Curiously, a 1990 Greater Vancouver decision to reject a regional WMI recycling proposal and opt for a sub-regional system was credited with saving many local businesses, including IPI, from bankruptcy.)

Seven contractors, including the Big Three, had responded to Winnipeg's request for proposals for an old newspapers contract. The Houstonians offered a drop-off operation and proposed a public awareness program publicizing the twenty-four-hour-a-day effort through the print and electronic media. The Waterworks, Waste and Disposal Division recommended BFI's plan. But before the city could act, opponents weighed in with a formidable array of objections.

The nay-sayers were a cross-section of Manitoba economic life: an Abitibi-Price paper mill in nearby Pine Falls which feared being driven under by the loss of their supply of old newsprint; a sheltered workshop whose severely handicapped workers sorted the paper supplied to Pine Falls; and the Recycling Council of Manitoba. As well, an out-of-town company was basing its proposal to invest $17 million to build a pulp molding plant on the availability of old newsprint. Some Works and Operations committee members saw in such an enterprise the value-added activity needed to break the boom and bust cycle of a hinterland economy.

Before the committee's final vote on whether to award BFI the contract, the debate degenerated to "name-calling and partisan politics."[11] As in the case of the earlier recycling debate in Vancouver, the background and corporate culture of the proponent became an issue. One councillor quoted an American environmental group on the Kohn, Savett cartelization case and said that the committee had to question the possible monopolistic impact on local recyclers if BFI was allowed to take old newspapers out of the province. Two right-leaning councillors who took a far more sanguine view of BFI's offer questioned both the need to dredge up a foreign court case and Duguid's judgement in allowing the introduction of such extraneous material.

Three councillors ended up storming out of the meeting. But when they returned, and decorum was restored, Duguid and his allies prevailed. A majority of the committee voted against awarding BFI the contract. Instead, they adopted a hands-on approach based on public depots, a mixture of public and private pickup, publicity and local re-use of the discarded urban ore.

But nobody assumed the matter would rest there. The Winnipeg electoral map recently had been re-drawn, dividing the city into larger wards and larger wards, favoured candidates with larger war chests. So as the ideological adversaries on the Works and Ops committee faced off against each other at the ballot box in coming years, money would play an ever larger role in determining who was to control old newsprint. It also would have its say in determining who would have responsibility for and control over such waste-related issues as our consumption habits, production methods and resources policy.

Chapter 9

Toronto: A Matter of Politics

*Be sensible: no sane businessman bids for a collection contract
that would be at the mercy of a landfill run by rivals.*

Waste Age, August 1978

*The question of what regulations and policies were needed had
become directly tied to the question of who would decide and on
what basis such decisions would be made. Garbage, an issue that
had generated a multibillion-dollar industry, had also become a
matter of politics.*

Louis Blumberg and Robert Gottlieb, *War on Waste*

Toronto's garbage story covers the gamut of waste disposal issues.
In the early 1970s the scene was a familiar one: the big waste
corporations rapidly closing in on the independents, either eating
them up or pushing them aside. The question was: Who would end
up controlling the Maple pits, the largest projected landfill on the
continent, and thus capture much of the refuse flow of Canada's
largest city? Just as it looked as though WMI was going to prevail,
various activist organizations pressured the administration of Metropolitan Toronto into recognizing the implication of a private-sector coup, and to expropriate the pits.

In the mid-1980s it became clear that even the Maple site would
not be vast enough to contain the metropolitan waste stream for
much longer, and a long public consultation had yet to reach any
consensus on alternatives. A business consortium tried to circumvent a public process and parley its political connections at the
highest levels of the governing Liberal Party into an unprecedented
private waste disposal monopoly. Its solution to the impending
waste crisis was to search for remote communities desperate
enough to welcome the city's refuse as an economic boon.

However, with the NDP's unexpected rise to power in 1990, partly as a result of waste issues, it looked for a while as though the process of public consultation and control would advance.

But the private sector did not sit idle for long, watching the monopoly revenues on 12,000 tons of solid waste per day disappear into the public purse. The haulers would eventually find their way back into the waste stream, and start to siphon off some for themselves, thus breaking the circle of public control needed to change the giant city's profligate waste habits.

MacLaren's Plan

The idea of using the Maple pits as a major garbage dump was first introduced in 1967, soon after the newly consolidated Municipality of Metropolitan Toronto was handed responsibility for disposing of Metro's solid wastes. Until 1966 Metro was made up of thirteen municipalities, each individually responsible for managing the wastes generated within its boundaries. Some owned incinerators, either individually or in consortium, others relied on land disposal. Smaller municipalities were dependent on neighbouring public facilities or private dumps. As refuse volumes grew, this chaotic, unplanned system was losing its capacity to cope. With the municipalities working at cross-purposes, it seemed increasingly likely that in the rush to find solutions, social and environmental costs would be ignored. Thus pressure for rationalization mounted. When the structure of Metro government changed in 1966, the thirteen municipalities were consolidated into the City of Toronto and five surrounding boroughs. Although Metro was made responsible for solid waste disposal under the new system, to a large extent this responsibility was a nominal one. The important power of licensing disposal sites continued to be exercised at the provincial level, while collection remained the business of the individual municipalities.

Metro took its new duty seriously however. It commissioned James F. MacLaren Limited, a firm of consulting engineers, to formulate a disposal plan based on the needs of the 26 municipalities within the 720-square-mile Metropolitan Planning Area. The MacLaren report and Metro's response to it marked the beginning of the scramble for disposal sites in the Toronto area. The central issues that would occupy the attention of Metro politicians and planners, provincial board members, garbage company executives, environmental activists, public employee unions, and local residents near proposed sites for the next fifteen years emerged at the same time. As the debate developed, these issues fell into two categories. On the one hand, there were the issues surrounding the impact of a large disposal site on the environment, its effect on the quality of life of people living near the site, and how best to minimize the damage. On the other hand, there were the issues of control: If garbage was indeed a resource, who should control its flow? In particular, debate focused on the wisdom of entrusting control of disposal in the Toronto area over the next several decades to a transnational waste management firm. While a number of proposed sites were involved in this debate, as time went on discussion increasingly centred on the largest of these, in the largest projected dump on the continent, the Maple pits.

In its master plan submitted in May 1967, MacLaren noted that "generally speaking, the Area municipalities had inadequate disposal facilities" to handle the more than 4,500 tons of refuse generated daily and recommended pursuing some mix of incineration and landfill until 1986. Although it handled the issue somewhat gingerly, the consulting firm suggested that Metro pay some attention to the question of flow control:

> The economics of this plan can only be achieved if Metro can successfully acquire and operate the long range disposal sites on which the plan is based ... In order to avoid unpredictable and undesirable fluctuations in refuse capacity requirements at the various disposal facilities, it will be necessary for Metro to make specific efforts to police the origin-destination of refuse. Any situation which might make it attractive to the collection and hauling agencies to deviate from Metro's desired delivery pattern should be avoided.[1]

With considerable naïveté, MacLaren maintained that Metro could rely on the use of market forces to realize the plan: "If the Metro disposal system is operated efficiently and charges made reflect only actual costs, much of the incentive to private competition should be removed."[2] In reaching this conclusion, the consulting firm did not foresee the emergence of waste management companies whose size rivalled even as large a public body as Metro and that were in a position to undertake private planning that could supplant the plans of public authorities and override the environmental standards of concerned communities.

MacLaren assigned the Maple pits a key role in its plan. Calculating on the basis of a 745-acre site, it estimated the capacity of the pits at 21 million tons which was a conservative figure compared to later ones. Its capacity was not the only thing that made the Maple pits an ideal site. Also counting in its favour were its topographic features, accessibility, earth-cover availability and low water-pollution potential (this last would be challenged in later studies). According to MacLaren's scheme, the site would come on stream during the 1976–1986 planning period. The owners of the pits were still removing aggregate in 1967 and seemed unwilling to consider garbage dumping for a number of years. Nevertheless MacLaren's recommendation that Metro acquire the pits aroused interest in the site. Because it lay beyond Metro's boundaries, in the jurisdiction of the neighbouring Town of Vaughan, Metropolitan authorities could not simply expropriate it. Hence Metro, the Town of Vaughan and former North York reeve Norman Goodhead's Disposal Services Limited, which already had a forty-three-acre disposal site in the pits, began jockeying for position.

In 1968 Metro Council authorized the purchase of the pits. The following year the town approached the Metropolitan Toronto and Region Conservation Authority (MTRCA) to consider joining it and Disposal Services in developing a disposal facility at Maple. The authority suggested including Metro. But the Metropolitan bureaucracy was already stirred with misgivings. One potential problem was developing a secure site in the sieve-like kame moraines; another was convincing the Ministry of the Environment to approve the site which was a source of recharge for the groundwater aquifers.

The dynamics of the situation were changed considerably by the arrival of WMI in 1972. The American waste managers moved quickly to consolidate a dominant position within the private sector, and their most important acquisition was Disposal Services, which they bought in August 1972. A few months later they added another local operator, York Sanitation Limited, to their network. When subsidiaries of WMI picked up four dump sites north of Maple, the smaller local companies were alarmed to find that 80 per cent of all licensed private dump space in the area was in the American company's landbank.

To help guide them through the political maze in Ontario, the men from Oak Brook could now count on Norman Goodhead. Goodhead remained with Disposal Services, became a director of York Sanitation, and became involved in Valeria Holdings Limited with the local district manager of Waste Management of Canada. Having settled for the role of Tory loyalist after his defeat in North York municipal elections, and allied with the darling waste manager of Wall Street, Goodhead would mastermind the scheme to make the Maple pits the largest privately owned and operated dump in the world.

It was also through Goodhead that WMI acquired access to the Maple pits. With a formidable assortment of well connected individuals, Goodhead purchased Superior Sand, Gravel and Supplies Limited for a reported $1.5 million in September 1972. The company owned 683 acres in the pits, and this site became part of WMI's landfill bank through a royalty arrangement. Goodhead's associates in the deal included his former Disposal Services partner, Max Solomon, who was now a WMI executive; Phineas Schwartz of the prominent Toronto law firm of Goodman and Goodman; developer Joseph Zentil; Edward and Tom DeToro, sons of road-paving magnate Johnny (Sir Bulldozer) DeToro; some anonymous Italian investors secretly moving funds to a safer haven; and race-horse owner Donald Godfrey, whose brother Paul had been a protégé of Goodhead's during the garbage contractor's active political days and was about to become chairman of Metropolitan Toronto.[3] The foundation was being laid for a large-scale private sector coup.

The investors who made up the Superior Sand consortium ran three major risks: the province could refuse a licence on environmental grounds, Metro could back some alternative system that would divert large amounts of refuse away from private facilities, or some public agency could expropriate the Superior Sand site. WMI's Max Solomon was prepared for this last possibility. He informed one Toronto reporter that "if they're going to expropriate me I'll go to the Privy Council of England to fight it ... They'll have a hell of a fight on their hands."[4] Goodhead added: "Metro had their chance. If they didn't want to take it that's their fault. Now we've got it."[5] But the danger that surfaced first, before WMI even formulated a plan for the Maple pits, was the threat of an alternative system. In November 1972 the Metro Executive Committee voted to sign a contract with Canadian Pacific, which would move about 400,000 tons of refuse a year in specially built railway cars to Hope Township. Goodhead's reaction revealed his conception of the relationship between public office and commercial waste management. He threatened to run for mayor of North York "to make my case heard against a Metro plan to ship garbage by rail for disposal in landfill sites outside the area."[6] But the opposition of Hope Township residents living near the proposed dump killed the plan, and Goodhead was spared the hustings.

In early 1973 consulting engineers engaged by the WMI-Goodhead group prepared a Solid Waste Management System plan. The pits were considered the key to solving the Toronto area's waste disposal problems. The plan included disposing of two million or more tons of waste annually for thirty years; building six recycling stations in Metro costing $30 million; recycling and segregating all reusable material; using shredded garbage to fuel Ontario Hydro generating stations; and transferring any surplus bales in covered freight cars along Canadian National tracks to the Maple property. According to an internal WMI document, the scheme "encompasses using Disposal's and Superior's property in the Keele Valley area [the Maple pits] as a landfill site for all of Metropolitan Toronto's solid waste." Explained Goodhead: "In the light of present knowledge, this is the ultimate solution, and if Metro does not want us to do it, I suggest they do it themselves and pay us a royalty for our facilities and landfill space."

Hurdles to Private Disposal

Use of the Maple pits as a dump site was firmly on the agenda in 1973. During the next seven years, the private sector attempted to pilot its potentially lucrative scheme through environmental hearings, rural opposition and scandal. The process of winning approval for the scheme went through three stages. The first was Disposal Services' attempt to obtain a licence for its twenty-acre site in the pits, which was considered a prototype for the entire Keele Valley facility.

After the prototype facility was approved in 1974, attention turned to Superior's mass-dumping application. A similar application was submitted by the other major quarry owner in the Maple pits, Crawford Allied Industries. The presence of two competing contractors in the pits was a serious complication. Superior and

Crawford did not agree on matters of design and operation or on how to manage, without destroying the delicate ecology of the site, the fifty to sixty million tons of solid wastes they expected to bury there. (This amount of waste was equivalent to twenty-five to thirty columns each having a football field as its base and rising as high as Toronto's CN Tower.) Though the companies shared a common boundary for 7,000 feet, they proposed different engineering techniques to seal the site. To prevent contaminated liquids from migrating into the groundwater, Superior proposed installing a clay liner and elasticized plastic sheeting. Crawford proposed installing purge wells at the edge of its site to draw in the leachate. When the applications were heard by the Environmental Assessment Board (successor to the Environmental Hearing Board) in 1976, opponents of the dump provoked each applicant into claiming that its own technology was the most suitable one, thereby casting doubt on both systems. Two years later, misgivings about the leachate control technology were a major factor in the board's decision to reject the applications.

Local residents' resistance to the Maple pits scheme was part of the larger movement that had begun to develop in the late 1960s wherever in rural Ontario the dumping of Metro Toronto's garbage was practised or projected. In Whitchurch-Stouffville, a group called Protect Our Water Resources (POWR) was formed when citizens became concerned about the effects of the York Sanitation dump on their drinking water. As the WMI subsidiary expanded its disposal activity in Whitchurch-Stouffville, the resolute citizens were waging battle on more than one front. They were up against not only corporate growth but also the Ministry of the Environment. What they called "pollution" the ministry called a "chemical imbalance." Elsewhere opposition to Metro's rural dumping grounds spawned groups such as Derail Dumps Today (DDT), Help Oust Pollution (HOPE), Group Against Rural Dumping (GUARD) and Group Against Garbage (GAG). In Maple citizens formed Maple Against Dumping (MAD) to fight the expansion of dumping in the pits.

When the Texas Department of Health granted BFI a permit to operate a dump in a predominantly black section of northeast Houston, local residents filed a lawsuit alleging racial discrimination. They maintained that dumps had historically been located in minority neighbourhoods. The principal minority that was affected by the projected dump in the Maple pits was the well-to-do. Among

the most active local opponents of the dump was R.J. (Dick) Hassard, a Bay Street lawyer whose country retreat adjoined the pits.
Another activist was Lyn MacMillan, a medical professor's wife
and the daughter of a British Raj army doctor who had tended to
the cares of maharajahs. "We have a place up there that's paradise
and those buggers are coming in there and ruining it," she said.
"Well you can't blame them I suppose. They are only businessmen." Also involved in the protest movement were the Redelmeiers, whose 973-acre Don Head Farms — by their count the
largest Jersey dairy farm in Canada — lay near Maple pits at the
headwaters of the east branch of the Don River. The leading opponent of the dump on Vaughan council was Dr. James Cameron, a
geography professor.

These activists had access to methods and resources that were
not available to the Houston blacks. During the Environmental
Assessment Board hearings, Hassard hired his own experts to go
through the applicant's geological and hydrological evidence. On
another occasion, Hassard and the legal counsel for the Redelmeiers
were able to obtain an audience with Premier Davis to talk about
garbage matters. Hassard also brought his considerable courtroom
skills to the hearings. In his summation he raised the question of
the profit potential of the Maple dump:

The total tonnage as I read the evidence sort of varies ... as I
understand it ... between 50,000,000 and 63,500,000 tons of
garbage.

There is a current dumping charge of $7 a ton. That means
there is about $350 million at stake.

As I recall the evidence in the '74 hearing, at the time, Disposal Services was trying to get $4 a ton and it only recently
raised it from $2.80 a ton, so in the last three years it has gone
from $2.80 to $4 a ton, up to I believe ... $6 a ton in early
'76 to $7 a ton in late '76.

So it seems, ... if this inflationary trend continues, the amount
at stake will be considerably in excess of the $350 million that
is presently before this Board and if one includes not only
inflationary trends but the fact that one of the applicants,
Superior, is in the hauling business, the transfer station busi-

ness, I suggest that there is probably in excess of $2 billion at
stake in this, if the applications are granted.

Lawyers for the Canadian Environmental Law Association also
attempted to ensure that the full implications of the Maple dump
were publicized. Among all the various entities affected by the
private sector's proposal to develop the Maple pits, perhaps the
most curious role was played by the Municipality of Metropolitan
Toronto. Despite its obvious interest in the question of where and
under whose control Metropolitan Toronto's garbage would be
dumped for the next quarter-century and its position on the side of
public ownership, Metro was not as effective an opponent of the
WMI-Goodhead plan as it might have been. To mount a convincing
resistance to the private-sector scheme, Metro would have had to
come up with an alternative plan. During the long period in which
the application was under consideration, this was something it
never did.

From 1973 Metro's administration was under the chairmanship
of Paul Godfrey, who grew up under the spell of his political idol,
Norman Goodhead. It was a source of frustration to opponents of
the pits development that they could make no connection between
the Godfrey-Goodhead relationship and Metro's attitude towards
the Superior/Crawford application before the Assessment Board.
"Goodhead's political and personal connections, in particular with
the Conservative Party in Ontario and with Paul Godfrey," wrote
Vaughan councillor James Cameron, "raise a number of interesting
but unanswered and perhaps unanswerable speculations and concerns among citizens in Maple who were opposed to Disposal's ...
activities and plans in the Maple area."[7]

Chairman Godfrey's efforts were directed towards establishing
a civic administration and network of commissions and boards that
interlocked with the provincial system.[8] Garbage, however, would
be an area of exceptional friction. Many of the anti-dumping activists resided in constituencies held by Conservatives, creating a rift
between the interests of the ruling provincial party and those of the
metropolitan government. As a result of local opposition, the province rejected Metro's 1972 proposal for hauling garbage by rail to
a site in Hope Township, despite the recommendation of the Environmental Hearing Board that the proposal be accepted and the
conclusion of the board chairman that because of groundwater
problems the Maple site was not an alternative. Godfrey reportedly

considered the province's attitude a betrayal. In the past Tory environment ministers had supported rail haul beyond Metro's limits, but by May 1974 a new minister would announce in a major policy speech that "Metropolitan Toronto should look after its own garbage."[9] The message was clear: Conservatives would not allow Metro to dump its trash in constituencies that faithfully re-elected their members to Queen's Park. The minds of Godfrey and his bureaucracy turned to more public-spirited solutions which, notwithstanding rumblings about Goodhead's political ties, were inimical to the WMI group's scheme.

A few days after the minister's address, Godfrey called for the establishment of a Crown corporation to deal with waste disposal. As a supra-regional authority, such an organization would transcend the self-interest of its constituent members, which Godfrey suggested should include Metro and the surrounding regions of Durham, Peel and York. The new garbage authority could stand up to the province, which was paramount in the licensing and regulation of disposal sites. Godfrey warned that "Metro's garbage problem is reaching crisis proportions and all available landfill sites will be full within nine months to a year.[10] In a submission to the Metropolitan Toronto and Region Conservation Authority, which had undertaken an inventory study of the Maple site, Metro's Deputy Commissioner of Works argued that to allow a single private operator to control the Maple site was to create the conditions for a private monopoly of a major and vital public service.

With the support of the conservation authority and the Town of Vaughan, Metro made the main case for public ownership and control. On 5 November 1974 Metro Council adopted a report from its executive committee which contained the following comment: "That preferably, the filling of the whole Maple site be under the direction of one Authority, with binding responsibilities for all environmental phases. This might be a Crown Corporation or Public Authority." The Godfrey administration also continued to generate an atmosphere of crisis. In June 1976 the Metro Executive Committee authorized its Commissioner of Planning to advise the approaching Environmental Assessment Board hearings that they would be out of disposal sites by 1982 or 1983.

But despite this atmosphere and the calls for supra-regional public planning, Metro remained curiously inert. No new efforts were being made to find other public sites. In its 1978 report rejecting the Superior and Crawford applications, the Environmental Assessment Board mentioned the torpor afflicting public administrators.[11] Because of this bureaucratic inertia, the board's rejection would be only a temporary setback for the WMI-Goodhead group, and the Maple pits would emerge as the preordained receptacle for Metro's refuse.

The Appeal

After the Ministry of the Environment accepted the Environmental Assessment Board's recommendation that the companies' applications be rejected, Superior and Crawford (which by now had also fallen into the WMI-Goodhead orbit) appealed. In 1976 the question of the Maple pits now went to the Environmental Appeal Board. But Tory Ontario's legislature so limited the mandate of the hearing process that economic issues were considered irrelevant. The Environmental Assessment Board hearings were held under the Environmental Protection Act (EPA), which requires a proposal to justify itself only in terms of technical and engineering feasibility.

But even leaving questions of exorbitant private profiteering aside, the ministry presented a brief expressing doubts about whether a safe site could be engineered in the pits: "Because of the technical and environmental constraints involved, this site is marginal."[12] Also questioned was the applicants' actual knowledge of the site's hydrogeology and their ability to cope with hundreds of thousands of gallons per day of contaminated groundwater.

At the highest levels, however, the provincial government felt that it could avoid an active role and let lower levels of public administration and the private sector fight it out. When Dick Hassard and the lawyer for the Redelmeiers met with Premier Davis, Hassard reported that "we came away with all the wrong answers. There was no government policy." No policy, however, was a policy of sorts. Its ultimate result was approval of the revised Superior/Crawford application in 1980.

The revised application had a number of factors in its favour that its predecessor lacked. One of these was an element of rationalization introduced when Crawford was bought out by the Goodhead group in July 1978.

Another factor favouring the private garbage forces was a weakening of the opposition. For unlike Norman Goodhead, the activists were distracted by other goals. The Canadian Environmental Law

Association moved to new fronts. Dr. James Cameron turned his energies to a book exposing a corporate fantasy factory — Canada's Wonderland — rising above the flat farmland on the other side of the embattled village of Maple. A Maple high school teacher, a founder of MAD, said in 1980 that "in the beginning MAD had a membership of five hundred. If you called a meeting tomorrow you'd be lucky to get six." The opposition had been unable to stop the dump, but its contribution would be visible in the stringent engineering and environmental conditions the Environmental Appeal Board attached to its approval of the joint Superior/Crawford proposal.

After the board's decision was ratified by the ministry in September 1980, all that remained was for the WMI-Goodhead group to fulfil those conditions and strike a deal with Metro.[13] Before this could happen, however, new circumstances arose that would derail the whole plan.

Metro's Best Interest

After the WMI-Goodhead proposal for the Maple pits was approved, WMI hired a senior Ministry of the Environment official to oversee the scheme, and earth-moving equipment began spreading the clay liner over 245 acres in the pits. Chairman Paul Godfrey recommended to Metro Council that the latest consultants' master plan be approved in principle. One of the plan's 21 recommendations called for a contract with WMI to deposit 500,000 metric tons yearly until 1990 at Maple. The scenario presented by the private waste managers, and warned against by opponents of the scheme, appeared to be coming to pass.

At least one interested party refused to accept its inevitability. Two days after Godfrey's recommendation to council, Locals 43 and 79 of the Canadian Union of Public Employees (CUPE), representing 10,000 metropolitan civic workers, called for "waste management as a public utility." The union had monitored the progress of the waste majors since the early 1970s, and was alert to manoeuvres that might result in irreversible shifts of economic activity from public to private sector control. In March 1981 the Metro Executive Committee heard CUPE's position outlined in what the *Toronto Star* described as an "unusually angry and lengthy" brief.[14] For the first time, serious opposition to the scheme was expressed that was not primarily argued on environmental grounds. The concerns about a private garbage disposal monopoly that the environmental boards had deflected were now placed by the union on the political agenda.

The CUPE analysis (which was based on the author's research) cut through to the monopoly basis of the WMI-Goodhead scheme. Like lawyer Dick Hassard, the union arrived at astronomical numbers when they calculated the potential revenues at the Maple pits. When the City of Kingston, against the recommendation of its civic workers, had contracted out the transferring and landfilling of municipal refuse to Tricil, costs had risen by more than 400 per cent between 1973 and 1979. Metro Toronto's tipping fees to private haulers at municipal dumps had risen by 231 per cent between 1971 and 1980. Assuming that the trend continued and that a publicly controlled Maple could charge commercial user rates as had been suggested by the consultants, the union estimated that the pits might yield billions of dollars in revenues. They called for expropriation of the site; by treating waste management as a regional public utility, Metro could realize an unanticipated financial boon. This was the lesson the new garbage chains had been teaching close observers of the business, and the union insisted that municipal administrators learn from the experience. If they did, "tax rates would be stabilized, Metro would not have to pay tipping fees determined by a private corporation that can simply wait until it receives the fees it dictates, a proper concern for the environment could be established, and garbage could be used as a resource to generate additional revenues."

The union brief helped crystallize opposition among municipal politicians and others who were wary of the private sector scheme. "There was some feeling on the part of the committee," Alderman June Rowlands (now mayor of Toronto) told CITY-TV reporter Colin Vaughan, "that the evidence from the union was probably correct." Rowlands, not known as one of the council's more radical members, thought that "there's cause for concern. There's no question about that at all." The president of the Consumers' Association of Canada wrote to the Metro Executive Committee that "we are impressed with the research [in the civic workers' brief], particularly the findings with respect to the structure of Waste Management . . . and the history of its business activities. Unfortunately, the frightening scenario painted of the takeover of the waste disposal industry by a few multinational conglomerates — with a record of disdain for the environmental and other laws — is all too true."

Despite all this, Paul Godfrey appointed a special task force to negotiate with WMI "one of the biggest and most difficult deals in the history of Metro politics." And a Metro works subcommittee authorized its staff to continue negotiations for the use of the Maple pits. But the negotiators could not get a deal with WMI. The municipality asked for a price of $7.25 per metric ton, which was consistent with the consultants' master plan. WMI could do no better than $7.75 per metric ton, and insisted on being guaranteed 525,000 metric tons. An intransigent company finally forced the hand of the metropolitan bureaucracy. Since the negotiations were being so closely scrutinized, they had to find an alternative to private dumping. With Metro having given up the search for landfill facilities long ago, leaving the Goodhead group alone in the field, there was only one way out now. On 16 June 1981, at a private meeting of the Executive Committee, chief Metro administrative officer John Kruger proposed that Metro buy the site.

The 1967 master plan had estimated that Metro could acquire, develop, operate and complete the Maple site for $11.2 million. Goodhead was prepared to break ranks, but at a price. He was asking for $45 million for the land alone. A two-hour secret Metro Council session debated the pros and cons of the deal. The prospective purchase offer was complicated by dozens of conditions. The engineering problems associated with the site were considerable and further testing would be required to ensure that Metro could comply with the provisional certificate of approval. There was also the question of whether the provincial government would transfer the licence. The transfer was crucial if Metro was to avoid hearings under far more demanding legislation than that which covered private dumping applications. Finally the deliberations ended. By a vote of twenty-two to nine, the councillors voted to purchase the empty pits. By a circuitous route Metro had finally come around to accepting the solution that had been urged on it for almost fifteen years and committed itself to becoming the owner of the Maple pits.

For the privilege of owning the 245-acre site which was to be developed following the revised Superior-Crawford plan with a 100-acre buffer, Metro agreed to pay the $40 million price recommended by Kruger. Without having dumped a single bag of trash, Goodhead and his co-owners would realize a handsome return on their original investment in Superior and Crawford. On the other hand, WMI was far from satisfied with the outcome of the Maple affair. As James Temple, district manager of Waste Management of Canada, lamented before the Ontario Industrial Waste Conference in 1982:

> Three years ago we at Waste Management of Canada had high hopes that our site at Maple would be one of the grandest and most celebrated landfills in the western world. So far there has been very little to celebrate. First there was a very long hearing before the Environmental Assessment Board which we lost. Then a hearing before the Environmental Appeal Board, which gave us the go-ahead, provided we lived up to nineteen conditions. And finally there was the sale of the site to Metropolitan Toronto. I must say with a sigh that that lovely big hole in the ground has just about become the grave of our dreams for a viable private landfill business in Ontario.

If the combined efforts of various groups could halt WMI's progress towards the pits, their real match would now prove the pits themselves. Great technical ingenuity would be required to prevent these vast excavations from becoming the nemesis of the anticorporate forces. Further testing revealed it might be impossible to seal the exhausted quarries. In the spring of 1983 the deal with the Goodhead group had still not been closed. Kruger, a renowned civic administrator, sought greater assurances that the site actually could be designed to meet community standards. He hedged Metro's investment by securing the vendors' agreement to return $19 million if the proposed Maple operation fell apart within a period of six years. The discovery of a second line of contamination (caused by previous disposal in the area) running beneath the site led to further delays. The indomitable Lyn MacMillan was still warning of the dire consequences of dumping over a vast reservoir. In a letter to a Toronto newspaper, she alluded to recent findings of a distinguished soil scientist who considered the idea of secure landfills a "figment of optimistic imaginations." It would indeed take extraordinary measures to protect the water-bearing formation; but the prospect that the enormous cash (and garbage) flows could provide public solutions to public problems seemed slightly brighter now that the pressure of private profit had been relieved.

Citizens Consider Alternatives

The struggle for control of the Maple pits, which finally opened as a publicly controlled dump in 1984 had less to do with ecological considerations than it did with political economy and ideology. Nevertheless, the shift to public ownership altered the dynamic of waste management planning and helped open (if ever so meagerly) the way towards a genuinely democratic approach. For control of waste disposal — and ultimately when they chose to exercise it, the economic wherewithal which flowed with it — now was in the hands of the public works bureaucracy and the elected council of Metropolitan Toronto.

From 1983, the Ontario government moved to close private dumps (or the owners closed them under threat of provincial action) and, in the next four years, the amount of waste going into Toronto's public sites tripled. But tipping fees remained low — a hidden subsidy to the generators of trash. Throughout the province, in spite of such innovations as the blue box recycling program (originally a private-sector initiative of Laidlaw's in Kitchener-Waterloo), Metro Toronto officials remained reluctant to use their power to control the price of disposal for any purpose other than the elimination of a private monopoly over an essential service.

One Pollution Probe activist recalls the glazed expressions in the eyes of Metro planners whenever he talked to them in the mid-1980s about waste management options. It was his impression that all the municipal engineers really wanted to do was to build incinerators along the Toronto waterfront, an engineer's homage to the industrious Japanese who relied heavily on incineration. Tokyo had built thirteen trash burners between 1960 and 1983 and dumped the ash in dyked areas of Tokyo Bay.[15]

However, an important piece of provincial legislation — the Environmental Assessment Act — began to apply to Ontario's municipalities in 1980. The law subjected public planners to an arduous approval process, requiring them to consult citizens before submitting any new waste project to the hearing process. As well, they had to study the relative advantages and disadvantages of proposed undertakings, and most crucially, they had to come up with possible alternatives to the preferred project.

This unique confluence — public control and the unavoidable obligation on the public sector to pursue the question of possible alternative waste strategies — led the public works committee of

Metro Toronto to invite ordinary citizens into its Solid Waste Environmental Assessment Plan (SWEAP) in 1987.

"SWEAP wasn't out of the blue," notes John Jackson, a respected Ontario grass roots consultant. "It was an attempt to do sincerely what the Environmental Assessment Act said everybody should be doing. But no one had figured out how to do it."

Public planners had been loath to describe alternatives to favoured landfill and incinerator schemes and, as a consequence, hearings boards were shooting down their proposals. Satisfying the act was becoming a Sisyphean task. The Region of Halton (to the west of Toronto) ran a decade-long hearings gauntlet during which it was forced to export its solid waste to an incinerator operated in New York. Metro Toronto, with this experience in mind, reckoned its own ability to negotiate the approvals minefield with new post-Keele Valley disposal projects would depend in large measure on its ability to play the public participation card.

In 1987, the bureaucracy sought to engage as its public participation facilitator for SWEAP a Rutgers University-trained psychologist who had written a thesis in learning theory. But before she would accept the appointment, Barbara Wallace insisted that the consultation program be a meaningful one. It was agreed it would but, as Dr. Wallace later recollected, she did not believe that the works department "really understood what that commitment meant."

Under the direction of Wallace and her principal collaborator John Jackson, the word "public" began to take on an entirely new meaning. It no longer referred to the random statistical man on the street but instead was taken to mean the stakeholder groups with an interest in the issues.

Various groups outside the traditional decision-making loop assumed a more dominant role in the quickly evolving program than politicians, industry and works department bureaucrats intended them to have. Each of the stakeholders (environmental organizations, the general public, government, politicians and industry) had a caucus which was represented on the Multi-stakeholders Committee (MSC) whose monthly meetings became the focal point of the entire consultative process.

Metro's primary focus (in the view of environmentalists) was on landfill and incineration. Only reluctantly did it agree to implement the blue box program. Its legal staff insisted — as Dr. Wallace remembers — that all the public consultation program had to do "is meet the legal requirements." But she had her own wider agenda. She conferred with whomever she felt had influence. Caucus committees and the half-dozen special task forces that she and her allies devised were exploring the terra incognita of at-source reduction, packaging and legal and regulatory changes. They sought to explore a whole range of options and opinions about what should be in Metro's master waste management plan.

The private waste managers caucus endorsed the primacy of market forces in developing any SWEAP programs and the view that as vital as recycling might be, it often only deferred ultimate disposal. Not surprisingly, the multi-nationals maintained low profiles throughout. Such a process — sans corporate jets, lobbying, global equity offerings, campaign contributions and expense account life styles — was not their natural habitat. Small independents, however, found themselves in accord with efforts by environmental groups to push the bureaucracy to undertake such things as a composition study of the waste stream.

How (they asked in unison) could Toronto hope to design a system without any idea of who was dumping what and exactly where it was coming from? Metro engineers dug in their heels, insisting for at least two years that this was too odious a task for anyone to undertake. Who (they demanded to know) could be found to sort through the green bags? But more pressure was applied and the public works department, caught up in the web of its own devising, eventually came through with new information. Sympathetic Metro functionaries (like Wallace and Drew Blackwell, who later was to be named by an NDP government to head a new waste reduction initiative within the provincial ministry of environment) even egged on activists, provoking them to demand increased resources from their bosses for such things as public education.

Slowly, the consultation process began challenging the status quo and all its assumptions. But meanwhile, the quantity of privately hauled industrial, commercial and institutional waste flowing into public landfills kept growing and, as it did, the accumulating tonnage shortened the life expectancy of the public's disposal assets (its transfer stations and dumps). Keele Valley had been supposed to remain open until 2004 but now seemed likely to be full by 1993. So what loomed as an immediate challenge for SWEAP — a Metro-only plan to cope with the rapid elimination of disposal options in the economic centre of Canada — translated from another perspective into the chance to make a real killing.

Envacc

While the cumbersome consultation process felt its way along a time line which kept lengthening, there was a rumour in the Toronto press that a consortium calling itself Envacc Resources Incorporated (coyly standing for ENVironmental ACCountability) had made a presentation to Premier David Peterson, whose Liberals had ousted the entrenched Tories in 1985.[16]

Envacc had been dreamed up by an out-of-work Canadian environmental and engineering consultant. On receiving a golden handshake from a firm in Michigan, Doug Edgcumbe had been asked by a former business acquaintance at the well-connected Toronto law firm of Gardiner, Roberts to help out a client who feared that a public landfill might go in near property he intended for development. What Edgcumbe came up with was a plan of somewhat Pharaonic proportions to re-direct the entire regional solid waste stream to government-owned property east of Toronto near the town of Pickering.

The lawyer was intrigued and his firm underwrote further research. Edgcumbe looked into systems in Holland, Spain, Germany and Japan. He even made some calculations on Seymour Cray's legendary super computer at Stanford. Soon thereafter, Gardiner, Roberts brought in a backer whose name meant nothing at the time to Edgcumbe. All he knew was "that's when things got moving at a political level."

Later on, Edgcumbe happened to read with fascination a newspaper exposé by the *Globe and Mail*'s Jock Ferguson dealing with the powerful influence of three developers. Marco Muzzo, Alfredo De Gasperis and Rudy Bratty, though virtually unknown to the public, apparently were extremely effective developers, long accustomed to having municipal councils around Toronto take notice of their development projects.

Muzzo, a long-time Conservative Party supporter, had changed horses, moving forcefully to the Liberals after they dislodged the long-reigning Tories. Businesses of Muzzo and associates made the largest donation from related companies ever given to a provincial political party.[17]

Now Edgcumbe thought he understood why everything seemed peaches and cream. Envacc's backer was none other than Marco Muzzo and, from what he could see, the whole thing had been fast-tracked at the highest levels.[18] Edgcumbe travelled with a Liberal member of provincial parliament who was promoting Envacc at Queen's Park and who accompanied him to Japan with provincial money to study waste technology. He had attended confidential meetings with the Liberal caucus and senior officials.

The consortium quickly grew to include Canadian Pacific, which took a 50 per cent stake for itself and, via Laidlaw (which it had acquired the previous summer), began gearing up to propose to design, finance and operate a scheme which seemed entirely to bypass the SWEAP process. In January 1989, John Jackson, now immersed in the public consultation as SWEAP's Multi-Stakeholders Committee facilitator, was shocked to be invited to meet with senior Laidlaw executives. At the meeting, Jackson was presented with a copy of their proposal which he figured was a token gesture to allow the consortium to claim he had been consulted. But unbeknownst to Jackson, the premier, the previous summer, had pushed the Muzzo group to involve environmentalists in their planning.[19] Laidlaw's proposal was more the by-product of private circumvention than of public consensus.

What Envacc proposed was an omnivorous plan to separate, recycle, recover, waste-product manufacture, product-develop, compost, landfill and sell methane gas. Jackson didn't find it serious on the question of reduction and recycling but noted that — as a possible hook to his constituency — it excluded any mention of the absolute demons of incineration and energy from waste facilities. That month, the *Globe and Mail*'s Michael Valpy was informed that Envacc was going to make a move and he used his column to sound an alarm. The mega-project was about to be pitched to the Metro Works Committee which under Ontario law was responsible for waste disposal. "What Envacc is proposing," he wrote, "is that it become the Ma Bell of garbage — totally in control of one of the most politically sensitive issues of the day." Seeing what amounted to a 12,000-metric-ton-a-day scheme, Valpy found it difficult "to see where the incentive would be for a private monopoly to attack the greatest problem with garbage, which is excess volume."[20]

The proponents appeared before the committee in a televised session and the audience included Edgcumbe who later asserted how shocked he had been (as were other officials and some municipal politicians) to hear a Laidlaw executive indicate Envacc's tipping fees could range as high as $300 a tonne.[21] At the time, Metro was charging haulers $84 to dump a tonne of rubbish at

Keele Valley. "In my opinion it was turning into a set up to bleed the public," said Edgcumbe. He was becoming increasingly disaffected with the approach adopted by his high-powered confederates. Not long thereafter, Edgcumbe found himself back on the street — and embroiled in legal conflict with his former associates.

Meanwhile, Jock Ferguson, having decided to extend his investigations into the area of garbage, came up with Edgcumbe's name. But before he could find him, Edgcumbe phoned and asked: "Are you interested in garbage?" "If it involves Marco Muzzo," Ferguson replied, "I am." The caller laughed. He claimed to the reporter that Muzzo had kicked in $300,000 to launch Envacc.

Edgcumbe agreed to provide documents including minutes offering an inside view of the group's pursuit of a possible $1-billion contract with a new waste authority about to be initiated by the Peterson government. The Solid Waste Interim Steering Committee (SWISC) was a provincial strategy designed to remove responsibility for waste disposal from Metro Toronto and place it instead with an inter-regional agency comprising all five regions of the greater Toronto area.

On 13 March 1989, the day before SWISC was announced at the Ontario Science Centre, excerpts from Envacc's minutes appeared in the *Globe*. The revelations included evidence of an aborted approach to Peterson's father-in-law in the hopes that in return for a piece of the action he might assist them "in selling the concept to the Premier."[22] A livid Premier Peterson denounced as nonsense and innuendo the muckraker's insinuation of favoritism towards the Envacc scheme. Two weeks later, Toronto councillor and former Canadian Federation of Municipalities president Richard Gilbert, a proponent of an all-encompassing public (rather than private Ma Bell) approach to the management of used materials, added his more measured denunciation. He charged that SWISC's approach (preemptively calling for private bids to long-distance haul the solid waste of the five lakeshore regions) was backwards.

Gilbert foresaw getting locked into high-tech plans into which enormous amounts of trash would have to be fed with the consequent cutting back on the 3 R's of recycling, reuse and reduction. "A call for proposals, in good faith, has to lead to a contract at the end. That means that Metro and the regions are letting private companies plan for their area's future."[23]

Willing Hosts? Orillia and Kirkland Lake

In the face of the difficulty of siting waste facilities under the existing assessment process and the constant air of impending crisis over what to do next, Peterson was probably hoping that the private sector could identify cities sufficiently distressed to volunteer themselves as a waste terminus.

The incineration vendor Ogden Martin targetted a community which had been the setting for humourist Stephen Leacock's *Sunshine Sketches of a Little Town*. Here in the resort town of Orillia between the shores of Lake Couchiching and Lake Simcoe, the Fortune 200 service company with 33,000 on its payroll made a sufficiently positive impression on the local Economic Development Commission to get itself invited to meet city council members to discuss "the concept of Orillia becoming the host community for a modern Ogden Martin Resource Recovery Facility."[24]

Ogden's track record (almost 20 per cent of the U.S. energy-from-waste market) seduced the local power structure which saw the project as a godsend. The committee of the whole city council, in recommending a Letter of Intent be prepared for submission to Ogden, informed the mayor that "Orillia's nearness to the Toronto area and good transportation routes make it an attractive site for this major industry. The benefits to the City of Orillia should a plant be established would include a major boost of industrial tax assessment, new permanent jobs, both directly and indirectly, opportunities to attract secondary industries and commercial operations as well as a long term solution to the Orillia and Area Waste Management and Recycling Programs."[25]

What Ogden desired was to ring Toronto with three $500-million plants. Each site would employ about 150 people. Trash would be rail-hauled in and each big burner would produce seventy-five megawatts of electric power, more than enough to meet the present needs of Orillia.

Hopeful that the public would also see in the giant furnace a form of economic deliverance, the council of the financially pressed city unanimously approved signing an "expression of interest" with Ogden in April 1990. Then the mayor informed Toronto of his support for Ogden Martin becoming the designated instrument for dealing with the Metropolitan garbage crisis.[26]

But reaction came quickly and it was negative. Local doctors used computers to search bio-medical journals published in seventy countries for information on the health aspects of incinerators. They broke up into committees to study what 166 articles and reports had to say about the current technology, its effects on water, the effects of particles on lung function and the impact of metal emissions. Their catalogue of concerns ran to twenty pages of single-spaced type and included such matters as the apparent fact that quench and waste waters of solid waste incinerators contain chlorinated benzene, the health effects of which were said to be "totally unknown." Nor was the report reassuring about possible dioxin, mercury and lead emissions. As for cadmium (for which there was said to be no safe level) the doctors expected the furnace to spew 558 pounds of the soft, bluish-white metallic element into their atmosphere every year.[27]

Other citizens, realizing that to be viable the Ogden furnace would need far more than Orillia's refuse, demonstrated at city hall. They said they were unwilling to become Toronto's garbage can.[28] At a day-long protest in a park, the local Progressive Conservative member of provincial parliament made common cause with the socialists. The Tory suggested the incinerator should be built in Toronto if it was so safe. Bob Rae also made light of the whole concept — though he hardly could have anticipated how significant a role dissatisfaction over the politics of waste was going to play in an election three months down the road.

Fifty-two of Orillia's fifty-four doctors ended up endorsing a report titled *Hazards of Incineration* which concluded that incineration is a processing technology and not "a total method of municipal solid waste disposal ... There is absolutely no place for heavy metals, chlorinated plastics, or bleached paper within the incineration process. Once one removes the paper and the packaging and the metal containing waste there is very likely insufficient fuel to be efficient in producing energy."[29]

The physicians moved on to make a crucial point about the primacy of planning — the very point that was being made by members of SWEAP, who looked on warily as the new SWISC authority, without anything like Barbara Wallace's consultative process, had gone ahead and issued its own world-wide call inviting corporate expressions of interest to develop a comprehensive long-term disposal system.

"The only efficient method of reducing the risks of incineration," the doctors noted, "requires that a broader system of municipal solid waste management be examined. This would require planners and managers to step back from their crisis mentality which is now dictating decisions and consider all steps in the product cycle, production, use, discarding, collection, recycling and in recovery, processing and ultimate disposal. *Comprehensive planning of this type can only be conducted on a regional or national basis rather than at a municipal level.*"[30]

Finally, in arguing that every effort be made in the interests of "this rather wonderful green and relatively unpolluted corner of a polluted world," the doctors recommended "that the current incinerator proposal for Orillia be stopped."[31] Nine thousand of the town's twenty-four thousand citizens backed them with an anti-incineration petition. Two days following the presentation of the signatures, and after three months of bitter debate, the city council cancelled the agreement, but held out the possibility of approaching Ogden Martin for a smaller burner in the future.

Ogden Martin's general counsel reacted with corporate culture's usual approach to conflict resolution. A belligerent lawyer's letter was sent to the doctors. What seemed on the face of it a legitimate act of self-defence became twisted in the eyes of the company into a claim that the physicians had intended to defame the firm by publishing baseless and libelous statements. Unless they saw the light, retracted them and notified the firm of their non-participation or non-endorsement of their report, the lawyer warned that Ogden Martin would consider filing defamation lawsuits.

"We're not playing hardball," an Ogden Martin vice president of marketing told *The Orillia Packet and Times*. He confessed that he was concerned lest other communities take the Orillia report as fact. "We're injured. You can't let a thing like this go on its course. It's too damaging."[32] The threat backfired, causing a fifty-third doctor to endorse the report and its recommendation. Then in August 1990, the Ontario Medical Association followed suit, coming out in defence of physicians "who stick their necks out for the good of public health — and, in particular 14 Orillia MD's who may be facing legal action." The OMA's executive committee passed a resolution supporting Orillia's doctors for having presented their report.[33]

Ultimately, along with Ogden Martin's, SWISC received another eighty-five responses to its call. The most outlandish may have been one proposed by a former Royal Canadian Air Force engineer who wanted to use Hercules-like planes to drop 10,000 tons of garbage a day in the bush north of Sudbury. "It would be comparable," he told a reporter, "to the Berlin airlift."[34] Thirty-three of the concepts called for incineration. Another twenty-one had landfill components. Eight considered finding remote host communities up north, including a controversial plan by a consortium involving Canadian National Railways and Bechtel to alter the traditional relationship of the city to the hinterland. Where once gold and iron ore had flowed south, now waste would go north.

The idea (enthusiastically backed by Metro officials who poured half a million dollars into geological, hydrological and hydrogeological studies as well as into public relations work) proposed to haul 30 million tonnes of trash in double-stacked sealed containers 600 kilometres north of Toronto. Once up there, the waste was supposed to re-vivify the town of Kirkland Lake's economy by nourishing the growth of state-of-the-art recycling companies or, alternatively, be buried in an abandoned 700-foot iron ore pit sitting in 8,000 acres of isolated bush.

Seven mines in Kirkland Lake had been closed and, with only 318 mining jobs remaining, 30 per cent of the work force was on the dole. Kirkland Lake's Director of Economic Development and Tourism told the New Democratic Party's northern caucus that the "the host communities [which also included Englehart and Larder Lake] look upon solid waste as a southern resource. This is an opportunity to reverse the traditional flow."

Notably absent from SWISC's roster of would be mega-managers was the name Envacc, though its presence lived on in the form of a proposal from Laidlaw. But as the provincially organized body began winnowing its list, SWISC's legitimacy came under attack. The Toronto Environmental Alliance pointed out that Metro generated over 58 per cent of inter-regional area waste yet all the proposed landfill and incinerator sites were beyond its borders. Obviously, therefore, the steering committee of the lakeshore regions really was nothing more than a device to circumvent the Environmental Assessment Act and export Metro's problem.[35]

Like many other environmentalists, the Alliance, believing that habits only could be modified by dramatically shifting waste management to the 3 Rs and making land burial difficult and burning impossible, opposed transporting waste beyond the area of generation. To be permitted to ship refuse to the internal Third Worlds was equated by Pollution Probe's David McRobert to "giving an alcoholic a still for Christmas." This challenge to the notion of a willing or happy host was to have repercussions when David Peterson called a snap election in the summer of 1990.

Crowning Glory: The NDP's Garbage Promises

In the midst of the 1990 campaign (with Metro now having to dispose of almost 80 per cent more waste than it did a decade ago), city planners were completing a secret list based on their search (which included newspaper ads in every community in Ontario) for volunteers to take the solid waste of greater Toronto. Richard Gilbert told his fellow councillors that "I just see us slipping into disaster. It has been clear for three years that we are in a dire predicament. It will take a miracle" to find a dump by 1993.[36] Out on the hustings, prospects of a solution to Toronto's dilemma were dimming every day. Opposition to its trash was a hot issue and social democrats were doing what they could to capitalize on the discontent.

The New Democratic Party (along with groups like Pollution Probe and the Association of Municipalities of Ontario) slammed the Liberal waste management strategy and renewed a long-standing commitment to a ban on municipal waste incineration. Its environment critic, Ruth Grier, called for the primacy of waste reduction over other options, and Bob Rae presented himself as the St. George who would slay the trash dragon. But as election day approached few realized the extent to which voters would seize on these promises.

Peter Leiss, an NDP activist, remembers being in the Rotunda campaign headquarters as the returns began coming in on the night of 6 September. At 8:15 newscasters had the social democrats leading in fifty ridings. Party workers imagined a computer glitch. Soon thereafter, however, the TV had them ahead in more than seventy races. Still, nobody believed it. But by 8:30, it began to hit. Ontario was about to make Bob Rae its first-ever social democratic leader.

The NDP realized its political ascent was in good part due to its success in playing the waste card. There were now about fifteen potential dump sites on the list being prepared for Metro's master waste plan and locked in the office of the Metro Works Commissioner. "Residents in almost all the listed communities voted New Democratic candidates to power," according to the *Toronto Star*'s Royson James, "after the party's promise to keep Metro's garbage out of their towns."[37]

Further proof of the role of waste and its discontents in bringing the NDP to power at Queen's Park came from the newly elected government. In a letter sent to Doug Edgcumbe, the NDP thanked the whistle-blower for what it saw as his contribution (through exposing the Envacc minutes) to the defeat of the Liberals.

But making good on its promises was going to prove to be an extremely taxing matter. The NDP had come to power as Ontario was being hit by the double blows of deep recession and a flight of capital initiated by the free trade treaty which the federal Mulroney regime signed with the United States. Even if the government knew what it wanted to do about waste (and, given the complexity of the issue, there was much doubt about how to balance issues of social equity and the environment) stout hearts would be required to challenge the status quo without offending the powerful.

Citizens in designated dumping grounds immediately began calling on the new government to make good on its promises. Ruth Grier, now suddenly the NDP Environment Minister, was allowed no time for considered moves. She opted simply to keep the faith and kill the hearing process on interim sites for Metro's waste, thus numbering the days of the Liberals' (and Metro officialdom's) willing host approach. Grier told Metro that henceforth it would be the province that would search for a site for Metro's garbage, so they should forget their pursuit of new dumps. But, that said, she also signaled to them that they continue to pursue the mega-project which excited them the most — the Adam's Mine at Kirkland Lake.[38]

Two months after arriving in her fifteenth-floor office at the Ministry of Environment, Grier announced the first of a series of major initiatives. A creature of the provincial government, soon to be called the Interim Waste Authority Limited (IWA), would be established to search for, acquire, construct and open three landfills in the greater Toronto area. No sooner had Grier spoken than Ontario's most important environmentalists (including Steven Shrybman of the Canadian Environmental Law Association and David McRobert of Pollution Probe) petitioned her to reconsider. These activists held disposal in any guise — be it public or private — an anathema and assumed (like many private contractors did) that Grier's new IWA represented a move towards the kind of publicly owned and operated program which a key NDP constituency, the public employees, wanted.

Fearful that such a utility model could end up incorporating the Kirkland Lake scheme, the environmentalists told Grier her new authority was a mistake. They argued that should she persist it would be fatal to invest this new disposal agency with responsibility for 3 Rs. "When mandates for waste disposal and reduction have been given to the same institution, the former has inevitably predominated."[39] Environmental activists regarded even the provincial environment ministry's existing Waste Management Branch as a backwater populated by retrograde advocates of private-sector disposal. They encouraged Grier to proceed with the Waste Reduction Office (which had been talked about during the election), stressing that it must be a serious force with the bureaucratic status necessary to make real progress in developing policy and 3 Rs initiatives.

Before the economy entered the depths of the recession, Grier did establish a Waste Reduction Office (WRO), appointing Drew Blackwell, the former Metro Works employee who had been so closely involved with the SWEAP process, to head the new office in February 1991. Many of those involved in Metro's consultation process (Barbara Wallace referred to them as the Sweapies) ended up being swept by Blackwell into the WRO, as did such prominent environmentalists as Pollution Probe's lawyer David McRobert, whose appointment signified that the WRO represented a break with the status quo.

"The Sweapies had to learn that this was no longer SWEAP," said Wallace. "It was a new office in the provincial bureaucracy." The new office amounted to a beachhead operation of outsiders within an old boys' network of civil servants who regarded the WRO with suspicion. Furthermore, when Grier stunned Metro Toronto's managers in April 1991 by doing a volte face and rejecting their Kirkland Lake project, she created yet another vector of tension.

Grier had stood in the path of building a northern garbage economy in the name of the ideological winds prevailing at the WRO. Accordingly, official Toronto was as disdainful of the WRO as was the in-house ministry fraternity, thus making its staff of low-tech upstarts more than ever isolated figures on the landscape.

Yet the reality was that the NDP's decision had been backed up with far more pragmatic analysis than its legion of detractors were to give it credit for. In fact, the numbers on the Adam's Mine Recycling and Solid Waste Disposal Project (what its promotor Gordon McGunity called a "world class waste management system") did not add up.

A Ministry of Treasury and Economics economic study of various alternatives for greater Toronto had concluded that "under no scenario is the 'Kirkland Lake' option favoured and under most scenarios the local option is considerably better. In the most favourable case to Kirkland Lake, this option would cost $650 million more than the local site(s) alternative."[40] Hauling waste up to Kirkland apparently made more sense as a public subsidy to the railroad than it did as sound waste management policy.

Whereas the engineer-driven ethos at Metro Works favoured megaprojects, Blackwell's staff tended to see the way out of the perpetual disposal crisis in terms of behavioural change. Export (the distancing of polluters from their pollution) was deemed to provide economic incentive and social sanction to an unsustainable system whose financially ruinous and environmentally unsound methods depended on the high volume of waste.

The NDP, in denying the go-ahead to supporters of the Kirkland Lake project in the affected communities and in Metro, subjected itself to intense public vilification. Hostile Metro councillors accused Grier of having undermined four years of extensive searching and $40 million of expenses, thus pushing the region towards a "garbage apocalypse." They demanded she seriously study incineration, knowing full well she was otherwise disposed.[41]

Toronto's dailies, not to mention others up north, railed against the decision which ruled out leaving the deal's fate to the public assessment process and which directed the new landfill search authority, the IWA, to limit itself to potential dump sites within greater Toronto.

One *Globe and Mail* business columnist whipped himself into a froth of incoherence. "As Newton or somebody once said, it is a law of metaphysics that matter that is not moved, destroyed, or stored is matter that will sit out on the front lawn and in the industrial parking lot from here to eternity," wrote Terence Corcoran, accusing Grier of "worshipping at the altar of the high priests of radical environmentalism. Through the miracle of the three Rs, environmentalists believe all matter can be reduced, re-used, or recycled, and ultimately the curse of garbage will be eliminated from the face of the earth. Forget Newton." [42]

David Lewis Stein saw in Greenpeace and ten other groups who rallied to Grier the deranged passions of the Spanish Inquisition. "I fear the NDP is listening now to people who want to save the planet with the same punishing fervour that an earlier generation of zealots showed when they saved immortal souls by burning heretics at the stake."[43] *The Financial Post,* far less histrionically, focused on the loss of $300 million in fees and other economic activity which Metro could have injected into a severely depressed economy. "Kirkland Lake was positively excited about receiving Toronto's garbage, calling it the town's 'crowning glory' — in the words of town mayor Joe Mavrinac. Good luck in beating that arrangement, Ms. Grier."[44]

On 11 April 1991, while still in the centre of the firestorm of abuse and in full face of the contrary desires of the Metro Works, Grier made a daring and provocative decision. She declared that Canada's largest province was going to be the first major jurisdiction in North America to ban municipal incineration as a policy option. "Incineration," she said, in words that must have deeply irked much of Toronto's waste officialdom "is an environmental sleight of hand which gives the illusion of making waste disappear when, in fact, it re-appears in different and often more hazardous forms."[45]

Many Metro politicians including East Toronto councillor Paul Christie (a supporter of the Kirkland Lake deal and what he called the happy host solution) could not accept the new WRO as a rival policy-making centre. Speaking of the likes of Drew Blackwell and Steve Shrybman (who now was an environmental advisor in the Cabinet office with ready access to the premier and his staff), Christie did not hide his outrage. "Their careers were based on their opposition to Metro's waste initiatives," he complained, adding that the whole new thrust of former Metro employee Blackwell was offensive to him. "I think Metro was on the right track."

Having boxed in the country's major metropolis, the NDP also had boxed in itself. Grier had begun to shift the entire issue via a 3 Rs strategy from a matter of pollution to one of resources. "Grier's is a bold experiment," wrote columnist Thomas Walkom. "She is trying to implement a real NDP policy, one significantly different from that of her predecessor Liberals. If she succeeds — and the odds are against her — it will be a coup."[46]

Flow Control

Initiatives and policies were one thing. But what environmentalists ultimately had to face up to were questions of power and political economy. Once control of landfill had been the key to a simple business; now what mattered was to define what waste is and what it is not, and then, having done that, to determine how waste would be handled and by whom, and likewise for what was deemed to be reusable materials.

In 1991, Metro had debated what would constitute the appropriate powers necessary for it to provide a comprehensive waste management system. These flow control powers (which had to be acquired from the province through a revision of Section 66 of the Municipality of Metropolitan Toronto Act) would have to include the power to compel use of its system; prohibit rival systems being created without its consent; designate facilities waste generators must use; make mandatory source separation and waste audits.

The prospect of such powers in public hands chilled the private sector. Former WMI official Jim Temple, director of the Ontario Waste Management Association, whose members included not only multi-national waste firms but also hundreds of others involved in the business of waste and recycling, said that "it would seem that Metro was trying to take over the private sector, and all we can draw comfort from, I think, are some rather polite reassurances that somewhere we fit into the structure."[47]

But before the Section 66 debate could fully play itself out, Metro's planning was to be blindsided by the second of two unanticipated occurrences. The first had been the provincial takeover of the landfill search process; now to that was added a sudden (and at first mysterious) drop-off in the quantities of waste flowing into Keele Valley and the other sites under its control.

In April 1991, as refuse being dumped in Metro-run landfills dramatically decreased, civic politicians debated why the garbage apocalypse they had been predicting suddenly seemed to be receding before their eyes. Some attributed the fall-off to the recession; some to the success of reduction and recycling efforts; and others blamed illegal dumping and burning. Richard Gilbert was the first councillor to intuit what was going on. The leakage was due primarily to the tipping fees.

Public disposal charges had been raised in the last three years from $18 to $150 a tonne to promote private sector waste diversion and pay for 3 Rs programs. By so doing, Metro began to reap the windfall revenues which had provided the private sector a king's ransom in cash flow and easy profits. But now rather than seeing the monopoly rents flowing into corporate coffers, the funds began to accumulate in a Waste Fund to finance a public program of blue box recycling, waste reduction grants, public education, facility construction and so on. Soon there was $200 million in the fund and, as Gilbert put it, "what has happened in reality is that Metro has stumbled into a wholly new form of taxation, a new form of sin tax. Sin taxes in the past have been on things that are damaging to the user, notably alcohol and tobacco. Now we should be moving quickly towards taxing things that are damaging to the environment."[48]

However, as the recession deepened, with rising joblessness and tightening federal restrictions on eligibility for unemployment insurance, Metropolitan councillors faced unprecedented welfare costs and a likely 25 per cent tax increase. Few politicians wished to saddle property owners with such a hike in an election year. By dipping into the Waste Reserve (for $55 million), they figured that they could confine the tax bill to 7 per cent, maintain police services and provide the needy their dole.

Ruth Grier objected to this raid on the fund, insisting that the Reserve was supposed to be for recycling and composting projects. Drew Blackwell reiterated her message to his former employers, the Metro Works Committee: The Fund should be available for the 3 Rs. Period. But councillors facing re-election understandably remained unmoved. "This is a rainy day fund, and it's raining," said Paul Christie, and he and his fellow councillors defied the province and sued the Reserve for the cops and the welfare cases.[49]

Later that year, however, as they sought monies for waste reduction efforts, the politicians were alarmed to discover their waste revenue was shrinking even faster than projected. What had happened was that various large American waste companies (who they are is not publicly known) had successfully challenged a 1983 U.S. Department of Agriculture ruling, which had permitted only the import of Canadian solid waste going to an incinerator. As a result of the new open door, Metro's planners were dealt a blow by the private sector as industrial, commercial, and institutional (IC&I) waste and revenues began flowing south.

Even had Metro wanted to retain the waste in order to recapture the cash flow, it did not possess the authority to do anything about such a diversion. Unlike residential waste collection, all IC&I had been contracted out to the private sector which was free to take the stuff wherever was most profitable. As well, flow control powers still resided with the province, and, to the extent waste was deemed to be an article of trade, they were shared with the federal government under the Constitution Act.

Ironically, while the export of waste subverted public planning it also alleviated pressure on the province to find new dump sites. At the same time, as Richard Gilbert put it, in spite of an annual revenue loss which he estimated to be in excess of $100 million to Metro alone, "there is a squeamishness on the part of the municipalities from appearing to be too concerned about revenue from waste." The private sector, however, exhibited no such misgivings.

The waste blitzkrieg (estimated to reach two million tonnes by 1993 if provincial action was not taken) was carried out by an army of garbage brokers and private waste haulers. The huge convoys, each semi weighing 80,000 pounds under a full load, transported Toronto's trash to cheaper dumping grounds in New York, Pennsylvania and Ohio. Substandard American sites offered going-out-of-business rates to haulers in anticipation of closing up because of their failure to comply with new EPA regulations. Even Indiana (whose conservative Republican senator Dan Coates was leading a fight against the waste management industry for the right of states to say no to waste importation) was being dumped on by Toronto. According to an aide to New York Congressman Bill Paxon, who introduced legislation to ban the transboundary waste trade, so long as Toronto's tipping fees remained so high "no point in the continental USA is immune from its wastes."

But to bow to external forces and reduce public disposal charges threatened not only those on the dole. Such a policy reaction also undermined the implementation of the mandatory recycling schemes necessary to begin transforming a consumer culture of profligacy. Metro's Waste Reduction Task Force was calling for changes in lifestyles, composters in every community, massive storage of recyclables and garbage police to halve the urban region's landfill requirements by 1993. But action was premised on making the cost of disposal not lower but higher, so as to act as a disincentive to waste and help finance the radical program of social reform.

The haemorrhaging of the regional wasteshed and its associated revenues was so great that by May 1992 the Commissioner of

Works was recommending that Metro forego its plan for new used-materials facilities until the province could control the export situation. Landfill diversion projects were going to be put on hold.

For Doug MacDonald, a key player on the Metro Waste Reduction Task Force, "the next logical step is to ban [out of province] export. You close off that option." Yet even if the government could deal with the powerful array of forces profiting from the waste export (and that was uncertain) it had to have a ready plan for what to do with the recaptured cornucopia of refuse.

Bill 143

Bill 143, the Waste Management Act, sketched out the rudiments of new planning powers. It had been drafted to assist the new government in moving beyond the willing host approach and to create a new framework now that the province had taken over Metro's and SWISC's authority. In fact, Ministry of the Environment planners were working on amendments to confer flow control on the regional governments when senior officials decided to back off because of the coincidence of the tabling of Bill 143 and municipal elections. Thus was an important policy thrust ended for fear of alienating, among others, lower-tier municipalities where the NDP had local power bases.

What remained of the bill finally introduced into the legislature in October 1991 was intended to confirm Grier's inchoate new vehicle, the IWA, as a temporary Crown Agency with powers to establish new long-term landfills inside the borders of greater Toronto by 1996; extend the life of Keele Valley; and amend the Environmental Protection Act to allow the province to mandate 3 Rs activities. At hearings on the bill before the legislature's Standing Committee on Social Development, the Canadian Union of Public Employees called on the government to expand the IWA into a sound waste reduction infrastructure and take over control of the IC&I waste flows currently being diverted southwards at such vast private profit. There are no figures on what the thousands of businesses within Toronto are charged by the waste industry, but the public employees estimated it might add up to half a billion dollars annually.[50]

This immense sum was seen as the rational funding source for a public utility approach. But the authors of Bill 143 were being rebuffed in merely attempting to enable the province to develop regulations on municipal accounting that would require the munici-palities to take into account the true cost of waste disposal. These powers were seen as indispensable for governing the manner in which municipalities carried out the financial management of their waste activities. Yet the Association of Municipalities of Ontario (not to forget the private sector which protested that "as far as this legislation is concerned, the existing private waste management industry simply does not exist") objected to what they saw as the sign of a unilateral takeover of waste management. By the time the Act was proclaimed on 27 April 1992, the government had given in and the bill came into force without the offending (but critical) accounting clause.

The waste convoy continued to flow south and as it did the various contending interest groups continued groping for their pre-ferred solutions. But the pressure for substantial reform was escap-ing like air from a punctured balloon. Metro Works Commissioner Bob Ferguson acknowledged that in so far as the export of waste to the U.S. was concerned "the private sector has turned us upside down."

A provincially appointed Waste Reduction Action Committee (which was influenced by private sector positions) offered what they called a "shared model" as an alternative to the public utility approach. But the export by private contractors of the waste crisis to small town America was lessening the urgency and the possibil-ity of true progress.

Some of Grier's closest advisors hoped almost wistfully that the U.S. Congress, in an election year where opposition to a continental waste market cut across the spectrum of elected officials (from an extreme liberal black woman to conservative good old boys) might vote to stop the import of Toronto's waste. By so doing, it would spare a beleaguered Ontario government from having to impose limits on the sovereignty of the refuse trade, and from being de-nounced as a fire-breathing communistic ogre. (In fact, as we shall see in the next chapter, Quebec's Liberal environment minister Clifford Lincoln had interfered with the "right" to import American solid waste into Quebec without causing his own government to be destabilized.)

Gilbert's view was that "there are times when you simply have to make decisions because the different interests are simply not reconcilable." That said, the maverick Gilbert (whose opinions were respected even by environmentalists who found unacceptable his apparently heretical willingness to consider incineration as a rational option) was not optimistic. He saw a further irony in the present situation: that under a social democratic government with the best of intentions a decade-long march towards greater public participation and control could be reversed.

"A trend that was begun by the Tories, sustained by the Liberals and may — not deliberately — but through an inability or unwillingness to grasp the reins of the issue — become unravelled through the present government. I don't think for a moment that the present government wants this to happen, I just don't see it having the will, or perhaps even the wit to stop it happening." Such was Gilbert's sad commentary in the spring of 1992 on the process begun almost ten years previously with the public supplanting of an emerging private waste cartel.

Chapter 10

Montreal: Privatization, Protest, and the Multi-nationals

Montréal, c'est une jungle de vidange [trash].
A head of a small garbage firm

Private contractors held out over the waste multi-nationals longer in Montreal than in most other North American cities, but for reasons quite unlike the ones advocates of free market competition were offering to justify their policies. However, by the mid-1980s, the Big Three had moved in and incorporated Montreal, then much of Quebec, into their continental operations. As well by the late 1980s, a new factor had entered Quebec's waste equation: American waste was pouring into the province's rural landfills. Once the environmental consequences provoked a mass movement of popular opposition, however, the concept of waste as a "good" or article of commerce that could freely cross borders was presented with one of its most serious legislative setbacks in the history of the waste trade.

Vindicating Savas

When E.S. Savas, the Columbia University professor, apostle of "privatization" and future Reagan administration official, was amassing evidence to demonstrate the superiority of the contract method of garbage collection in the late 1970s, he did not have to look far to find a functioning example of his prescriptions. Just an hour's flight north of his New York City office was Montreal, which had been contracting out its garbage collection for more than two decades.

Montreal's waste industry was indeed an unusual institution, but not entirely for the reasons stressed by the advocates of privatization. While the leading waste disposal corporations were rapidly rendering competitive capitalism irrelevant as a theoretical framework for the industry in the rest of the continent, they had made little headway throughout the 1970s in Montreal. The city still boasted its own home-grown firms and they had characteristics to which the Savas team chose not to pay too close attention. As in many other metropolitan areas, the Teamsters' imposition of their labour contracts on all significant contractors, when added together with the property rights phenomenon, made the local business more a matter of self-regulation than of competition. But while private waste managers elsewhere tended to be embroiled in conflict with trustbusters and environmentalists, Montreal's trash-hauling fraternity had attracted involvement by individuals whose legal and financial troubles came from outside the world of garbage.

Collection by Contract

In March 1978 E.S. Savas, along with his assistant Eileen Berenyi and their National Science Foundation program manager, travelled to Montreal to study the city's garbage industry. On their four-day agenda were talks with city officials and private carters, including Sanitary Refuse Collectors Incorporated (Enlèvement sanitaire de rébuts Inc.), the region's biggest garbage hauler. The case study Savas and his associates produced from their visit concluded that Montreal was well and cheaply served by a complex bidding system that encouraged vigorous competition. Predictably, their preliminary findings were that contract collection cost less than collection by the city's blue-collar workers (who worked the most difficult routes): $27.60 per ton compared to $36.19. Free enterprise was so healthy in the Quebec metropolis, Savas and Berenyi inferred, that small haulers could hold their own even against a transnational like BFI, which had commercial and industrial accounts in Montreal. They noted that one (unidentified) national firm actually withdrew from bidding on residential contracts because it could not compete with the low prices submitted by the small haulers.[1]

When these claims were reported to the owners of one "mom and pop" firm that had been around since the 1950s, "Pop" simply laughed. "Mom's" gut reaction was to wonder how the $560,000 National Science Foundation grant could have produced conclusions so far removed from her own perception of the business in Montreal. How convinced would the Columbia University researchers have remained had they stayed to discover some of what lay behind the innocent-looking corporate logos that the local operators presented to the casual observer of the city's yellow pages?

Montreal's contract system was developed during the first "reform" administration of Mayor Jean Drapeau in the mid-1950s. Until the city began phasing them out with open dump trucks during the Second World War, household trash had been hauled by municipal garbagemen in horse-drawn carts. In 1955, a salesman for an American firm that built compactor trucks tried to interest city officials in replacing the trucks with his elephantine packers. They weren't interested but they did informally give the company he formed (Sanitary Refuse) the right to pick up domestic refuse in the city's East end. By so doing, public administrators made possible what was to become a three-decade-long reign over the local trash business. Soon about 25 per cent of Montreal's total residential waste collection was being handled by Sanitary Refuse and a few other firms. When smaller companies and individual haulers complained about this unfair arrangement, the collection system that was to attract the Savas team's attention began to take shape.

The small operators knew that they would be quickly dealt out of the garbage game if the city handed out pickup contracts in large population blocks. But the city wanted a minimum total cost ensured by maximum competition. Montreal's roads department divided up the entire city into routes that could easily be handled by a single rear-load packer, and agreement to privatize garbage pickup was secured from the city's blue-collar workers (or *cols bleu*) in return for certain concessions. Now a hauler could bid on dozens of contracts, or on just one. By 1967 a little more than 90 per cent of the city's refuse pickup was farmed out. The remaining routes handled by municipal workers were on congested streets scattered throughout the city, the ones for which the highest bids had been received. Over the years, about three dozen firms were kept alive by this system, but that number got smaller and smaller. In 1972 only nine of the thirty-seven haulers who submitted tenders obtained contracts for five or more areas; in 1977 of thirty-five firms submitting tenders only seven got contracts for five areas or more.

Sanitary and its corporate affiliates were clearly the beneficiaries of the system. In 1972 they were awarded 65 of the city's 180 contracts. By the mid-1970s the company that described itself as "the largest single refuse collection company in North America" was running a fleet of 150 rear-loaders day and night, collecting from nearly 1.5 million residents in Montreal and 25 suburban communities. Sanitary had 600 employees, a Teamster local, 5,000 steel box containers and 15,000 commercial and industrial customers.

In 1972, with the continental shopping spree of the "Big Two" at its peak, Sanitary Refuse was an obvious candidate for a takeover. Both BFI and WMI sent their emissaries to Montreal. The major firms' approach was to operate from a position of strength based on control of disposal. Having conceived a strategy based on integration of waste handling services, they tended to be uninterested in being mere collectors. Sanitary Refuse had its own dump in south-shore Caughnawaga (now famous for its mayor's desire for an 18-hole golf course) and some recycling facilities, but the Montreal region's most promising landfill sites, the giant quarries on the island, were already in the hands of construction conglomerates. The city had recently built an incinerator to burn 1,200 tons of refuse a day. Thus control of disposal seemed out of the big multi-nationals' reach, and this made the prospects less promising in Montreal than in Toronto, where BFI and WMI bought up the two major independents.

WMI's interest in Sanitary was more serious than BFI's, but the deal it held out to major shareholder Maurice Courtois was still the standard share exchange. Courtois was uninterested in talking shares, and a far more avid suitor than WMI was waiting anxiously in the anteroom with an offer of bags full of cash. In September 1972 Courtois sold his business for $2 million to Belgium Standard Limited of Waterloo, Ontario, a small manufacturing firm with grand pretensions. At the time the firm's earnings were less than $100,000.

Glad Tidings on the Stock Market

Belgium Standard was soon destined to become a private waste manager like none other. Its public face was to bear some resemblance to the new image of the industry. But behind the public relations and the annual assurances to shareholders, the public company was offering its investors a decade of uneven performance. Unlike the fast-growing refuse megacorporations, Belgium Standard had begun life not as a trash hauler but as a manufacturer of truck bodies, compactors and, later, side-loading refuse collection vehicles. In time the dissimilarities between Belgium Standard and the Big Two would become extreme. By the early 1980s, the Canadian company was managing to lose money, while the waste giants had discovered a formula for virtually printing it.

The company's misfortunes were directly related to the flashy career of Montreal stock promoter Irving Kott. The first tie was made in 1970 when a Kott associate joined Belgium Standard's board of directors. In March 1971 a director and vice president of Kott's Onyx Investments Limited, a consultancy firm that would promote Belgium Standard as a waste manager, became a vice president of the manufacturing firm. In late 1972 Belgium Standard acquired Sanitary Refuse through Onyx-Forget, an alliance between Kott's investment firm Onyx, and L.J. Forget & Company, Montreal's oldest stock brokerage house.

Things got off to a rosy enough start. Belgium Standard's 1972 annual report assured shareholders of the company's glorious future in the brave new world of "privatized" waste management:

> Within the short period of one year, Belgium Standard Limited, through internal growth and acquisition, has become a major fully integrated solid waste systems corporation ... Belgium Standard is a leader of the many revolutionary changes now encompassing the solid waste industry. The industry is being modernized, dumping at sea is now largely against the law and open dumps are being closed down by pollution conscious municipalities ... As a result, a highly fragmented number of small local operators is being consolidated through acquisition by more efficiently operated and well financed publicly-owned solid waste collection specialists that take a professional "systems" approach to the functions of the industry.

Belgium's entry into the waste management business was accompanied by a steep rise in the price of its stock. The glad tidings about Belgium Standard spread by the Onyx-Forget network pumped up its share value on the Canadian Stock Exchange in Montreal. However, the trading in Belgium Standard and other Kott stocks did not appear to reflect the normal demand-supply relationship which was supposed to determine the value of a security traded in a public-auction market. *The Financial Post* reporters Amy Booth and Philip Mathias, writing in September 1972, described this activity as smacking of some kind of "artificiality."[2]

Soon afterwards the accumulation of rumours and allegations about insider manipulation appearing in the daily press knocked over the first domino that sent L.J. Forget tumbling down.[3] A shock wave of selling (which left thousands to stand their losses) was followed by the appearance on the scene of the commercial fraud section of the RCMP. In April 1973, not long after the firm's hundredth anniversary party, the RCMP raided Kott's offices. Following that, Quebec Securities Commission chairman Robert Demers closed down Forget and suspended trading in Quebec of all of Kott's group. Forget was left holding Kott-promoted stock certificates that had been bought on margin with unpaid (and now uncollectable) balances. The brokerage firm was ordered liquidated by the Quebec government, and most of its salesmen had their licences permanently lifted.

The next few years saw Kott being dragged through one legal battle after another, and his name kept popping up in places that Belgium Standard directors and shareholders might have found unsettling. He was convicted, and then acquitted on appeal, on a charge of having filed a false prospectus. He was convicted and fined $500,000 for stock fraud in a case involving Somed Mines.

The embattled financier's name also surfaced when police tape recordings of conversations between Vic Cotroni of the well-known Montreal "family" and Paolo Violi, a presumed Mafia chieftain (murdered in 1978), were introduced as evidence in a bizarre extortion trial. Cotroni and Violi had been seeking information about a bogus plot in which their names had been used without their prior knowledge. Extortionists had succeeded in getting a large cash payment from Toronto associates of Kott on the promise they would be spared the physical reprisals of certain "people in Montreal" for money lost in the collapse of Forget. Police overheard Cotroni tell Violi he had contacted Kott to get to the bottom of the scheme, and portions of the transcribed eavesdrop appeared in *The Financial Post* in late 1976.[4] However inconclusive the affair, the financial establishment had been made more wary of Kott.

For Belgium Standard, the Kott connection was becoming an increasingly serious liability in the investment and banking communities. By late 1974 Kott stocks had become the dogs of a bad market. After hitting a high of $27 in 1972, Belgium Standard was now going for $1 and change. Although its chief asset, Sanitary Refuse, was still Montreal's leading garbage contractor, in the latter part of the decade Belgium Standard was a company with seriously undervalued stock and dubious bankability. While Kott's association with the company was receding, various moves to eliminate what company directors had referred to as his "occult presence" did not succeed in improving the company's performance as an aspiring waste manager. Three dissident shareholders, who had themselves been directors in the past, were appalled and outraged by continued transactions with Kott and "related persons and corporations," and by the bad publicity their company had received during a campaign by *cols bleu* opposed to contracting out. The dissidents formed themselves into a committee soliciting support for a completely new board of directors.

A deal with Highland Knitting Mills Limited, a subsidiary of Cecil Kott's Berncam International, had left them feeling that "things are unusual and unsatisfactory. The outside shareholders are being treated with contempt" and that their company was "in a worse financial crisis even than appears from the statements." The takeover of Highland had cost more than $1 million, but by October 1982, with Highland losing more than $800,000 yearly and Belgium Standard experiencing record losses, the shareholders learned that the men's clothing manufacturer was being jettisoned. The dissident shareholders succeeded in placing a nominee on the company's board in 1983.

The company pressed on, seeing its salvation in foregoing the bizarre entrepreneurial union of trash and fashion for strict specialization in refuse. Teamster union muscle (applied on Sanitary's behalf) and a provincial government *décret* imposing wage parity based on the Teamster collective agreement made it difficult for other contractors to undercut Sanitary by reducing labour costs. Sanitary was still dominant in the suburbs and had the largest share of residential collection in the city. In the late 1970s, however, changes in the industry — such as the new provincial legislation making it mandatory for suburban municipalities to tender their garbage contracts and the strategy introduced by some smaller contractors of turning their drivers into self-employed *artisans* — had threatened to throw the status quo into disarray.

The Mayor

Like Norman Goodhead of Toronto (see Chapters 4 and 9), J. Aldéo (Léo) Rémillard turned his energies to the garbage business after his career in municipal politics floundered. It was the voters of North York who decided they no longer wanted Goodhead as their reeve; the man who would become Rive Sud's most prominent founder and principal owner was bounced from municipal politics by a special act of the Quebec legislature. Pierre Sévigny, who served as associate minister of national defence in John Diefenbaker's cabinet, once observed that Rémillard "was a product of the streets. If only his athletic prowess and leadership qualities had been better directed during his youth, Rémillard might not have found it far more attractive to seek immediate riches from illegal activities than from more patient but quite commendable undertakings."[5]

In the early 1950s, in the last years of Camillien Houde's lengthy tenure as mayor of Montreal, a commission of inquiry headed by Judge François Caron exposed the extent of underworld vice in the city. On the heels of the investigation Jean Drapeau, who had distinguished himself as a crusading lawyer at the commission's hearings, was elected to succeed Houde in 1954, and as a result many illicit operations were driven into the suburbs, where mobsters found shelter and more accommodating régimes. Nowhere did corruption take root more deeply than in Ville Jacques-Cartier, a "town of 10,000 shacks" at the foot of the Jacques Cartier Bridge which journalist Boyce Richardson described as "the most scandalously unplanned, exploited and corrupted of all the municipalities during those corrupt and awful times."[6] In 1960 Rémillard got himself elected mayor of Ville Jacques-Cartier.

Léo Rémillard, whose acquaintances included various dubious characters and, by his own account, the Cotroni brothers, was prominent among this new breed of suburban politicians. The subsequent reign of terror in Ville Jacques-Cartier eventually aroused the ire of the labour movement, which proved to be the nemesis of

the Rémillard régime by forcing government action. Trade union-
ists, and especially the 175,000-member Montreal Labour Council,
found two incidents — Rémillard's refusal to recognize the right
of the Fraternité Canadienne des employés municipaux to negotiate
for his city hall workers, and his harassment of an aircraft worker
who dared defy the mayor — particularly galling.

A young schoolteacher named Raymond Laliberté was so appalled by Rémillard's heavy-handed control of the local school
commission that he decided to make a career of trade unionism.
Laliberté, who became the head of Quebec's largest teacher's union
and leader of the Quebec wing of the New Democratic Party, would
confess that "without doubt, it was Léo-Aldéo Rémillard who gave
me the impetus to go into trade unionism."[7] Equally horrified was
Louis Laberge, chairman of the Montreal Labour Council (and later
president of the Quebec Federation of Labour). In a telegram to
Premier Jean Lesage, Laberge demanded the government's "immediate intervention ... to put an end to the reign of terror in Ville
Jacques-Cartier." He deplored the methods used by "Mayor Rémillard and his band of recidivist scoundrels and criminals to keep
control of the town administration and the school commission. We
regret your silence in the face of these billyclubbers and your
abandonment of an entire population of 50,000 souls to the hands
of bandits who are unscrupulously and publicly defying the courts
of justice, the government and the laws."[8] Gérard Filion, the pub-
lisher of *Le Devoir*, added his voice to the chorus demanding
Rémillard's head: "To say that municipal administration in Jacques-Cartier is in the hands of blackguards is not a figure of speech.
It is a known fact."[9]

In July 1962 the provincial Liberal government rather illiberally
moved to end His Worship's political career by refusing to accept
his argument that his debts to society for crimes committed in his
youth had already been paid. The Cities and Towns Act was
amended to bar from municipal or school board office for twenty
years persons found guilty three times of offences punishable by a
five-year jail term. Having been convicted of theft, receiving, as-
sault, perjury and complicity in running a still, Rémillard qualified
for banishment.[10] It was rumoured that he had support at the federal
level, from Pierre Sévigny and former secretary of state Noel
Dorion, that could lead to Ottawa's overriding the provincial legislation by granting him an absolute pardon. Laberge wrote to
Prime Minister Diefenbaker that it would be scandalous and revolt-

ing for his government to take any such action, and if it did the only conclusion one could draw was that organized crime had its spokesmen within the federal cabinet. In the end, Rémillard got no help from Ottawa. He gave up the fight and handed in his resignation on 19 February 1963.

From Ville Jacques-Cartier City Hall, Rémillard was drawn to the world of trash. Around the time of his forced resignation, small haulers such as Metropole Refuse Disposal and Service Sanitaire Gi-Gi had just entered the market in the face of almost total dominance by Sanitary Refuse. Metropole, starting off with only two trucks, was able to make the deepest inroads; the firm would emerge as the region's number two solid waste carrier, with subsidiary operations in Saint John and Moncton. In September 1966 a former Metropole vice president joined Rémillard and two other partners in a new enterprise, Service sanitaire de la Rive Sud.

By 1972 Rive Sud's packers were busy hauling refuse both on and off the island. During the night-time "blitz" when all of Montreal's domestic trash was picked up, they worked the city streets. Daytime found the ten-wheelers in suburban Longueuil on the south shore, where Rive Sud shared residential pickup equally with Sanitary. Another south-shore community in which Rive Sud hauled garbage was Saint-Hubert, where Rémillard was on good terms with the election organizers of Mayor Aldas Boileau. It also carted away the trash from the Saint-Hubert military base and had pickup contracts with the small communities of Saint-Amable and Sainte-Julie.

Sanitary and the Little Guys

Meanwhile in December 1972, the municipality of Lachine had just signed a new five-year contract with Sanitary Disposal. Sanitary had been collecting all of Lachine's household garbage since 1959, but Lachine mayor Jean G. Chartier decided to use his veto to end the company's monopoly. At a special meeting of the Lachine city council he listed among his motives for a veto on the new contract the fact that the council had refused to consider any other contractor. Nevertheless on 26 March 1973, with the mayor dissenting, the councillors voted to give Sanitary a one-year contract, the Quebec Municipal Commission having warned that it wouldn't accept anything longer. But the matter was not allowed to rest. Throughout the spring and summer, insisting that tenders should be called, Chartier said he was going to make a political issue of garbage collection. Council and the civic bureaucracy continued to resist. On 28 May finance director Donat Beauchamp wrote to the mayor and councillors, solemnly declaring that "no other tendering party than Sanitary Refuse Collectors Inc. has deposited a tender with me." Then Beauchamp went on to describe the reality that had allowed Sanitary to build up its local garbage empire by means of a de facto suburban franchise. He asserted there were two dozen municipalities that objected to the calling of public tenders because they didn't want to be "at the mercy of incompetent contractors." Sanitary had provided these services satisfactorily since 1959, and he could not see how others could give the same value for taxpayers' money. "This opinion is shared unanimously," wrote the administrator, "by all managers of the 25 municipalities within the island of Montreal which are served by the same contractor."

Beauchamp's reasoning, which was an implicit argument for garbage collection as a "natural monopoly," was not in step with the prescriptions that would be issued a few years later by E.S. Savas. Lachine voters appeared to agree with Beauchamp and defeated Mayor Chartier at the polls in November 1973. Further light on the standards of civic life in Lachine was cast in 1978, when a construction contractor went to the police with information that certain Lachine city officials were trying to peddle their influence with council. Quebec police laid a trap and ensnared roads engineer Tony Pellegrino and councillor Victor Trimbo (who back in 1973 had seconded the motion to sign a new contract with Sanitary in the face of Chartier's veto). Both Pellegrino and Trimbo received prison sentences. In his testimony before the court, Pellegrino said that "it's commonly known that if you pay the councillors, if you 'grease' them, things will happen. I told that to Jean-Louis Pilote [the contractor] several times before the November 1977 elections."

After the law was changed to make public tenders mandatory, the contract to collect Lachine's household trash went to tender for the first time in November 1979. Two contractors submitted bids — Sanitary Refuse and Société Sanitaire Laval (SSL), which had been gaining ground with contracts from the municipalities of Montreal, Laval, Roxboro and Terrebonne as well as from CNR, CPR, various government buildings and Dorval and Mirabel airports. But Sanitary won the day and held on in Lachine.

In some other suburbs Sanitary did not fare as well. In the Town of Mount Royal, Sanitary lost two of its three contracts. It tried to make up for the loss of its secure position in the suburbs by low-balling all the competition for the eighty-two three-year contracts the City of Montreal let out in 1980. In late 1979 "Pop" of the "mom and pop" firm we were introduced to earlier attended a contractors' association meeting and heard a Sanitary official exhort the assembled haulers to keep ahead of inflation in bidding for Montreal's contracts. Then Sanitary expanded its City of Montreal business at the others' expense by coming in with bids beneath them all and winning more than 60 per cent of the contracts. With Sanitary and two other Belgium Standard subsidiaries awarded fifty-four of the eighty-two contracts, and Léo Rémillard's Rive Sud taking fifteen, only thirteen were left for all the other operators. Consternation was general. When the bids were opened at City Hall, one hauler who insisted on anonymity later remembered: "It was a shock for everybody. Some people were crying in City Hall." His associate added: "Some people said, 'Tomorrow I'm going on welfare.'" And the penny-ante contractor, one of the presumed beneficiaries of the city's system of periodic competition, asked: "If I have a $75,000 truck and I didn't get the contract ... *what the hell am I going to do with a $75,000 truck?*"

The Rise and Fall of Gi-Gi

Rive Sud's fulfilling its fifteen contracts depended on its being able to subcontract to self-employed owner-operators. And this in turn depended on its being able to hold at bay the Teamsters, who were determined to fight this non-union *artisan* ploy with all the considerable means at their command. Unfortunately for Rive Sud, it came off second best in its struggle with the Teamsters, and let go of its Montreal contracts in January 1981. The abandoned routes were inherited by Service Sanitaire Gi-Gi, one of the small operators that Sanitary had forced out of the game in 1980.

Gi-Gi's owner, Robert Nantel, was another product of the streets — especially the streets of Saint-Henri, the low-income neighbourhood in the southwestern part of Montreal that spawned the Dubois brothers, the ruling family in a French-Canadian gang that by the mid-1970s was considered a serious rival to the Sicilian and Calabrese clan surrounding the Cotronis. Fearless and hardworking, he tried to make it in two tough occupations, the bar business and garbage. In both trades he was eventually the victim of higher forces.

In his day, Nantel had worked in clubs where violence was not uncommon: the Café du Palais, the Pagoda, the Mocambo and Vic Cotroni's Vic Café. Then in 1967, having made a stake for himself in refuse removal, he opened up Robert Bar Salon in Saint-Henri. Not unlike his contracting business, this venture would also be subject to territorial imperatives. After enduring a nightmare of extortion attempts, a ransacking and kidnapping at gunpoint, Nantel sold out to a buyer Raymond Dubois had waiting. The price was $25,000, although the contractor had once refused an offer of $60,000. According to the Quebec government commission of inquiry into organized crime, CECO (before which Nantel testified in camera in 1975), it was common knowledge in the underworld milieu that Robert Bar Salon had come under the protection of the Dubois.[11]

Nantel's Service Sanitaire Gi-Gi held municipal contracts in Montreal's west end throughout the 1970s, in addition to carrying on a commercial pickup service. In 1980, the year of Sanitary's lowball bids, Gi-Gi lost all its west-end contracts to the dominant firm. Nantel got rid of seven trucks, keeping just two to do some commercial pickup. But the next year an opportunity for a comeback arose when the Rémillards of Rive Sud ran into their troubles with the Teamsters. A Montreal Executive Committee resolution dated 28 January 1981 approved the transfer of Rive Sud's fifteen Montreal contracts to Gi-Gi. With the company logo slashed vertically across their doors, Gi-Gi's thirteen new ten-wheeler trucks with their eighteen-cubic-yard bins were soon racing east across town to their night-time routes. But the windfall soon proved no windfall at all. Working at Rive Sud's prices proved ruinous, and in August 1981, Gi-Gi forfeited its surety deposits and bowed out without having secured a firm enough toe-hold in the waste heap even to be of interest to the acquisitions departments of the advancing waste multi-nationals.

Understandably, this portrait of the dark side of the model prescribed by Professor Savas benefited from the fact that more than four days were available to explore behind the smiling mask of entrepreneurial efficiency. But in 1984, as two major waste contractors appeared in Quebec, the academic recommendations of the New Yorkers seemed even less worthy of export. For from that date the privateers were far more powerful, and their presence gave birth to a new movement of citizen activists who saw the waste contractors in all their various guises as being more a part of the problem than of the solution.

The Big Three Poised

The Big Three drew Quebec more fully within their orbit in 1984. That year, world leader WMI, presumably capitalizing on the recent exposure of the lingering Kott association, acquired Sanitary Refuse from Belgium Standard. Laidlaw, for its part, bought out two lesser lights, Metropole and Services Sanitaires Laval. By year's end, *La Presse* observed that the new arrivals accounted for 75 per cent of the city of Montreal's residential trash pick-up.[12]

Two years later, in settlement of a five-week strike, Montreal accorded its own *cols bleus* half its residential collection, much of which ended up being burned in the city's incinerator. But, as far as the twenty-seven remaining Montreal Island municipalities were concerned, the private sector continued to haul all their refuse, much of which ended up in the city of Montreal's east-end Miron quarry. The site was so widely renowned for its ludicrous tipping fees, the lowest in North America, that haulers came from as far as the U.S. to dump into the two-hundred-foot pit, until it was a swollen, sometimes mobile, toxic monster.

In 1987, when the new reform administration of Mayor Jean Doré first tried to raise dumping charges at least to reflect social costs, other municipalities of the Montreal Urban Community (MUC) objected. They raised such a ruckus the intermunicipal commission blocked the threatened price hike.[13] The disagreement was symbolic of the emerging Balkanization of waste management policy. On one hand was the city of Montreal itself, with the progressive Montreal Citizens' Movement in power; on the other, were the antediluvian administrations of the remaining twenty-seven island communities, which faced the closing off of their Miron option. They would come together in a Régie intermunicipale de gestion des déchets (intermunicipal waste management authority) to determine their own waste future.

Foster Wheeler's Burning Plan

Urban affairs supposedly had come a long way since underworld types had acted as intermediaries on local incinerator projects, but secrecy and controversy still surrounded the politics of waste into the late 1980s. The Régie quickly decided to farm out management of its entire waste stream in one global contract, putting out a call for proposals. To ensure that its constituents would be locked into any deal struck, the Régie succeeded in having a law slipped through the provincial legislature in late 1988 extending from five to twenty-five years the agreement tying the municipalities to the waste authority.

Bids came in from the likes of Ogden Martin and from WMI which was fanning out across Quebec. But the Régie's ultimate decision in November 1989 was to go with another member of the municipal-industrial complex: Foster Wheeler, a U.S. multinational which had constructed 160 waste fuel plants in North America and operated in 12 countries. Les Chaudières Foster Wheeler had had a presence in Quebec for six decades and, as Andre Noël pointed out in *La Presse* June 1990, the company was linked through joint ventures to SNC, the giant Quebec engineering and construction firm. SNC had provided the Régie's selection committee with technical expertise and the current director-general of the Régie had managed the waste division of SNC/Foster Wheeler.[14]

A dissident mayor, Ed Janiszewski of Dollard des Ormeaux, protesting against what he saw as an unalloyed backroom deal, revealed that in spite of having been the Régie's treasurer for two years he never had been asked to sign a cheque, even as the inter-municipal waste management board paid out millions.[15] Still, twenty-three of the twenty-six island mayors voted in favour of the refuse-burning complex which included a de rigeur recycling component and was to be capable of generating thirty-five kilowatts of electricity annually, making the trash burner the largest independent producer of electricity in a province not known for its dearth of energy.

Such was the apparent rush to burn on the part of the consenting city fathers that by 1992 the board reportedly was spending far less on consulting fees and environmental impact studies than on public relations, using tax dollars to sell voters on the proposed complex which was going to cost them about $250 million.[16]

When in the summer of 1992 the Régie sought a green light from Quebec City to proceed with the signing of a contract, Janiszewski, who had claimed that "environmentally, it's completely unacceptable, and financially, it's completely irresponsible," made two striking announcements.[17] He was quitting as the Régie's treasurer and might pull his town of 46,000 and its trash out of the Foster Wheeler project.

Leaked documents indicated that the firm Econosult had ranked an incineration-recycling complex as its ninth choice in a 1988 study for the environment service of the Urban Community of Montreal. Furthermore, and equally worrisome, *Le Devoir* learned from sources within the Quebec Ministry of the Environment that a "put or pay" clause (wherein the operator had to be paid a tipping fee whether or not an agreed quantity of waste was actually delivered to the burner) in the still-to-be-signed contract might possibly fly in the face of federal plans for a 50 per cent reduction in the municipal solid waste stream by the year 2000.

The Régie was preparing to guarantee Foster Wheeler half a million tonnes of waste every year, scaled down to 400,000 in subsequent pronouncements. Given that the island municipalities (excluding the city of Montreal itself) generated only some 600,000 tonnes of residential, commercial and industrial waste, any serious shortfalls in the waste fuel supply, either by reason of mandated waste reduction, defections from the Régie or competition from other public or private waste managers threatened taxpayers who found themselves having to foot the bill and pay off the debt which was going to be incurred in building the big burner.[18]

Like everyone else, citizens and environmentalists alike, the Quebec Public Interest Research Group (PIRG) at McGill University had been cut out of the information loop on the Montreal-Est complex. So its activist members had little alternative but to scan the horizon for other experiences with Foster Wheeler that might serve as a guide to what Montreal might be facing. As chance would have it, they did not have to look far to find what they took to be parallels (and lessons to be learned) in an on-going incineration and legal battle being waged in a rural dairy farming region of New York state.

Hudson Falls

Just ten miles from the Lake George resort popular with Quebecers, what might be called the usual bunch of suspects — a local garbage contractor and a group of bankers, underwriters, lawyers, consultants, lobbyists and state officials — had targeted some of New York's poorest counties as host for a Foster Wheeler plant. But, as we have seen repeatedly, a decision by the well-connected and powerful to burn trash in someone else's backyard is always a provocative one. Given the substitution of public relations for consultation and consensus, court conflict is inevitable, forcing judges to act as the ultimate arbiters of waste policy.

Contracts were approved by the elected supervisors of Washington, Warren and Essex County in December 1984, and what followed became a caricature of the social distress latent in such an endeavour. For the Foster Wheeler waste-to-energy facility in the village of Hudson Falls became "one of the most litigated trash plants in the country."[19]

In April 1988, Essex County voted not to landfill the incinerator's ash (soon to be ruled a hazardous waste in Illinois, Indiana and Wisconsin) and pulled out. This left two counties and an apparent reduced supply of fuel for the plant. So Hudson Falls, fearing the importation of out-of-county waste to meet the shortfall, sued claiming the burner's specifications would have to be rewritten to account for the changed situation. The case was won only to be reversed on appeal. The Industrial Development Agency (IDA) of the two remaining counties proceeded to authorize issuance of the required bonds and in February 1989, on the eve of the sale by the underwriters, Smith Barney, of $75 million in bonds to pay to build the plant, another lawsuit was launched.

The plaintiffs, the Greenwich Citizens Committee and Concerned Citizens of Hudson Falls as well as 328 citizens, viewed the project as an undemocratic scheme to enrich an inter-connected old boys' network rife with conflicts of interest. They were suing the two counties and the IDA to halt construction, charging no proper public hearings had been held nor had any studies been made of the impact of going forward without Essex's waste. The timing of this intervention stung the promoters to the quick. After all, selling bonds is arguably an incinerator's *raison d'être* and the legal action forced the sale to be delayed and the bonds subsequently to be devalued and discounted. Foster Wheeler reportedly had had to pay almost $1.5 million to Smith Barney "to discount the bonds without the approval of either county or the IDA."[20]

A Kafkaesque twist was given to the conflict when the IDA and one of the counties accused the citizens of "malicious interference" in their bond negotiations and counter-sued each of them individually, for $1.5 million in damages. Revealingly, the essence of the sabotage was purported to be calls made to the bond rating agency Moody's, to *The Bond Buyer* (a paper relied on by bond buyers), as well as to at least one institutional buyer, advising them the project violated the law, would be sued and never built, thus placing prospective purchasers in jeopardy.[21]

The defendants characterized the counter-suit as an example of a Strategic Litigation Against Public Participation: "While it is not unusual for developers and corporations to file SLAPP suits, it is rare for local governments to attempt to intimidate their citizens in this manner. What is even more outrageous is that this SLAPP suit appears to have been an attempt by the two governmental entities to recover funds on behalf of the developer."[22]

Eventually, after ten months, during which the opposition was threatened with financial ruin, an appellate court threw out both claim and the counter-claim and, as if foreordained by an implacable deity, the incinerator continued to rise above its scaffolding in a gully down river from Hudson Falls.

As it did, an architect of the opposition movement, a retired math teacher named Robert Daly, received an unsolicited phone call from an ex-student, someone he had known for twenty-five years. He knew the caller to be a private eye and took it on good faith he was, as he claimed, working for a client opposed to burn plants who wanted to nail Robert Barber, the owner of North American Recycling Systems. Barber, the contractor instrumental in bringing the incinerator to Hudson Falls, was a minority partner with Foster Wheeler in the plant. Daly provided five pages of hand-written notes to the detective only to see them used against him more than a year later when Barber, his partner and their wives sued him for libel and slander.

Controversy surrounds exactly what the teacher alleged and to whom, but the charges were based on the notes where references are made to crime families and, if nothing else, testify to the somewhat demonic aura (in the eyes of put-upon citizens) of strangers who deal in waste. The actual complaint made mention of a statement accusing the contractors of "gradually obtaining a monopoly on garbage hauling in the area north of Albany. This is the way the Mob generally operates."[23]

The libel suit accused Daly of having relayed the allegations contained in the notes to the groups opposed to the Foster Wheeler burner as well as to two residents of Hudson Falls. "I was set up," says the retired teacher, "it was a sting." Barber refused comment when asked by the *Post-Star*'s David Blow if it was he who had hired the detective. [24]

Having worked to expose what he saw as a financial drubbing about to be inflicted on county tax-payers, Daly now found himself being sued for $6 million. This sum was to compensate the aggrieved businessmen (who sold out the waste-hauling portion of North American Recycling Systems to the omnipresent WMI in October 1992) for the damage they said Daly had done their good names, business reputations and social standing. As well, further damages were being sought on claims by the waste entrepreneurs' wives that undue stress on both men "has caused the women to 'lose the services' of their husbands."[25]*

Barber assured the *Post-Star* he would "drop the suit if Daly will publicly apologize," but Daly refused.[26] After gathering eighteen sworn affidavits, asserting he never had made such allegations, the former teacher filed for summary judgement only to have a judge deny his request. The case moved to an appellate court. But with the incinerator now complete, the retiree did not await his judicial fate passively. Many locals continued to fear a stack which was permitted to emit nearly four tons of lead and 1300 pounds of mercury a year. So Daly and other citizens decided to slap back.

A constitutional lawyer was retained and he prepared a $32-million lawsuit against the authorities who had sought to shut up his clients. Filed some months after the incinerator started up in February 1992, this latest lawsuit asserted that the incinerator funding agency's counter-suit had been part of a campaign "to intimidate

---

*   The stress level increased late in 1992 when a grand jury charged Barber with allegedly having bribed Washington County's Solid Waste Chair to help navigate the burn plant project through the shoals of public opposition. For his part, Barber accused District Attorney Robert Winn of "prosecutorial abuse" and stated "the truth is going to come out and when it does we will be totally exonerated."

and deter the citizens from exercising their constitutionally protected rights to freedom of speech, association, and to petition the
government for redress of grievances."[27]

"It must be noted," stated the federal civil rights action, "that
since the filing of the original suit against the two counties and the
IDA, most of the citizens' concerns as expressed in that suit have
in fact been realized. The plant was over-sized and over-priced."[28]

Faced with a shortfall, Foster Wheeler had indeed turned to new
sources of garbage on the spot market and succeeded in securing
New York City waste for disposal at far less than what locals were
being charged to burn theirs. What had been predicted by the
opponents of the plant appeared to be coming to pass. County
officials now faced the galling prospect of being inundated with
imported waste of unknown provenance and being unable to meet
ruinous bond payments should locally generated trash continue to
prove insufficient.

According to *Waste Not*, the project's proponents originally had
estimated tipping fees at between $5 and $10 per ton. Then, eight
years later at start-up time, they were set at $75, the sum locals
continued to pay even as Foster Wheeler began importing spot
waste to burn at $40. The IDA (Industrial Development Agency)
tried to prevent this undercutting, but backed off when challenged
by Foster Wheeler.[29] Richard Swift, Foster Wheeler Power Systems' chief executive, stated to the finance committee of Warren
County: "We are going to bring in trash to pay the trustee. The IDA
is telling us we can't, but we are going to do it." [30]

To meet their monthly bills, newly elected supervisors (the ones
responsible for the bond repayments) were forced to begin using
tax money to subsidize the incinerator and the generators of the
imported waste. As they did so, they too began talking to lawyers
and pondering whether to try to renegotiate the contract. But, for
David Blow, whose newspaper was suing the IDA to release the
names of the bond-holders and who had watched the deal get
rammed past an unsophisticated rural community, Foster Wheeler
had won this round and was "in the catbird seat." Should the IDA
default on its bond payment obligations, Foster Wheeler's executive Swift warned: "There is a trustee in New York that has to
protect bondholders and believe me, ladies and gentlemen, they will
do that. Ten days from now, if this money is not sent to the trustee,
the trustee is going to come back and he has the right to do a lot of
things."[31]

The Catbird Seat

Promoters of the Foster Wheeler project for Montreal Island had so insulated themselves behind closed doors it is unlikely that their wives were yet in a position to sue anyone for being deprived of their husbands' services. However, by the summer of 1992, cracks were appearing in the grand design.

With municipalities suggesting they might bolt from the Régie, the question of waste availability and flow control powers became as critical as it was in Hudson Falls — especially since the Montreal complex was to be three times the size of the one in Washington County, PIRG's Aaron Freeman noted in a report on Foster Wheeler's track record that "the Régie's proposed burner is so large that already they have admitted that they will have to negotiate for commercial as well as industrial waste, or import garbage from the City of Montreal or Laval."[32]

However, local boosters were mesmerized less by details than by scale. With apparent pride, the Régie's chair, La Salle Mayor Michel Leduc, told reporters the new complex would be "the biggest in Canada." But before they could build their incinerator in economically devastated working class Montreal-Est, a typical precinct for such a garbage colossus, the politicians still had to face what they feared most — the community and environmentalist opposition banding together in a coalition of fifteen citizens groups called Action RE-buts.

The Régie won its first round just before the summer recess of the National Assembly where minds already had turned to cottages and lakes. A Liberal member introduced a bill (Bill 221) to allow the Régie to sign a contract with Foster Wheeler without prior approval by the provincial environment ministry. Yet, in spite of the private bill's curious timing, and the fact such bills are rarely opposed, two Parti Québécois deputies mounted a rudimentary protest.

Columnist Jean Denis Girouard had reported that the secret deal with Foster Wheeler contained a clause requiring the Régie to pay the company a $2.5-million penalty should necessary environmental permits not be forthcoming.[33] So the further the project got, the more unstoppable it would be.

Environment critic Denis Lazure called on the Minister of Municipal Affairs, Claude Ryan, to bring sanity to waste planning on Montreal Island. Should Bill 221 pass, the way would open for not one but two burn plants in the east end — the Régie's and the City of Montreal's, which now faced a repair bill of between $60 and $100 million. Lazure spoke of the necessity of requiring the rival island authorities to work out one common plan. Furthermore, regarding the Régie's possibly having broken Quebec law by cavalierly having dispensed $9 million on the project without any public oversight, Lazure argued that passage of the bill would be "completely unacceptable: we are being asked to endorse illegality, the lack of openness and non-respect for the most elementary democratic rules."[34]

The Péquiste deputy also found it noteworthy that Foster Wheeler was appointing a former provincial Liberal cabinet minister, Fernand Lalonde, to head its Quebec division. Lalonde had been a key supporter of Claude Ryan for leadership of the governing party and his presence would provide yet another catbird seat, this one offering the company a commanding view of its political surroundings and adversaries in Quebec.

Joining the chorus alongside Lazure and Action RE-buts to contest the bill was the local waste entrepreneurs' association. As in the Akron, Ohio, case and so many other instances involving incineration, the haulers, recyclers and landfill operators did not look forward to seeing the island's refuse going up in flames in the Foster Wheeler plant. Adopting a decidedly public-spirited view, the group's president told the parliamentarians considering the bill that "the locomotive of the [Régie] has lost its wagons and cannot stop by itself ... The lack of co-ordination (with the city of Montreal, among others) in the management of waste risks to lead to irrational and costly solutions."[35]

Notwithstanding the protests, the bill passed, leaving opponents one last forum to make their case at hearings of the Bureau d'audiences publiques sur l'environnement (BAPE) scheduled for the fall of 1992. But to prevail, activists like Jacqueline Mayrand of Action RE-buts recognized they must come up with a strategy for convincing the political establishment of the wisdom of considering solid waste incineration in the context of a far more all-encompassing approach.

Saint-Etienne-des-Gres

The absence of an overall strategy had been underscored by Jean-Benoit Nadeau in *La Presse* in August 1989 where he noted the government's laissez-faire attitude towards Quebec's seventy-one landfill sites. For Nadeau, the real scandal had less to do with pollution than with official nonchalance towards the price war raging between rival dumps. Operators admitted to him that so long as the law of the market was in force, wastes would flow to the cheapest sites which never have the wherewithal to conform with existing barely regulated environmental standards.[36]

Simultaneously, waste treatment and disposal was being taken over by multi-national corporations. Railways had cornered liquid chemical wastes: Stablex (controlled by the giant Conrail) handled inorganic elimination; Tricil (controlled by Canadian Pacific) specialized in the destruction of organics. As for solid wastes, BFI, WMI and Laidlaw were completing what reporter Louis-Gilles Francoeur described as "their strategy of encirclement."[37] While politicians pursued their various agendas, the refuse of the metropolis began flowing farther and farther afield to small-town and rural Quebec where the biggest waste firms were setting up shop.

One of Quebec's leading environmental activists, Pierre Morency, saw in this trend a threat to rational planning and spoke out against the menace of monopoly. Morency estimated that between the summer of 1990 and early 1991, the major firms and their local affiliates bought up forty to fifty landfill sites.[38]

In early 1989, WMI moved to impose its own rationalization of the province's garbage economy by buying Sani-Pare, one of Quebec's biggest remaining independent haulers. As well, it took over a giant landfill site (big enough for the region's needs for twenty to thirty years) twenty kilometers north of Trois-Rivières near the town of Saint-Etienne-des-Gres. Soon thereafter, however, WMI's bid on the Montreal Island contract (the one eventually won by Foster Wheeler) sparked an intense popular reaction. The prospect that every year for the next twenty years hundreds of thousands of tons of Montreal's waste might be buried in this remote village gave birth to Groupe d'action pour le respect et la défense de l'environ-ment (GARDE), a citizens' group which in its analysis and pre-scriptions would go far beyond the not-in-my-backyard phenomenon.

But before GARDE could exert its influence, WMI also succeeded in provoking anger in official quarters when the firm tripled
disposal fees for municipalities using Saint-Etienne. Quebec law
requires proposed new prices be preceded by an announcement and
WMI had run its notice in Montreal's *Le Devoir*. This rather improbable choice is read mainly by Quebec's intellectual class and
enjoys limited circulation among WMI's rural clientele.

The regional municipality of Centre-Mauricie took exception
and went to court, arguing the announcement had escaped its attention, and as a result, the new charges had not been challenged in
the prescribed period of time. A lower court judge proved sympathetic, but the case was lost when the Quebec Court of Appeal
disagreed.[39] But by the time the Supreme Court of Canada refused
to hear a final appeal, events had far overtaken a mere dispute over
a distant waste corporation's pricing régime. WMI's presence in
Saint-Etienne had turned the community upside down. At one municipal meeting, the mayor, fearing verbal warfare might escalate
into bloodshed, had called in the Sureté du Quebec, the provincial
police.

GARDE eventually succeeded in unseating Saint-Etienne's municipal council, then moved on to participate in the search for
solutions. Aware of a U.S. EPA study in which fully 90 per cent of
the landfills reviewed had contaminated the groundwater, GARDE
concluded that only a public utility concept breaking the link between unrestricted mass dumping and the profit motive could provide the requisite level of public security.[40]

Under GARDE's influence, Saint-Etienne proposed creating its
own intermunicipal Régie and abolishing WMI's monopoly
through expropriation. Such was the concern over becoming a
dumping ground for imported waste as well as over being gouged
by an uncontrollable waste company that forty-two municipalities
in the regional communities of Francheville, Mekinac and Centre-
Mauricie, including Trois-Rivières, offered moral and financial
support.[41]

Maintaining their sang-froid, WMI's local officials looked on
the optimistic side and foresaw the opportunity of a partnership
with a new intermunicipal authority. To that end, the company
began what the president of Quebec's federation of professional
journalists, Andre Noel, described as "a vast public relations campaign."[42] The waste firm financed a radio program on the environment, bought ads and paid for Mauricie region reporters to visit

some of its New England sites. But Saint-Etienne's mayor, François Chenier, remained unmoved. The new mayor continued to hold the view that the public interest demanded expropriation.

In June 1991, Chenier, whose pursuit of a regional utility had subjected him to ridicule in the local media, signed a protocol for a new regional public waste authority with himself as its first president.[43] And in spite of having been thrown out of court, public officials continued their resistance, refusing to pay WMI its new tipping fees. In addition, the new Régie now had a mandate to pursue the expropriation of the WMI company.

The political culture of the Quebec collectivity might in some ways be on the other side of the moon from such other sites of WMI's operations as "live free or die" New Hampshire, but the company still had room to manoeuvre on the banks of the Saint-Maurice. The long and costly court battle it now faced could well resolve the conflict in the firm's favour should the growing opposition to the notion of a free flowing continental waste trade prove unable to translate abhorrence into alternatives.

Half Victory

As we have seen in the United States, insofar as waste was concerned, individual states continued to be subject to the sovereignty of the interstate commerce clause. In Quebec, however, in spite of its having been integrated into the marketing strategies of the continental waste disposal corporations, unfettered market forces proved unable fully to withstand public reaction against the dumping of American solid waste. Waste still might be a good like any other in the eyes of constitutional lawyers, but intense popular reaction had propelled public officials to just say no.

In the summer of 1988, the magnet of cheap rates was attracting an estimated two hundred metric tons a day of refuse into southern Quebec from the U.S. Construction rubble and incinerator ash from the Boston region as well as from Ohio, Vermont, Massachusetts, and even Kennebunkport, Maine, summer residence of President Bush, were crossing the border and being dumped in St-Denis-de-Brompton and Magog townships. Residents of the bucolic countryside long ago settled by United Empire Loyalists fleeing the American Revolution were outraged. After a concerned customs officer alerted citizens to the scale of the shipments, the Eastern

Townships witnessed what must have been "the quickest creation and growth of a protest movement in its history."[44]

Within a few months, an anti-import coalition coordinated by Ayer's Cliff councillor Pierre Morency came into being, comprising eighty-six labour unions of the Confederation Syndical National, Université de Sherbrooke students, doctors, business and tourism groups as well as 126 municipalities, many of which passed resolutions demanding a halt to importation. At first their pressure yielded little more than automatic federal excuses about jurisdictional complexity and assurance from provincial environment minister Clifford Lincoln that trash-laden cargoes entering the province underwent customs and police surveillance. However, a border stake-out by Morency recorded by a Radio-Canada T.V. crew belied the claim, casting doubt on whether anyone had the foggiest notion about the contents of the 200-odd dump trucks coming in every week.

Finally, just before Christmas 1988, Lincoln tried to calm the outcry, announcing that he would modify an article of the quality of the environment law. Henceforth Quebec landfills would no longer be permitted to accept solid waste from outside the province. But though Pierre Morency at first declared the ban an immense victory, he later backed away, preferring instead to claim "half-victory." Within Quebec itself, haulers remained free to import wastes to any privately owned landfill in any region of the province.

In spite of having accomplished its original objective — the ending of transborder solid waste shipments — the movement did not disband. Like so many other such groups around North America, once standing, it found itself fulfilling a necessary role as part of the permanently assembled citizens' opposition to the continental waste trade.

But the government of Quebec, through its public pension fund investment agency, the Caisse de dépôt, had a stake in the multinational disposal-for-profit model which the citizens had unalterably opposed. And Quebec's stake was immense. As of May 1991, the Caisse owned almost $300 million worth of Laidlaw shares and $400 million worth of its parent, Canadian Pacific.[45] To say such an investment raised questions of conflict of interest for a custodian not only of the environment but also of the public interest in waste policy is an understatement. It is also a reminder of the warning of the U.S. Congressman who had concluded the disposal industry now constituted a shadow government.[46]

Chapter 11

As Long As It Rains

A popular government, without popular information, or the means of acquiring it, is but a prologue to Farce or Tragedy ...
James Madison

The analogy between England's great water supply monopolies (see Chapter 2) and the modern waste disposal industry is more apt than it ever was. The former enterprises were royally chartered and profited their powerful patrons even as their methods gave rise to an historic reform movement which ultimately would bring about radical change in the nature of public administration. Today, as we have seen, the ideology of privatization has given rise to a new form of public service monolith, the multi-national waste management company, with ties to today's political lords of the earth — be they in Washington, London, Beijing or Jakarta.[1]

Thirty years after the Milwaukee County civil action for monopolistic practices launched against an assortment of obscure regional haulers including WMI's Dean Buntrock, Waste Management International successfully raised nearly $800 million in one of the largest initial global equity offerings of early 1992. The shares had been listed on the New York and London stock exchanges and a gratified Buntrock wrote the Securities and Exchange Commission's chairman to commend his staffers on their role in coordinating their activities with their London counterparts. One might have assumed an old complaint about a waste collectors' cartel in Wisconsin to be ancient history.[2] After all, by now Buntrock's company was one of the corporate success stories of the times. Its chairman, Buntrock himself, sat cheek by jowl on WMI's board of directors with a former White House Chief of Staff to Ronald Reagan and a former Secretary of Commerce of the United States.

Yet, in spite of this evolution, some waste industry adversaries and its opponents remained fixated on the past, expending energy and resources seeking out evidence of criminal connections to explain the phenomenal rise to dominance of the world's leading corporate waste manager.

So, even as international investors were engorging WMI's coffers, the company found itself having to face its ghosts. In 1991, the San Diego County Board of Supervisors, for instance, in reviewing the waste giant's application to develop a landfill along the San Luis Rey River expressed concerns about numerous allegations against the company including the charge of organized crime connections, and asked District Attorney Ed Miller to examine the company's record. When Miller and WMI discussed the terms under which WMI would co-operate with and pay for such an investigation, the D.A. realized that these terms could mean that his office might not be free to openly discuss the conclusions they reached. Miller opted to go it alone on the public purse.

His report (which an international law firm, retained for the purposes of rebuttal by WMI, found in a counter-report to be harsh, one-sided, inaccurate and, in a number of instances, flatly wrong) reflects the limits of time and resources to which law enforcement agencies are subject.[3] Miller painted in broad strokes the now familiar "property rights" landscape and provided an account of behind-the-scenes skirmishing for the high ground on the local landfill deal. Some old charges were recycled, such as one that the 1962 Wisconsin complaint had described "behaviour and methods most typically associated with organized crime operations."[4] (In late 1992, WMI sued the district attorney claiming that he had violated the firm's civil rights by not affording it the opportunity to defend itself against the published allegations.)

In concluding its investigating sketch the D.A.'s office speculated on the possibility that WMI might be behaving like a law unto itself. "Waste Management has been capable of absorbing enormous fines and other sanctions levied against it while still maintaining a high earnings ratio. We do not know whether these sanctions have had any punitive effect on the company or have merely been considered as additional operating expenses."[5] It warned that in dealing with WMI the county should proceed with caution. A local editorialist noted skeptically that "(t)here's not much the report does not insinuate. Mob connections, political corruption. Nobody has been fitted for concrete shoes, but maybe that's in the sequel."[6]

Such was the Mafia's all-pervasive mystique that as late as the summer of 1992, and as far away from San Diego as Forbach in

France, where WMI was seeking to install an incinerator, American grass roots activist Brian Lipsett of the Citizens Clearinghouse for Hazardous Waste found himself being questioned by activists and reporters on what possible links might exist between the world's biggest waste disposal corporation, WMI, and organized crime.

Underworld/Upperworld

Few observers of American society better understood where the economic underworld ended and the upper one began than did Walter Lippmann. The renowned journalist once observed that it was in the lower reaches of capitalism that competition laws "run counter to the invincible necessities" of order and security. The small and disorganized industries of large metropolitan areas were vulnerable to all the hazards of the open market. Consequently, it was among these industries that a demand arose for a service criminals might provide — the protection of weak economic agents from unwanted rivals. Lippmann clearly saw how the "underworld through its very crude devices serves that need for social organization which reputable society has not yet learned to satisfy. Indeed, one might go further and at least inquire whether certain forms of racketeering are not the result under adverse conditions of the devotion of legislatures, courts, and public opinion to the philosophy of laissez-faire."[7]

Lippmann's observation that the underworld phenomenon went far beyond mere criminality was made in 1931, at a time when Prohibition had given the criminal class an unusually large role. In Lippmann's view, the underworld was a giant catering service providing liquor, prostitution and gambling to otherwise law-abiding citizens, and its growth was a direct result of law and social policy. Legislators had made these activities illegal, thus removing them from the region of social control. As a result, vast money-making opportunities were there for those prepared to live beyond the pale of respectability. The economy of the underworld was the inevitable byproduct of the conflict between liberalism and puritanism, a conflict which resided deep within the American personality. On one hand, Americans insisted sin be proscribed. On the other, they proved steadfastly unwilling to institutionalize the level of repression needed to eliminate what the law prohibited. Thus was a dangerous and, even more crucially, a criminally (rather than publicly) regulated economy created.

Fulfilling the "need for social organization" was precisely the function the underworld had performed in the waste disposal industry. Lippmann would have recognized in the industry's own characteristic racket — "property rights" — an example of the "perversions of the search for economic security."

In the period examined in *Giants of Garbage*, the industry moved from the lower to the upper reaches of the economic system, but understandably, given the cultural roots of the industry, the old stigma lingers. In the early 1980s, during a Toronto police investigation of an independent garbage company with dubious associations, a cop appearing in the local office of one of the waste multi-nationals was surprised by the reaction of a company official. "We are not the Mafia," the executive exclaimed. "You know that, don't you?" This assertion is true enough, but it reflects a certain defensiveness about what distinguishes the new industry from the old.

One important change is that the need for order and security is now being fulfilled by different means. In the process of development, therefore, mob protection as a condition for survival was replaced by the creators of the new industry with newer, stronger, more stable forms. The transformation of the refuse removal business into the waste management industry brought with it improved organizational control and higher levels of financial and technical resources, some of whose dimensions were described in the exploratory voyage carried out by the Philadelphia lawyers in the course of their class action discussed in Chapter 7.

Clearly, there is overwhelming evidence to suggest that though the new waste giants are creatures of capitalism their business practices in many respects defy conventional notions of free and open market behaviour. Although a company like WMI can point to its periodic and mandatory antitrust compliance seminars for line officers, as well as to its written and audio-visual antitrust educational materials for all employees, evidence presented in this book has shown that the present industry bears a strong family resemblance to the old one. In 1980, a full decade after the advent of the continental industry, a New Jersey deputy attorney in charge of garbage investigations could still argue that property rights "exist for the life of the individual or the company, and this is a proven fact, and it's more pervasive than just New York or New Jersey. In fact it's probably at work in most metropolitan areas in North America."[8] Then more than a decade later, with the industry gone global, the Kohn, Savett case and the Canadian Competition Tribunal inquiry into the automatically renewing (evergreen) service agreements used by the majors raised further challenges to the self-advertised image of the waste companies as conventionally competitive business enterprises.

With the disappearance of Boston's SCA, a company which proved what a hindrance perceived Mafia connections were in a publicly financed industry, the mobster had become a dinosaur in the waste disposal industry. Financial muscle had replaced the physical kind. However, and crucially from the perspective of public policy, the industry had not outgrown some of the practices originating in the era when mobsters had a grip on segments of the business, and above all, it had not outgrown the need for order that strong arm types had once provided.

Critics of the industry, as a new millennium approaches, do not consist only of not-in-my-back-yarders. They now also include independent and community-based recyclers, public employees, grass roots activists, environmentalists, and inquiring reporters the likes of which we encountered in the Channel 4 investigation of Attwoods. But they are well advised to base their critique elsewhere than in insinuations of organized crime connections.

Fast Bucks

A *Business Week* piece on WMI's mismanaged Chicago incinerator is more to the point. The hazardous waste burner, once proudly shown off as a model facility, was proving no model at all. Looking for some explanations for "a disturbing series of allegations and documented instances of management, environmental and worker-safety problems," the article did not finger the phantoms of a secret association with *la cosa nostra* but far more prosaically pointed to "pressure that headquarters put on plant managers to achieve high profits."[9]

Furthermore, questions in the business press about the waste industry's accounting practices reveal how prone some of these companies can be to overstating their earnings prowess. For example, Leland Montgomery, reporting in *Financial World,* noted that "the small but well-regarded Chambers Development admitted it had been cooking the books for years. When restated, 1991 operating earnings for Chambers were cut nearly in half."[10] Montgomery quotes Stephen Schweich of Alex. Brown & Sons as claiming that the "Chambers debacle ruined the credibility of the industry and has put into question the accounting practices of all the companies."[11]

That said, the obsession with short-term profits is hardly unique to the waste industry. It is an impulse — as points out Hilmar Kopper, the chief executive of Deutsche Bank, one of Germany's financial powerhouses — endemic to American business culture as a whole.

For Kopper, the U.S. economy, to its disadvantage, is more a "quarterly performance-driven economy" than many others. Its myopia is made more chronic by the fact that insurance companies, pension funds and other institutional investors suffer from the same condition.[12] Such investors (who own over half of WMI's outstanding shares and hold many hundreds of millions of dollars in the other waste industry majors) live for quarterly corporate results which as Kopper tells it means "they must go for the fast buck." With money managers continuously comparing their performance to other institutional investors, a premium is placed on today's rather than tomorrow's results. "In turn, these people are driving U.S. industry crazy to do the same thing."[13]

If being driven crazy is something the waste industry has in common with other American businesses, what makes it unlike most industries is that the consequences of its activities have to be measured on a time scale without historic precedent. For example, its short-run perspective continues to make extravagantly profitable landfilling the preferred waste management method even though even less is known of the health effects of waste burial than of burning. Since major waste depositories most likely will require oversight for periods ranging from several generations to forever, the windfall profits of corporate dumping are privatized while longer-term liabilities are socialized. All this in the name of a presumed superior efficiency, which may not amount to much more than the rapacity with which the biggest waste companies seek to extract monopoly rents from captive markets.

No more compelling example of the gap between private gain and public risk can be found than in the case of WMI and its Emelle, Alabama, depository (see Chapter 4), which was receiving 17 per cent of all the commercially landfilled hazardous wastes in the U.S.

The highest U.S. court rejected the state's right to tax WMI's toxic inflows in the face of the fact that no federal government comprehensive strategy for addressing long-term post-closure concerns at permitted hazardous waste facilities had been developed. The General Accounting Office, an agency which reports to the U.S. Congress, underscores this blind spot in rational planning by reporting that in its view "the potential exists that efforts to address this issue will continue to be deferred as other environmental concerns arise, and actions needed to ensure that post-closure liability problems do not occur may be too little, too late."[14]

Yet, even as WMI's officers and its shareholders were cashing in on their mega-dump, the state of Alabama helplessly looked forward to the day its taxpayers were saddled with "all of Chemwaste's responsibilities after the post-closure period expires."[15] This period is thirty years. After that, the problem is Alabama's. When asked how long seventy monitoring wells already in place at the giant dumping grounds would have to be monitored, Rodger Henson, the Emelle facility's former manager and a Chemwaste vice president, answered: "Those wells will be monitored in perpetuity."

"In fact, all of those things that we have described, the continued monitoring, the continued pumping, the gathering and collection and hauling away and disposal of leachate, and the security maintenance of the facility will have to be maintained at some expense in perpetuity?"

"That's correct." Henson went on to make the staggering admission that these costs "must be incurred 'as long as it rains.'"[16]

If the magnitude of discrepancy between profit and responsibility were not sufficient argument against a business-as-usual approach to the waste industry, there is a further compelling one. Unlike most forms of legitimate corporate activity, privatized waste management is uniquely distinguished by the public reaction to it. For the industry, as we have seen, has given rise to a spontaneous coalescence of ideologically diverse citizens opposed to its methods.

Everywhere groups have sprouted up in response to some specific waste industry-related issue, and then, once assembled, have recognized that the price of vigilance is a permanent presence. Thus, People Against Hazardous Landfill Sites Inc. (PAHLS), formed in 1982 as an act of self-defence when WMI began accepting hazardous wastes in Wheeler, Indiana. Since then, it has taken wing, growing into a multi-faceted grass roots' resource, linking citizens' groups and providing skills-training and technical assistance to communities with concerns about landfills, incinerators and water quality. Twice monthly, from its presses in Valparaiso, Indiana, the *PAHLS Journal* reaches out beyond the American heartland to readers in forty-five U.S. states, Europe and Asia.[17]

As well, local groups now find support at the regional and national levels from organizations like the Front commun québécois pour une gestion écologique des déchets solides in Montreal, the Ontario Environment Network, Work on Waste USA, the Environmental Research Foundation in Washington, D.C., and the Citizens Clearinghouse for Hazardous Wastes Inc. in Falls Church, Virginia.

The major waste firms arose as purely commercial or opportunistic responses to the coming of mass environmental consciousness and the first wave of clean air, water and waste legislation, and in so doing, gave birth, in their turn, to a social counter-movement that has grown in reaction to their corporate practices. Perceiving that government and its regulatory agencies are increasingly becoming captives of industry, ordinary citizens are devising various forms of self-defence, with the result that waste policy is more and more the by-product of social collision, or, more precisely, the political clash between contrasting cultures.

If one culture represents the essence of democratic participation, wherein citizens take it upon themselves to acquire understanding and then act directly in matters of compelling interest, people of the other culture (in their executive suites) are so insulated by high salaries and perks that their participation in the exercise of democracy is only ritualistic mimicry. In a country already noted for the extreme discrepancy between what chief executives pay themselves and what they pay their workers, the waste industry's top managers are among the highest paid businessmen in the world. Kohn, Savett came up with $54 million as the amount, including the exercise of stock options, paid to WMI's top three officers in the period 1987–89.[18]

If these companies, in becoming universal cash flow machines, did no more with their windfall wealth than extravagantly reward their officers, their behaviour might provoke little else than the resignation with which we greet news of the public gougings carried out by other global cartels in modern day staples, be they in sugar, grains, oil, cement, or pharmaceuticals. But the fact is waste profits end up being used not only to deflect citizens' opposition with an army of attorneys but to shape the terms of political debate over waste policy, law and regulation. WMI's political action committee, for instance, had pockets deep enough to pay out election campaign contributions in the U.S. alone of more than $1 million in a four-year period.[19] One can only imagine what gets doled out off-shore to friends of the waste multi-nationals as they race to make new inroads in eastern Europe and Asia.

Political reporter William Greider, in his book *Who Will Tell The People*, focuses on how such resources can make a charade of public participation. Using for illustrative purposes the story about Bill Ruckelshaus and the corporate counter-attack against U.S. Superfund legislation which assigned liability for toxic clean-ups to responsible corporations, Greider sees what he calls "mock democracy" in the way the big business coalition sponsored analyses on the workings of the new law. He states that in its resistance to the spirit of the law "an informal alliance was being formed by two important players — government and business — to massage a subject several years before it would become a visible political debate. There was nothing illegitimate about this. After all, it was only research. But the process that defines the scope of the public problem is often where the terms of the solution are predetermined. That is the purpose of deep lobbying — to draw the boundaries around the public argument."[20]

Such reasoning is of a piece with the proposition that the waste industry now constitutes a veritable shadow government, in opposition to which citizens not only feel compelled to defend themselves but also duty bound to resist the destructive powers of a misbegotten bottom line. Luke Cole of the California Rural Assistance Legal Assistance Foundation (which represents Latino farm workers in their quest for meaningful inclusion in the assessment of a major hazardous incinerator WMI's Chemwaste seeks to put up in the San Joaquin Valley) found himself opposing not only the "company town" of Kings County (where WMI already had a major landfill) but a company fully prepared to out-manoeuvre and outlast all opposition. It put five attorneys at a time on the case whose successful outcome represented a facility capable of burning two hundred million pounds of toxic waste per year at prices estimated to be "as high as $1000 a ton."[21]

One might justifiably frighten oneself about the capacity of society to make rational environmental choices in circumstances where economic pay-offs and potential consequences of miscalculation are of such staggering dimensions. The proposed Chemwaste burn plant is to be the largest commercial toxic incinerator west of Kansas, and to rise up "within shouting distance of the California Aqueduct which supplies the majority of water for the Los Angeles metropolitan area."[22]

The possibility of avoiding dangerous social choices is further undermined because what often passes for reality (and our range of options) is in fact carefully crafted for public consumption by public relations experts. In Ontario, for instance, WMI, in its controversial pursuit of a landfill near Lake Simcoe, engaged Hill and Knowlton, the kind of PR firm high-rollers seek out when playing for large stakes. One particularly persuasive example of Hill and Knowlton's artfulness in the service of the powerful came when the firm was hired by the Government of Kuwait during the build-up to the Gulf War. The PR firm successfully helped demonize the Iraqi invaders, and thus helped set war drums beating wildly in the public breast.[23]

In such a manipulated mediascape as ours, where information about transnational industry's business practices and stratagems fall inside the jealously guarded province of professional secret, corporations are the masters of the facts and the public (not to mention government agencies themselves) are left to surmise based on an unsatisfactory admixture of isolated data, recurrent patterns and reasonable extrapolation.

In the summer of 1989, New Hampshire's leading weekly sounded a warning about WMI when it asked whether or not the state should allow a single corporation, in this case WMI's incineration arm, Wheelabrator, "control over half of the state's solid waste disposal market?" The article made mention of one research group's conclusion that Waste Management and BFI "together controlled 47 per cent of our nation's waste hauling market." A WMI vice president, in seeking to erase the unflattering portrait, claimed that the 47 per cent claim was ludicrous. However, he offered no alternative figure as a contribution to popular information.[24]

Furthermore, to make the world's biggest waste firm loom far less largely on the continental horizon, the waste executive argued that the "metropolitan New York City market alone is estimated at over $1 billion annually, and Waste Management is not in it." However, given what we now know, the remarks seem somewhat disingenuous. For even as the WMI official was rejecting the 47 per cent claim, his company had its sights set on the gargantuan waste flows of New York City.

In a 1985 deal, Wheelabrator's predecessor company, Signal Environmental Systems, had been guaranteed a reported eighteen million tons of the City's trash for the proposed Brooklyn Navy Yard incinerator. After further shufflings, Wheelabrator (of which WMI acquired its first stake in 1988) emerged as the contractor chosen to erect the giant burn plant.[25] Should the so-called municipal-industrial complex succeed in overcoming the intense political opposition provoked by the unpopular project (and by early 1993, this seems a distinct likelihood), WMI will have succeeded not only in storming the old-style industry's last remaining bastion, but in becoming a major player in this market.

As many American cities face the closing of their community dumps in anticipation of the latest regulations coming into effect in 1993, municipal managers face with uncertainty the prospect of negotiating with the dozen or so companies which have cornered the national landfill market and which keep their financial data secret. For along with the burial facilities themselves, knowledge about the economics of disposal and its high gross margins (revenues before taxes and corporate overhead) has been privatized. Minneapolis councilman Steve Cramer, who heads the National League of Cities's task force on garbage issues, complained to the *Wall Street Journal* that civic officials were finding it hard to get the information necessary to negotiate beneficial dumping deals with private waste managers. [26]

Mock Democracy

Neither has public knowledge (particularly in the United States) been served by the further privatization of waste policy and practices through the use of the courts as the ultimate arbiters in disputes between citizens and the waste industry, government and the industry as well as between waste firms themselves. For these disputes often as not touch on matters of general community concern and, though relevant to policy formulation, end up being resolved privately. Though the courts have come to represent a kind of ersatz public forum, tens upon tens of millions of dollars (earned through private control of vast waste flows) are available to the multi-national contractors to settle complaints out of court and seal away from public view the information with which citizens might measure the extent of their control and judge their suitability for custodianship of the environment.

If any lawsuit demands full public airing it is the Cumberland Farms class action — which may be considered to have been a form of privatized prosecution. In fact, such was the scope of the case, pieced together by Kohn, Savett from millions of pages of documents, that it far surpassed in scale any government inquiry into the business culture and practices of this industry. The resulting thesis (though untested in a court of law) strongly suggests the possibility of an emergent waste cartel which, if left unobstructed by any new public policy approach, might well evolve into a small number of de facto continental utilities. These economically unregulated corporations would be at one and the same time creatures of environmental regulation and economic self-regulation — which is to say, in many domains, as the San Diego district attorney's report so clumsily suggested, economic laws unto themselves.

Thomas Jorling, New York's Commissioner of Environmental Conservation, recognized this eventuality when he explained in early 1992 that "it's not difficult to project a situation in the future where very few firms could have regional or statewide control on the management of public wastes. If that occurs, it might be necessary for some kind of public utility regulation so that the public is not ripped off."[27] Others, such as Richard Gilbert, currently Director of the Canadian Urban Institute, also have argued for public waste management, though crucially his utility model would be mandated to do more than opportunisticly "control" waste flows. Gilbert proposes a used (rather than waste) materials authority which begins from the ethical assumption that where disposal is concerned there is "no 'somewhere else.'" His agency would focus not on for-profit disposal but on reducing and eliminating waste. In seeking a fair and efficient distribution of the burden of disposal, Gilbert's approach holds out the possibility (in a way globalized corporate waste management never could) of a generalized democratic coming to terms with the cultural and social dimensions of waste.

That said, the public's role remains as much a question mark as ever it has since the first wave of green legislation. In spite of the important implications of the Kohn, Savett complaint, the public has not had the benefit of their singular efforts. Payments in excess of $50 million (paid out by the Big Two) had the effect of locking away the mass of evidence from public view. Reasonable minds remain in the dark and the power of money to insulate the powerful waste corporations from public scrutiny remains for many a source of legitimate apprehension.

When boards of directors move, as the board of at least one major waste manager recently did, to decrease limits on company directors' liability to the company and its shareholders (so-called "raincoat provisions"), it underlines the urgency of facing up to the immense disequilibrium of private profit and social accountability. After all, originally, the corporation had far more limits placed on its activities than it does today. In the last century, however, business increasingly began to acquire — as Dr. Peter Montague of the Environmental Research Foundation puts it — "the rights of individuals without the responsibility of individuals, and yet they are far more powerful than any individual."

Agora — The Public Space

In late 1991, when Ontario environment minister Ruth Grier appointed a task force of business and environmental organizations to draft an Environmental Bill of Rights, she was moving to redress the imbalance between rights and responsibilities. Various jurisdictions (including Michigan, Minnesota and Connecticut in the U.S. and the Yukon and the Northwest Territories in Canada) already had enacted such laws as a means of entrenching the public's right to a healthy environment. When Ontario's turn came there was a sense that, because previous such legislation often amounted to not much more than make-work projects for lawyers, a real role must be found for the public beyond the court room. Crucially, Grier's task force chose to steer as clear as possible of the customary American model which roots environmental protection in the protection of private interests. The writers of the new bill insisted the environment be seen not as a private but as a community issue. What they said they sought were reasonable and affordable mechanisms of public intervention based on principles of accountability and transparency.

The first draft of the bill was presented for public debate in July 1992 and the accompanying task force report described the new tack as follows: "This approach invites residents to engage the government decision-making process and the political process, rather than the judicial process. Residents of the Province would have an opportunity to become involved in the process that generates decisions that affect our environment."[28] The court was seen not as a first but a last resort.

Without a doubt, this attempt to develop new forms of policy-making forums beyond the court house is indispensable to progress. One of the philosophical underpinnings of the new bill of rights is that government's responsibility in waste policy is the primary one. But the authors of the draft law make the unexamined assumption that the key decisions affecting waste management in Ontario naturally get made by government. No suggestion is made of the unelected government of transnational waste managers, a closely guarded, macho corporate culture for whom accountability and transparency tend — if these pages are anything to go by — to be quite alien notions. It is doubtful any meaningful balance of rights and responsibility ever will be achieved without a sweeping public inquiry into corporate concentration in the waste industry.

While the settlement of the Kohn, Savett lawsuit may have satisfied the plaintiffs in the case, privatized prosecution of serious allegations with public policy implications is insufficient. For the public truly to be admitted to the process of waste policy-making and the consequent making-over of the basic nature of our society, forms of traditional democracy must be reinvented, some approximation of the Greek agora — the democratic coming-together of citizens to resolve issues that define the future character of society. Without popular access to information possessed by the major private waste managers, the government of waste can only be — to borrow from James Madison — prologue to Farce or Tragedy.

Questions raised by Kohn, Savett and the public-spirited but highly circumscribed Canadian Competition Tribunal's inquiry into the big three's service agreements cry out for answers that are arrived at publicly. These answers are vital to understanding the political economy of waste disposal. Presumably, given the considerable financial and legal resources necessary for such a task, what is called for in Canada is the striking of a Royal Commission and in the U.S. a Congressional investigation.

Such inquiries could complete the explorations begun by Kohn, Savett, mapping out the existing structure of the waste economy. They would include detailed information about the extent of corporate vertical and horizontal integration, regional and continental waste flows, collection and disposal market shares, rate of customer turn-over, pricing strategies, the role of regionally and nationally mandated price and profit mechanisms, comparative profit levels for various services and disposal methods. The most perfect environmental bill of rights ever written is no substitute for such a process because without such information there is no way for elected governments or citizens' coalitions to comprehend and account for the role of a key — if not *the* key — decision-maker in the waste economy.

After Montreal mandated its Bureau de consultation (a modern facsimile of the agora) to begin a public consultation process in late 1991, the Bureau heard from seventy-four participants. Out of that process the provincial environment minister was requested to begin a public inquiry "on the issue of waste elimination (incineration and land-fill) in the over-all context of solid waste management."[29] At a minimum what the Bureau was hoping to forestall was a ludicrous planning process (reminiscent of the ancient water supply monopolies) which might lead to rival incinerators on the island of Montreal and a "number of new and important problems for both human health and the ecosystem."[30]

Any more logical and communitarian approach than the present one to our waste crisis, begs for public investigation of the most wide-ranging and all-inclusive kind. Reasonable minds (of all political persuasions) should demand nothing less. For waste that is truly waste is not a good like any other and our attitude to it speaks not only to the value we place on our earthly future as a society but also to the individual character of our being.

Appendix

Rules of the Chicago and Suburban Refuse Disposal Corporation

Rules of the Chicago and Suburban Refuse Disposal Corporation, as enumerated in the antitrust complaint lodged by the office of Illinois Attorney General William Scott in 1971:

a. All member contractors are to refrain from soliciting the customers of other member contractors.

b. If one member contractor does obtain the customer of another member contractor (by solicitation or otherwise), he is required to either return the particular customer's account to the previous contractor or to "give value" for the account, that is, either pay a sum representing the current value of the business or transfer a comparable account.

c. If a customer serviced by one member contractor attempts to hire another member contractor, the latter will either refuse to deal with the customer or quote a price higher than that presently charged, thereby preventing customers from switching to or obtaining the services of another member contractor.

d. If bids are to be let by municipalities or other governmental units, or other companies or prospective customers, member contractors agree among themselves which scavenger is to submit the lowest bid.

e. If a member contractor wishes to raise prices charged to a particular customer, other member contractors contacted by the customer will either refuse to deal with the customer or quote a higher price.

f. If a building or business serviced by one member contractor acquires new owners or tenants, the latter must accept the services of that contractor and other member contractors collectively refrain from soliciting that account and refuse to deal with the prospective customer or otherwise offer services at competitive prices.

g. When a new commercial stop opens for business the member contractor who services the customer on the day on which he opens has the right to the account, and other members collectively refrain from soliciting said account and refuse to deal with the prospective customers or otherwise offer services at competitive prices.

h. If a customer or stop closes down, the site is regarded as the customer of the contractor then servicing it for a period of three years (excluding time for rebuilding or remodelling) and any new tenant or owner is restricted to the services of the member contractor previously serving it.

i. When a member contractor acquires a new customer, he is prohibited from raising prices for a period of four years, after which time he may raise prices ten per cent per year. If he attempts to violate this rule, the customer may be solicited by other member contractors.

j. When a contract is to be let by a municipality or other government unit, if there are member contractors already servicing a portion of same, the one doing the greatest volume of work is entitled to the contract and bids will be fixed in order that the contract be awarded.

Additional monopolistic practices described in the complaint as having been engaged in by certain of the co-conspirators included:

1. They have reported to each other the acquisition or loss of scavenger services customers, locations, and identity of their customers, prices paid by their customers for scavenger services, and other conditions concerning the servicing of their customers.

2. They have agreed with each other to bill customers for scavenger services not rendered by the billing scavenger but rendered by another scavenger.

3. They have sold to or exchanged with each other stops for which they agreed not to compete in connection with such sales or exchange.

4. They have refused to deal or have threatened to refuse to deal with suppliers of scavenger service equipment, with the intent to influence such suppliers not to deal with nonmember scavengers.

5. They have influenced or attempted to influence the International Brotherhood of Teamsters, through certain of its local unions, officers, agents, and members, to discourage customers from dealing with non-member scavengers and to interfere with the right of non-member scavengers to do business.

6. They have joined together in the ownership and operation of landfill and incinerator sites and have refused to open such sites to use by non-member scavengers or have charged unreasonable fees for the use of such sites, with the purpose and effect of restraining competition with themselves by non-member scavengers.

7. They have threatened physical and economic harm to customers using or attempting to use non-member scavengers.

8. They have colluded to rig bids or to refrain from bidding for scavenger service bid awards.

9. They have used predatory practices, including, but not limited to, unreasonably low price bids and unlawful disparagement of non-member scavengers, with the purpose and probable effect of inducing customers not to deal with nonmember scavengers.

Notes

Chapter One: The Changing World of Waste

1. U.S. Environmental Protection Agency, *The Private Sector in Solid Waste Management* (Washington, D.C.: 1974), p. 79.
2. E.S. Savas and Christopher Niemczewski, "Who collects solid waste?" *International City Management Association, 1976 Municipal Year Book* (Washington, D.C., 1976), p. 167-72. 3. *The State of New York* v. *A.B.C. Rubbish Removal Co.* Supreme Court of New York, 1973. Indictment No. 5314/73, p. 1-3.
4. Nicholas Gage, "Carting in Brooklyn is Linked to Crime," *New York Times*, 19 March 1974; Frank J. Prial, "55 Carters Are Charged With Brooklyn Monopoly," *New York Times*, 29 March 1974. For the expansion of carting companies controlled by members of the Vito Genovese and Carlo Gambino Mafia families, see Ralph Blumenthal, "Westchester Grip Tightened by Mob," *New York Times*, 13 October 1974; and for the more recent branching out of criminals into the toxic-waste industry, see Ralph Blumenthal, "Illegal Dumping of Toxins Laid to Organized Crime," *New York Times*, 5 June 1983.
5. John D. Hanrahan, *Government For Sale: Contracting-Out, The New Patronage* (Washington, D.C.: American Federation of State, County and Municipal Employees, 1977), p. 60.
6. Stewart E. Perry, *San Francisco Scavengers: Dirty Work and the Pride of Ownership* (Berkeley and Los Angeles: University of California Press, 1978), p. 38.
7. Thurlow & Associates, *A Preliminary Overview of the Solid Waste Problem in Canada*. A report submitted to the Resources Research Centre, Policy & Research Coordination Branch, Department of Fisheries & Forestry, April 1971, p. 60.
8. *Waste Age*, 3, no. 4 (July-August 1972), p. 28.
9. Keith Schneider, "Rules Forcing Towns to Pick new Dumps or Big Costs," *New York Times*, 6 January 1992.

Chapter Two: Public vs. Private Enterprise

1. Sidney and Beatrice Webb, *English Local Government: Statutory Authorities For Special Purposes* (London: Longmans, Green, 1922), p. 431.
2. "The Water Monopoly And The Sanitary Movement," *The Times*, (London), 25-28 December 1849.
3. Webb, *English Local Government*, p. 444.
4. Lewis Mumford, *The City in History* (Harmondsworth: Penguin Books, 1961), p. 542.
5. Quoted in "Contracting out: Private profit at public expense," a brief submitted to Donald Johnston, president of the Treasury Board, Ottawa, by the Public Service Alliance of Canada, the Professional Institute of Public Service, and the Economists, Sociologists and Statisticians Associations, July 1980.
6. A lively narrative describing the attempt to "privatize" Petro-Canada is contained in the (undated) special supplement "The Petrocan Connection," published by *The Democrat*, official publication of the British Columbia New Democratic Party.
7. Jack Kemp, House of Representatives Subcommittee on Employee Ethics and Utilization of the Committee on Post Office and Civil Service, 28 and 31 March 1977. The New York congressman addressed the hearings on contracting-out of jobs and services.
8. An important perspective on New York City's cash flow crisis was offered by a report in the *New York Times* (29 May 1975) which pointed out that almost 40 per cent of the $1 billion the city needed to avoid bankruptcy was to cover real estate taxes it had levied and spent but could not collect from landlords. The city had a longstanding practice of basing expenditures on what it legally might collect from property owners instead of what it actually expected them to pay.
9. E.S. Savas, "Municipal Monopoly," *Harper's Magazine*, December 1971, p. 56.
10. Stewart E. Perry, *San Francisco Scavengers: Dirty Work and the Pride of Ownership* (Berkeley and Los Angeles: University of California Press, 1978) p. 190.
11. Perry, p. 188-89.
12. Nicholas Gage, "Carting in Brooklyn is Linked to Crime," *New York Times*, 19 March 1974. There is evidence suggesting that

during the 1970s gangsters had exported their regulatory techniques and monopolistic practices beyond the New York City and New Jersey area. In July 1983, government prosecutors were preparing to try various refuse carters linked to New York crime families for having acquired and maintained control of the private sanitation industry in the booming retirement area of west Florida. According to unidentified Florida authorities cited by the *New York Times*, refuse carters formerly based in Brooklyn had succeeded in driving out local competition and seizing control of landfills throughout Florida by means of threats, extortion, beatings, pistol whippings and the burning of garbage trucks. See Ben A. Franklin, "Mafia Link Seen In Trash Carting In West Florida," *New York Times*, 3 July 1983.

13. Frank J. Prial, "55 Carters are charged with Brooklyn Monopoly," *New York Times*, 29 March 1974.

14. David Bird, "Public vs. Private Collection of Refuse: In Some Cities, It's No Longer a Debate," *New York Times*, 10 July 1975.

15. *Solid Wastes Management*, April 1980.

16. Eileen Berenyi, Senior Research Associate, Columbia University, Center for Government Studies, interviewed January 1982.

17. E.S. Savas, "Solid Waste Collection in Metropolitan Areas," in Elinor Ostrom, ed., "The Delivery of Urban Services: Outcomes of Change," *Urban Affairs Annual Review*, vol. 10 (Beverly Hills: Sage Publications), p. 215.

18. E.S. Savas, *The Organization and Efficiency of Solid Waste Collection* (Lexington, Mass.: D.C. Heath, 1977), p. 134.

19. Savas, *Solid Waste Collection*, p. 202.

20. E.S. Savas, E.M. Brettler, and J.A. Berenyi, "Solid Waste Collection and Disposal: The Economics and Financing," *The Daily Bond Buyer*, Special Conference Supplement No. 1, 70th Annual Meeting of Municipal Finance Officers of U.S. and Canada, Public Finance, San Francisco, 2-6 May 1976, p. 19.

21. E.S. Savas, "Intracity Competition Between Public And Private Service Delivery," Center for Government Studies, Graduate School of Business, Columbia University. An unpublished report prepared with the support of the applied Social and Behavioural Science Program, Division of Applied Research, National Science Foundation, p. 4-5.

22. Savas, *Solid Waste Collection*, p. 142-43.

23. These changes undermined the Savas studies' theoretical edifice which took the basic production unit in refuse collection to be the truck, whereas it was fast becoming the disposal facility.

24. Ralph Nader, Ronald Brownstein, and John Richard, eds. *Who's Poisoning America* (San Francisco: Sierra Club Books, 1981) p. 25.

25. Peter Moon, "Private waste disposal becoming U.S. preserve," *Globe and Mail* (Toronto), 22 April 1974.

26. Ken Romain, "Trash business lucrative for Laidlaw," *Globe and Mail* (Toronto), 11 January 1982.

27. Moon, "Private waste disposal."

28. Quoted in Greater Vancouver Regional District, *Report on Alternative Methods for Disposal of Mixed Municipal Refuse: Technical Status, Expected Costs and Preliminary Evaluation of Possibilities for Application in the Greater Vancouver Region.* Prepared by W.A. Melcher, Sr., Assistant Engineer, May 1980, p. 6-1.

29. Janet Marinelli and Gail Robinson, "No Room at the Bin." *The Progressive*, December 1981, p. 25.

30. Marinelli and Robinson, p. 23-24.

31. Richard Goodacre, *Some Potential Strategies For The Recovery and Reduction of Municipal Solid Waste* (Vancouver: Recycling Council of British Columbia, 1978), p. 15.

32. Thomas G. Donlan, "Garbage Into Energy," *Barron's*, 21 July 1980, p. 5.

33. Marinelli and Robinson, "No Room at the Bin," p. 25.

34. *Hybud Equipment Corp. et al.* v. *City of Akron et al.* U.S. Court of Appeals, Sixth Circuit, 31 March 1980, Appellant's brief, p. 40-41.

35. A Mussolini-era statute decreeing no raw refuse be dumped on land around Rome gave Italians a head start in developing the modern garbage processing factory.

36. *Rachel's Hazardous Waste News* #289, "The Recent History of Solid waste: Good Alternatives Are Now Available," 10 June 1992. Published by the Environmental Research Foundation, Box 5036, Annapolis MD 21403-7036.

37. Claire Pool, "Burn This," *Forbes*, 25 April 1988. Quoted in Louis Blumberg and Robert Gottlieb, *War on Waste: Can America Win Its Battle With Garbage* (Washington, D.C., Covelo, California: Island Press, 1989) p. 49.

38. Newsday, *Rush to Burn* (Washington, D.C.: Island Press, 1989) p. 7-8. "In this atmosphere of crisis, a kind of municipal-industrial complex is in the midst of a mad, perhaps, misguided, dash for

salvation. It is called resource recovery — a euphemism that implies environmental virtue but that tends to obscure persistent questions of safety, competence, economics and the environment itself."

39. *Newsday*, "Rush To Burn," p. 192.

40. Dr. Paul Connett, "Waste Management: As If The Future Mattered," 1988 Frank P. Piskor Faculty Lecture, 5 May 1988, St. Lawrence University, p. 15.

41. Dr. Paul Connett, p. 16.

42. Greenpeace Toxics newsletter, 1990.

43. *Rachel's Hazardous Waste News*, "The Recent History of Solid Waste ..." #289.

44. Louis Blumberg and Robert Gottlieb, *War on Waste*, p. 53.

45. Matthew Reiss, "The Garbage Broker, Norman Steisel and the Art of the Done Deal," *The Village Voice*, 26 November 1991, p. 30.

46. Smith Barney, Harris Upham & Co., "Hazardous-Waste Update, Part 1," *Pollution Control Monthly*, May 1989, p. 6.

47. Matthew Reiss, p. 32.

48. Matthew Reiss, p. 35.

49. Matthew Reiss, p. 33.

50. Newsday, *Rush to Burn*, p. 7-8.

51. Michael W. Anderson, "Will Solid Waste Management & Resource Recycling be Oligopolized in the 1990s." Anderson's 1990-91 writings are disseminated by Garbage Reincarnation, Inc., P.O. Box 1375, Santa Rosa, CA 95402.

52. *Rachel's Hazardous Waste News* #93, "What We Must Do — Part 5: Winning Corporate Strategies," 5 September 1988.

53. Jim Sibbison, "Revolving Door At the E.P.A.," *The Nation*, 6 November 1989, p. 527.

Chapter Three: BFI: The Pathbreaker

1. Ida Tarbell, *The History of the Standard Oil Company* (New York: Macmillan, 1925), p. 634.

2. *Waste Age*, July-August 1972, p. 8.

3. "Garbage gets a glamour image," *Business Week*, 4 March 1972, p. 44.

4. Quoted in John Hanrahan, *Government for Sale* (Washington, D.C.: American Federation of State, County and Municipal Employees, 1977), p. 61.

5. *Waste Age*, July-August 1972, p. 40.
6. Quoted in Stewart E. Perry, *San Francisco Scavengers* (Berkeley and Los Angeles: University of California Press, 1978) p. 196-97.
7. Perry, p. 119.
8. Paul Musgrove, "B.C. businesses face death at hands of U.S. garbage giant," *Vancouver Sun*, 22 November 1975.
9. Quoted in "Empire of Waste," *The Clarion-Ledger* (Jackson, Mississippi), 3 December 1980, p. 16.
10. Stephen P. Coelen, "Refuse Collection: The Price Is Not Right," *Waste Age*, August 1978, p. 38.
11. "Empire of Waste," p. 32.
12. Jeff Blyskal, "Glittering, glamorous garbage," *Forbes*, 8 June 1981, p. 158.
13. "Empire of Waste," p. 16-17. See also Carlos Byars, "Toxic Oil Waste Also Sold to Firm in La.," *Houston Chronicle*, 19 June 1979.
14. *The Wall Street Transcript*, Volume LXXXIX, Number 7, 14 February 1983, p. 9.
15. *The Wall Street Transcript*.
16. *Forbes*, 24 June 1991, p. 132.
17. R. Miner, "The Sweet Smell of Success — Industry Report," Paine Webber Inc., 28 November 1989, p. 14-15.
18. Louis Blumberg and Robert Gottlieb, *War on Waste*, p. 54.
19. Bernie Kohn and Janet Williams, "Chambers, BFI end legal tussle," *The Pittsburgh Press*, 7 June 1989.
20. See *Chambers Development Company Inc.* vs. *Browning-Ferris Industries Inc. etc.*, In The District Court for the Western District of Pennsylvania, Civil Action No. 83-2384.
21. *Chambers Development Company Inc.* vs. *Browning-Ferris Industries Inc. etc.*, p. 11-12.
22. Ralph Haurwitz, "DER offical walks tall in face of attacks, death threats," *The Pittsburgh Press*, 1 May 1988.
23. Haurwitz, "DER offical walks ..."
24. Haurwitz, "DER offical walks ..."
25. Paul Marniak, "Landfill operators to open books to U.S. investgator," *The Pittsburgh Press,* 11 November.
26. Haurwitz, "DER offical walks ..."
27. Bill Moushey, "Grand juries probe trash business," *Pittsburgh Post-Gazette*, 6 June 1987.
28. *Chambers Development Company Inc.* vs. Browning-Ferris Industries Inc. etc., U.S. District Judge Gerald J. Weber Memorandum and Order, 14 July 1987, p. 2.

29. *Chambers Development Company Inc.* vs. Browning-Ferris Industries Inc. etc., p. 3-4.

30. Stuart Brown, "The Wild World of Waste," *Executive Report, The Pittsburgh Region's Business Magazine,* March 1989, p. 21.

31. Stuart Brown, "The Wild World of Waste," p. 20.

32. Conversation with Jamie Whitten of Lipsen, Whitten & Diamond, 14 January 1992.

33. Jim McKay, "Browning-Ferris, Chambers drop criminal charges," *Post-Gazette,* 7 June 1989.

34. Jim Sibbison, "Revolving Door At The E.P.A.," *The Nation,* 6 November 1989, p. 524.

35. Jim Sibbison, p. 524.

36. Len Colodny and Robert Gettlin, *Silent Coup, The Removal of a President* (New York: St. Martin's Paperbacks, 1991), p. 363.

37. Jane Novack, "A New Top Broom," *Forbes,* 28 November 1988, p. 200.

38. Joani Nelson-Horchler, " 'Mr. Clean' turns 'Garbage Man,' " *Industry Week,* 17 July 1989, p. 15.

39. Joani Nelson-Horchler, p. 15.

40. A 27 July 1987 letter from Union Carbide vice president Cornelius C. Smith, Jr. to Superfund Alternative Task Group.

41. Undated Natural Resources Defense Council news release.

42. Undated Natural Resources Defense Council news release.

43. Jeff Nesmith, "Ex-EPA chief said trying to soften Superfund law," *The Atlanta Constitution,* 10 December 1987.

44. Michael Cinelli, *The Houston Post,* 29 April 1990.

45. Report to the Board of Directors of Waste Management Inc. by Karaganis, Gail & White Ltd.

46. Report to the Board of Directors of Waste Management Inc. by Karaganis, Gail & White Ltd.

47. "Can Bill Ruckleshaus Clean Up Browning-Ferris' Act?" *Business Week,* 14 October 1991.

48. Robert Johnson, "Browning-Ferris Plans to Leave Business of Hazardous Waste and Take Charge," *Wall Street Journal,* 6 April 1990.

49. Abraham J. Briloff, "Recycled Accounting, It Enhances Waste Management's Earnings," *Barron's,* 6 August 1990. Briloff's warning about what he considered to be WMI's profit-inflating hazardous accounting techniques echoed in the 1992 news that Chambers had been "cooking the books for years." See Leland

Montgomery, "Down in the dumps," *Financial World*, 23 June 1992.

50. *Cumberland Farms Inc. et al.* v. *Browning-Ferris Industries, Inc. et al.*, plaintiffs' Memorandum In Opposition to defendants' motion for summary judgement, 27 July 1990, p. 2.

51. Jeff Bailey, "Browning-Ferris Fires General Counsel, Chief Financial Officer Over Stock Sales," *Wall Street Journal*, 27 September 1991.

52. Barnaby J. Feder, "Browning-Ferris Unnerves Wall St.," *New York Times* 5 September 1991.

53. Jeff Bailey, "SEC Reviewing Browning-Ferris Stock Sales," *Wall Street Journal*, 24 September 1991.

54. Barnaby J. Feder, "Browning-Ferris Unnerves Wall St."

55. Barnaby J. Feder, "Browning To Drop Waste Unit," *New York Times*, 6 April 1990.

56. Leland Montgomery, "Down in the dumps," p. 32.

Chapter Four: WMI: The Global Empire

1. See *The State of Illinois* v. *Chicago and Suburban Refuse Disposal Corporation et al.* Circuit Court of the 18th Circuit, DuPage County, Illinois, 29 April 1971. Final Judgement and Consent Decree.

2. John Gault, "Watch Paul Godfrey Grow," *Toronto Life*, February 1972, p. 38.

3. Ron Haggart, "Should a reeve be in the garbage business?" *Toronto Star*, 25 November 1964.

4. During an 1973 interview, Waste Management's Harold Gershowitz explained: "More and more public agencies are looking to private enterprise to solve their disposal problems, as well as their collection problems. The areas of civil systems ... really represent astronomical potential for future growth for our company. Unparalleled, I think, in American business today. And I think that those will be the battlegrounds on which competition will continue to play a significant role." *Environmental Science & Technology*, April 1973, p. 46.

5. *Waste Age*, September 1980.

6. Paul Lieberman and Jerry Schwartz, "Trash Firms Targets of Grand Jury Probe," *Atlanta Constitution*, 9 February 1979.

7. Suzanne Garment, "Sifting Through the Rubble of EPA," *Wall Street Journal*, 14 March 1983.

8. "Mrs. Gorsuch Pollutes the E.P.A.," *New York Times*, 16 February 1983.

9. "Poison At The EPA," *The New Republic*, 24 March 1982, p. 8.

10. "Leader in Toxic Dumps Accused of Illegal Acts," *New York Times*, 21 March 1983. p. D10.

11. *Newsweek*, 7 March 1983, p. 23.

12. Jerry Brown, "Waste firm hid leak, says Lamm," *Rocky Mountain News*, 15 September 1982.

13. Sharon Sherman, "Lowry Landfill Lobbying Begins," *Denver Post*, 8 January 1983.

14. "Leader in Toxic Dumps ...," p. 1.

15. "Leader in Toxic Dumps ...," p. D10.

16. Raymond Bonner, "Big Waste Hauler Closes Site," *New York Times*, 22 March 1983, p. 1.

17. "Waste disposal's aggressive No. 1," *Chemical Week*, 12 August 1981, p. 42.

18. J. Stanley, *Wertheim Schroder Report on Waste Management Inc.*, 8 August 1990. Emphasis added.

19. J. Stanley, *Wertheim Schroder Report on Waste Management Inc.*

20. Velma Smith, Director of Groundwater and Drinking Water Project, Environmental Policy Institute, *Memorandum*, 2 July 1988.

21. Velma Smith, *Memorandum*.

22. Jim McNeill, "Protective Instincts at the EPA," *In These Times*, 11-17 October 1989.

23. Ben Gordon, *Greenpeace Toxics Campaign Memorandum*, 4 April 1989.

24. Gordon, *Greenpeace Toxics Campaign Memorandum*.

25. Jim McNeill, "Protective Instincts at the EPA."

26. See *Rachel's Hazardous Waste News*, # 156 and #157.

27. *Rachel's Hazardous Waste News*, "Reilly plans investigation of himself," #157.

28. William Sanjour and Hugh B. Kaufman, *Memorandum on possible criminal and ethical violations by the Administrator and Regional Administrator to John C. Martin, E.P.A. Inspector General*, 17 May 1989.

29. Sanjour and Kaufman, *Memorandum*.

30. "The Waste Management Connection," *The Amicus Journal*, Winter 1990.

31. Letter of J. Richard Wagner to Honorable John D. Dingell, House Committee on Energy and Commerce, Washington, D.C., 18 October 1989.

32. *Rachel's Hazardous Waste News*, #157.

33. "The Waste Management Connection," p. 9.

34. *Rachel's Hazardous Waste News*, #157.

35. See David White's two-part series in *The Birmingham News*, 26 and 27 November 1989.

36. A frequently cited 1987 study by Charles Lee, *Toxic Waste and Race In The United States*, observed a national pattern in which race proved the most significant factor in siting hazardous waste facilities and that 40 per cent of the U.S.'s estimated hazardous waste landfill capacity was sited near three predominatly black or Hispanic communities in Louisiana, South Carolina and in Sumter County, Alabama. Available from Commission for Racial Justice, United Church of Christ, 105 Madison Avenue, New York, New York 10016. Also see Jane Kay's four-part "Special Report: Toxic Racism" in *San Francisco Examiner*, 7-10 April 1991.

37. William Slakey, "Justice to enter view on Emelle," *Waste Tech News*, 2 December 1991.

38. *Guy Hunt, et al.* v. *Chemical Waste Management,* In the Supreme Court of Alabama, On Appeal from the Circuit Court of Montgomery, Brief and Argument of Appellant Guy Hunt, Case Nos. 190-1043 & 190-1044, p. 68.

39. *Guy Hunt, et al.* v. *Chemical Waste Management* In the Supreme Court of Alabama, p. 55.

40. See 584 *Southern Reporter*, 2d Series, 1367 (Alabama, 1991) *Hunt* v. *Chemical Waste Management*, p. 1375.

41. See 584 *Southern Reporter*, 2d Series, 1367 (Alabama, 1991), p. 1374-5.

42. See 584 *Southern Reporter*, 2d Series, 1367 (Alabama, 1991), p. 1382.

43. See 584 *Southern Reporter*, 2d Series, 1367 (Alabama, 1991), p. 1387.

44. See 584 *Southern Reporter*, 2d Series, 1367 (Alabama, 1991), p. 1388.

45. See 584 *Southern Reporter*, 2d Series, 1367 (Alabama, 1991), p. 1390-1.

46. *Just Say No,* Dakota Rural Action (Box 549, Brookings, SD 57006) November, 1991.

47. *Just Say No.*

48. Paul Barrett, "High Court to Enter Waste-Disposal War," *Wall Street Journal*, 23 March 1992

49. *Chemical Waste Management, Inc., petitioner* v. *Guy Hunt*, In the Supreme Court of the United States, October Term, 1991, Brief For The United States As *Amicus Curiae* Supporting Petitioner, Kenneth Starr, Solicitor General et al., p. 1

50. *Chemical Waste Management, Inc., petitioner* v. *Guy Hunt*, *Amicus Curiae*, p. 14-15.

51. *Chemical Waste Management, Inc., petitioner* v. *Guy Hunt*, *Amicus Curiae*, p. 15.

Chapter Five: SCA: The Price of Scandal

1. Robert Windrem, "The Mob Comes to Wall Street," *The Village Voice* (New York), 13 November 1978.

2. Nancy Pomerene, "Boston garbage: Cash in the trash," *Boston Phoenix*, 15 June 1976.

3. *Waste Age*, August 1976, p. 47.

4. Bernard Shakin, "No Want of Waste," *Barron's*, 14 May 1979.

5. Jock Ferguson and Michael Keating, "America's Wasteland," *Globe and Mail* (Toronto), 3 December 1980.

6. Bob Dearing, "Waste Firm Battles to Bolster Image," *Buffalo Courier-Express*, 24 September 1980.

7. "Now to Clean Up the Cleaners," *New York Times*, 22 December 1980, p. 22.

8. Jock Ferguson and Michael Keating, "Organized crime invading toxic-waste field, U.S. panel told," *Globe and Mail* (Toronto), 22 December 1980.

9. Jim Tharpe, "State Becomes garbage dump for the nation," *Greenville News*, 21 October 1984. First article in "The Dumping Ground: Hazardous Waste In South Carolina" series.

10. Jim Tharpe, "State Becomes garbage dump ..."

11. Jim Tharpe, "State Becomes garbage dump ..."

12. *The Wall Street Transcript*, Volume LXXXIX, Number 7, 14 February 1983, p. 11.

13. *The Wall Street Transcript*, p. 22 .

14. *United States of America* v. *Waste Management Inc. and WM Acquiring Corp.* Civil Action No. 84-2832, Complaint for Injunctive Relief, U.S. District Court for the District of Columbia, 12 September 1984. By squaring the market share of each firm in the

market and then summing the resulting numbers, the Herfindahl-Hirschman Index (HHI) approaches zero when a market is occupied by a lot of firms of relatively equal size and reaches its maximium as the number of firms decreases and the disparity in size between them increases.

15. "How Waste Management Inc. Avoided Antitrust Problems in Buying SCA," *The Hazardous Waste Consultant*, January/February 1985.

16. U.S. Department of Justice press release. 12 September 1984.

17. Edwin Chen, "Waste Hauler Fined $1 Million in Price-Fixing Case," *Los Angeles Times*, 14 March 1989, p. 1, and *Rachel's Hazardous Waste News*, #141.

18. Edwin Chen, "Waste Hauler Fined $1 Million ..."

19. Edwin Chen, "Waste Hauler Fined $1 Million ..."

20. Edwin Chen, "Waste Hauler Fined $1 Million ..."

21. *U.S.A* v. *GSX*, United States District Court for the Central District of California, Information. Filed 19 January 1989.

22. *The People of the State of California* v. *Waste Management of California, Inc. etc.*, Felony Complaint for Arrest Warrants, Case No. A 952588, 8 June 1987

23. Dermot Foley, "Corporate History of Wastech-Genstar," *Report of Citizens' Action Network*, Vancouver, B.C., April 1989.

24. Cecil Foster, "Laidlaw acquires GSX Corp. for $513 million," *Globe and Mail*, 22 July 1986.

25. Raymond Klempin, "Fatjo Pulls Out of Fitness Chain, Returns to Trash," *Houston Business Journal*, 6 February 1989.

Chapter Six: Laidlaw: The Canadian Player

1. Paul Kidd, "The Man who Bought the Ticats," *Hamilton Spectator*, 19 May 1973.

2. *The Financial Post*, 18 May 1974.

3. Paul Musgrove, "B.C. Businesses face death at hands of U.S. garbage giant," *Vancouver Sun*, 22 November 1975.

4. Gail Allison, Steve Mooser and Patricia Taylor, *Beyond The Trash Can*. An Oil, Chemical & Atomic Workers Solid Waste Educational Program Publication, August 1973. According to this union handbook, "sanitation work is nine times more hazardous

than the average industrial occupation, and second only to logging in the likelihood of injury."

5. Richard Starks, "Ottawa garbage contract raises more questions," *The Financial Post*, 25 October 1975, p. 32.

6. Gwen Smith, "Ontario's controls on waste called 'a game of sham'," *Globe and Mail* (Toronto), 26 August 1980.

7. John Jackson, Phil Weller and the Waterloo Public Interest Research Group, *Chemical Nightmare* (Toronto: Between The Lines, 1982), p. 47.

8. Eugene Forsey, "A slick way to skin the public," *Maclean's*, 11 February 1980, p. 6.

9. Robert Rickles and Harold Holzer, "Agent Orange," *Rolling Stone*, 4 March 1982, p. 11-12.

10. Ken Romain, "Trash business lucrative for Laidlaw," *Globe and Mail*, 11 January 1983.

11. Bruce W. Piasecki and Gary A. Davis, *America's Future in Toxic Waste Management: Lessons From Europe*, (New York: Quorum Books, 1989), p. 194.

12. Alan Block, *Defending The Mountaintop: Research in The Public Interest: A Corporate Profile of Attwoods PLC* (Arlington, VA: Citizens' Clearing House for Hazardous Wastes Inc.), p. 17.

13. "A Special Relationship." Documentary film produced by Box Productions, London, U.K., 1989.

14. "A Special Relationship."

15. "A Special Relationship."

16. See *Cumberland Farms, Inc. et al.*, v. *Browning-Ferris Industries et al.*, plaintiffs' Memorandum In Opposition To Defendants' Motion For Summary Judgment, In The United States District Court for the Eastern District of Pennsylvania, Master File No. 87-3717, p. 72-73.

17. See the 20 September 1991 report on Waste Management Inc. prepared for the Ventura, California, Board of Supervisors by the Ventura County Sheriff's Department.

18. John Plender, "Thatcher link with U.S. waste company scrutinised," *Financial Times*, 4 July 1989 and "A Special Relationship."

19. "A Special Relationship."

20. "A Special Relationship" and Alan Block, *Defending The Mountaintop*.

21. *Marion County, Florida* vs. *Urban Waste Disposal, Inc., et al.*, Complaint for Violations of the Florida Racketeering Influenced Corrupt Organizations Acts, Fraud, Abatement of a Nuisance, Neg-

ligence, Breach of Contract, Injunctive Relief and Damages, In The Circuit Court of the Fifth Judicial Circuit, In and for Marion County, Florida, Case No. 8700719-CA-A.

22. Adam Mayers, "DeGroote took Laidlaw from molehill to mountain," *Toronto Star*, 31 March 1988.

23. James Daw, "Investor scramble starts for Laidlaw," *Toronto Star*, 31 March 1988.

24. Cecil Foster, "DeGroote plan may have been doomed," *Globe and Mail*, 12 May 1988.

25. Richard Siklos, "Why Laidlaw was too big for CP to swallow whole," *Financial Times*, 16-22 May 1988.

26. Cecil Foster, "Analysts Say CP Ltd. May Sell Laidlaw School Bus Unit," *Globe and Mail*, 12 May 1988.

27. Diane Francis, *The Financial Post*.

28. Harvey Enchin, "ADT lashes back at Laidlaw," *Globe and Mail*, 12 July 1991.

29. "Laidlaw hit by ADT news," *The Financial Post*, 29 October 1990.

30. "Laidlaw seeking control despite pact, ADT claims," *Toronto Star*, 3 April 1991, and Mathew Horsman's *The Financial Post* articles on 8-9 April 1991.

31. *First Marathon Research*, Volume 2, Number 4, 22 May 1991.

32. Zuhair Kashmeri's *Globe and Mail* articles of 15 and 17 December 1990.

33. William Fox, "Lobbyist told feds Rogers took money on tax cut issue," *The Greenville News*, 11 January 1991, and Cindi Ross Scoppe, "Rogers' friends now witnesses," *The State*, 23 January 1991.

34. Zuhair Kashmeri, "Laidlaw lobbyist cited in U.S. indictment," *Globe and Mail*, 8 January 1991.

35. Zuhair Kashmeri, "FBI probes full extent of lobbying by Laidlaw," *Globe and Mail*, 9 January 1991.

36. Eric Reguly, "DeGroote," *The Financial Post*, 16 September 1991.

37. Cecil Foster, "Standing in the shadow," *The Financial Post*, 25 March 1991.

38. "A Special Relationship."

39. "A Special Relationship."

40. "A Special Relationship."

Chapter Seven: Derelict Conduct?
Captive Markets and Class Action

1. *Cumberland Farms, Inc., et al.,* v. *Browning-Ferris Industries, Inc., et al.,* Master File No. 87-3717. Plaintiffs' Memorandum In Opposition To Defendant's Motion For Summary Judgement. In The United States District Court For The Eastern District of Pennsylvania. 27 July 1990, p. 75.

2. Barnaby J. Feder, "'Mr. Clean' Takes on the Garbage Mess," *New York Times,* 11 March 1990, Section 3.

3. *Cumberland Farms, Inc., et al.,* v. *BFI, et al.,* p. 77.

4. *Cumberland Farms, Inc., et al.,* v. *BFI, et al.,* p. 77.

5. *Cumberland Farms, Inc., et al.,* v. *BFI, et al.,* p. 81.

6. *Cumberland Farms, Inc., et al.,* v. *BFI, et al.,* p. 82.

7. *Cumberland Farms, Inc., et al.,* v. *BFI, et al.,* p. 31.

8. *Cumberland Farms, Inc., et al.,* v. *BFI, et al.,* p. 31.

9. *Cumberland Farms, Inc., et al.,* v. *BFI, et al.,* p. 31-2.

10. *David Yeager* v. *Waste Management, Inc. et al.,* Complaint With Jury Demand Endorsed Hereon, Case 89-0983, In The Court of Common Pleas of Lucas County, Ohio, p. 5.

11. *Cumberland Farms, Inc., et al.,* v. *BFI, et al.,* p. 32.

12. *Cumberland Farms, Inc., et al.,* v. *BFI, et al.,* p. 34.

13. *Browning-Ferris Industries Inc., Derivatively by Sally M. Yeager, and on her behalf and on behalf of all others similarly situated* v. *William D. Ruckelshaus et al.,* Civil Action No. 91-6251, Shareholder Derivative Action, Complaint, In the U.S. District Court for the Eastern District of Pennsylvania, p. 14-15.

14. *David M. Yeager* v. *Waste Management, Inc. et al,* Case 89-0983, Complaint With Jury Demand Endorsed Hereon, In The Court of Common Pleas of Lucas County, Ohio, p. 15.

15. *The People of California* v. *Laidlaw Waste Systems Inc.,* Case No. 632530, Complaint for Injunction, Civil Penalties and Other Equitable Relief, and also Zuhair Kashmeri, "Laidlaw settles California fraud suit," *Globe and Mail,* 11 January 1991.

16. Competition Tribunal, Reasons for Order, In The Matter of certain practices by Laidlaw Waste Systems Ltd. in the communities of Cowichan Valley Regional District, Nanaimo Regional District and the District of Campbell River, B.C. Between The Director of Investigation and Research and Laidlaw Waste Systems Ltd., Ottawa, 20 January 1992.

17. Competition Tribunal, Reasons for Order, p. 29.

18. Competition Tribunal, Reasons for Order, p. 39 and 40.

19. Competition Tribunal, Reasons for Order, p. 96.

20. Competition Tribunal, Reasons for Order, p. 101-103, and R.H. Bork, *The Anti-Trust Paradox*, (New York: Basic Books, 1978), p. 347-348.

21. Competition Tribunal, Reasons for Order, p. 101-102.

22. *David Yeager* v. *Waste Managment, Inc. et al.*, Case 89-0983, Complaint With Jury Demand Endorsed Hereon, In The Court of Common Please of Lucas County, Ohio, p. 16-17.

23. Attorney General Anthony J. Celebrezze, Jr., *Fact Sheet, Browning-Ferris Industries, Inc. et al.* 15 August 1988.

24. *State of Ohio* v. *BFI, Inc., et al.* Civil Action C 86-7387, Antitrust Complaint, In The U.S. District Court for the Northern District of Ohio Western Division, p. 13.

25. *BFI of Ohio and Michigan* v. *Yeager*, Case No: 90-2491, Affidavit of David M. Yeager, In the Court Of Common Pleas Lucas County, Ohio, p. 6.

26. *BFI Inc., Derivatively by Sally M. Yeager, and on her behalf and on behalf of all others similarly situated* v. *William D. Ruckelshaus et al.*, Exhibit B.

27. *Cumberland Farms, Inc., et al.,* v. *BFI, et al.*, p. 4.

28. *Cumberland Farms, Inc., et al.,* v. *BFI, et al.*, p. 1.

29. *Cumberland Farms, Inc., et al.,* v. *BFI, et al.*, p. 19.

30. *Cumberland Farms, Inc., et al.,* v. *BFI, et al.*, p. 20.

31. *Cumberland Farms, Inc., et al.,* v. *BFI, et al.*, p. 30.

32. *Cumberland Farms, Inc., et al.,* v. *BFI, et al.*, p. 99-100.

33. *BFI of Ohio and Michigan* v. *Yeager*, Case No: 90-2491, Motion of Plaintiff for Summary Judgement on Counts IV and V of Defendant's Counterclaim, p. 19-20.

34. *Cumberland Farms, Inc., et al.,* v. *BFI, et al.*, Defendants' Further Memorandum In Response To Plaintiffs' Discovery Proposal, p. 5.

35. *Cumberland Farms, Inc., et al.,* v. *BFI, et al.*, Memorandum In Support Of Motion To Permit Release of Grand Jury Transcript of Bruce Ranck, p. 8.

36. *Cumberland Farms, Inc., et al.,* v. *BFI, et al.*, Memorandum of Waste Management In Opposition To BFI's Interference With Waste Management's Settlement with Plaintiffs.

37. *BFI of Ohio and Michigan* v. *Yeager*, Case No: 90-2491, Opinion and Judgment Entry, 3 May 1991.

38. Jeff Bailey, "Browning-Ferris Directors Reject Doubt About Ranck and Name Him President." *Wall Street Journal,* 6 November 1991.

39. *BFI Inc., Derivatively by Sally M. Yeager, and on her behalf and on behalf of all others similarly situated* v. *William D. Ruckelshaus et al.,* Exhibit C.

40. Bailey, "Browning-Ferris Directors Reject Doubt About Ranck and Name Him President."

41. Bailey, "Browning-Ferris Directors Reject Doubt About Ranck and Name Him President."

42. *BFI Inc., Derivatively by Sally M. Yeager, and on her behalf and on behalf of all others similarly situated* v. *William D. Ruckelshaus et al.,* p. 59.

43. *Wall Street Journal,* 3 October 1991.

Chapter Eight: Winnipeg: The Quest for Urban Ore

1. *The Queen against Haul-A-Way Waste Services, Acme Sanitation Services Ltd.,* and *Browning-Ferris Industries of Winnipeg (1974) Ltd.* Provincial Judge's Court (Criminal Division) Winnipeg, 9 January 1980. Transcript of evidence and proceedings, p. 80. According to Omiucke, his direct superior "told me that he was advised that we were not making any money with the prices that we were charging and that it was necessary to stop the war, and there was no question that it had to be done otherwise ..."

2. Consumer and Corporate Affairs, *Annual Report,* Director of Investigation and Research, Combines Investigation Act, for the year ended 31 March 1976 to the Hon. Anthony Abbott (Ottawa: Ministry of Supply and Services, 1976), p. 15.

3. Geoffrey Stevens, *Globe and Mail* (Toronto), 6 March 1979.

4. *U.S.A.* v. *Waste Management, Inc. and EMW Ventures Inc.* United States District Court, Southern District of New York, Opinion, 29 April 1983. So that their client's role would seem less dominant, defence lawyers argued for the widest possible definition of geographic and product markets. They proposed all trash collection service be included in one market — containerized and non-containerized, commercial and residential and, for good measure, self-hauling and recycling. For its part, the government attempted

to Balkanize the product market into four distinct submarkets, each based on the particular type of truck used (i.e., front-end, rear-end, roll-off, and side-load). For whatever reasons, customers were assumed to be reluctant to shift from their preferred market to another even when faced with significant price increases. Judge Thomas Griesa found the truth lay somewhere between the positions staked out by each side. He ruled there are really two markets, residential and commercial (front-end and roll-off combined). Thus defined, he concluded the WMI/EMW merger had substantially lessened competition in the commercial trash collection market in Dallas, but not in Houston. While not requiring the total divestiture of Waste Resources, Griesa did order Waste Management to rid itself of its Dallas subsidiary.

5. Wanda McConnell, "Skowron defends garbage collection contract decision," *Winnipeg Herald*, 20 January 1988.

6. "Guests of a garbage monster," *Winnipeg Free Press*, 28 January 1990.

7. Donald Campbell, "Memphis junket's accent on junk," *Winnipeg Free Press*, 24 January 1990.

8. "Guests of a garbage monster," *Winnipeg Free Press*.

9. Donald Campbell, "Citizens fume over landfill plan," *Winnipeg Free Press*, 9 February 1990.

10. Donald Campbell, "Citizens fume over landfill plan."

11. Bruce Owen, "Recycling proposal prompts catcalls," *Winnipeg Free Press*, 11 March 1992.

Chapter Nine: Toronto: A Matter of Politics

1. James F. MacLaren Ltd., in association with Black and Veatch of Kansas City. *Report on Refuse Disposal for Metropolitan Toronto*. Commissioned by Metropolitan Toronto and submitted on 19 May 1967, p. 19, 22.

2. *Report on Refuse Disposal*, p. 23.

3. Peter Moon, "How to make a million in garbage," *Globe and Mail* (Toronto), 23 April 1974.

4. Moon, "How to make a million."

5. Moon, "How to make a million."

6. "Garbage plan criticized for lack of public tender," *Toronto Star*, 9 November 1972.

7. James M. Cameron, *The Pits At Maple*, unpublished manuscript. With the generous permission of York University professor Cameron.

8. Here I am indebted to CITY-TV reporter and former Toronto alderman Colin Vaughan who presented this analysis during a panel discussion titled "Getting the Goods at City Hall " at the Annual Convention of the Centre for Investigative Journalism, 20-22 March 1981.

9. Quoted in *The Pits At Maple*.

10. Quoted in *The Pits At Maple*.

11. Environmental Assessment Board, *Landfilling And Resource Recovery Hearing* (Maple), unpublished report, 5 April 1978, p. 19. Copies available from Secretary to the Board, Ministry of the Environment, Toronto.

12. *Landfilling And Resource Recovery Hearing* (Maple), p. 28.

13. The Metropolitian Toronto and Region Conservation Authority, *Maple Area Study: Stage I — Inventory,* unpublished report, August 1974, p. 64.

14. Jack Cahill, "Garbage: Multi-million-dollar headache," *Toronto Star*, 17 May 1981.

15. Ellen Schwartzel, "Burning Desires," *Probe Post*, Summer 1991. The article refers to a trip made to Japan by Metro Toronto councillor Richard Gilbert whose own findings were summarized in *Waste International West Magazine*. Gilbert, disputing the myth that Japan recycles 50 per cent of its waste, says it's probably more like 6 per cent. He believes that the misunderstanding may arise from a mistranslation of "incineration" or "diversion from landfill" as "recycling."

16. Michael Valpy, "Imagine a Ma Bell in charge of garbage," *Globe and Mail*, January 1989.

17. Jock Ferguson, "Liberal backer on inside track on dump stakes," *Globe and Mail* 13 March 1989.

18. Interview with Doug Edgcumbe, 25 May 1992.

19. Jock Ferguson, "Liberal backer on inside ..."

20. Michael Valpy, "Imagine a Ma Bell in charge of garbage."

21. Michael Valpy, "CUPE scores points on garbage issue," *Globe and Mail*, 23 March 1989.

22. Jock Ferguson, "Liberal backer on inside track ..."

23. Michael Smith, "Councillor warns about private waste plans," *Toronto Star*, 2 April 1989.

24. Committee of the Whole Council Memo to Mayor and Members of Council, City of Orillia, 21 March 1990.

25. Committee of the Whole Council Memo to Mayor and Members of Council, City of Orillia, 21 March 1990.

26. Mayor John R. N. Mayor letter to Councillor Dale Martin, Metro Toronto Council, 2 May 1990.

27. *Hazards of Incineration: A Report to the City of Orillia by the Physicians of Orillia*, 26 June 1990.

28. Rudy Platiel, "Small town in turmoil over rubbish," *Globe and Mail*, 5 July 1990.

29. *Hazards of Incineration*, p. 18.

30. *Hazards of Incineration*, p. 19. Emphasis added.

31. *Hazards of Incineration*, p. 20.

32. Mark Bisset and Randy Richmond, "Ogden Martin threatens lawsuit against doctors," *The Packet and Times*, 31 July 1990.

33. *Waste Not: The Weekly Reporter for Rational Resource Management*, (published by Work On Waste USA Inc., 82 Judson, Canton, NY 13617), # 116, 13 September 1990.

34. "Big plane would 'bomb' North with garbage," *The Times-News*, 22 January 1990.

35. Gerard Coffey and Franz Hartman, "Solid Waste In Somebody Else's Community: An Examination of the Solid Waste Interim Steering Committee," Toronto Environmental Alliance.

36. Royson James, "Metro facing dilemma as trash piles up," *Toronto Star*, 18 August 1990.

37. Royson James, "Rouge on secret list of dumps," *Toronto Star*, 11 December 1990.

38. Royson James, "Metro's Garbage: Is Doomsday Near?" *Toronto Star*, 6 April 1991.

39. 3 December 1990 letter to the Honourable Ruth Grier from David McRobert (Pollution Probe), Steven Shrybman (Canadian Emnvironmental Law Association), Tim Grant (Environmental Action Ontario), Gord Perks (Greenpeace), Gerard Coffey (Toronto Environmental Alliance).

40. See summary of *Economic Analysis of Solid Waste Management Options For The Greater Toronto Area (GTA)*. A study by Russ Houldin of the Ontario Ministry of Treasury and Economics.

41. Royson James, "Metro faces 'garbage apocalyse' council says," *Toronto Star*, 11 April 1991.

42. Terence Corcoran, "Ontario flapping toward garbage crisis," *Globe and Mail*, 4 April 1991.

43. David Lewis Stein, "Burying taxpayers under pile of NDP garbage," *Toronto Star*, 5 April 1991.

44. "Wrong decision on waste disposal," *The Financial Post*, 24 April 1991.

45. "Municipal Waste Incineration Banned In Ontario, Canada," *Waste Not*, #146, 10 April 1991.

46. Thomas Walkom, "NDP keeps its promise, gets dumped on," *Toronto Star*, 6 April 1991.

47. Testimony of Jim Temple before the Standing Committee on Social Development, Legislative Assembly of Ontario, 22 January 1992.

48. Richard Gilbert, *Metro Report*, No. 98, April and May 1991. Also see his unpublished "A Used Materials Management Authority For The Toronto Region," 14 January 1988.

49. Royson James, "Councillors set to defy province over trash," *Toronto Star*, 23 April 1991.

50. Submission by the Canadian Union of Public Employees on Bill 143 before the Standing Committee on Social Development, Legislative Assembly of Ontario, 22 January 1992, p. 27.

Chapter Ten: Montreal: Privatization, Protest, and the Multi-nationals

1. Eileen Berenyi and E.S. Savas, *A Case Study of Montreal, Canada*, (unpublished) preliminary draft, October 1979. This, and other Savas group refuse collection studies, are available from Center for Government Studies, Graduate School of Business, Columbia University, New York City.

2. Amy Booth and Philip Mathias, "The tale of two CSE stocks that smack of 'artificiality,'" *The Financial Post*, 30 September 1972.

3. W. Stewart Pinkerton, "Canada's Irving Kott Enjoys Great Success as Promoter, but his Methods Spark Probe," *Wall Street Journal*, 9 May 1973.

4. John Whitelaw, "Street-level crime linked to stock fraud in Toronto trial," *The Financial Post*, 30 October 1976.

5. Pierre Sévigny, *This Game of Politics* (Toronto: McClelland and Stewart, 1965), p. 96.

6. Boyce Richardson, *The Future of Canadian Cities* (Toronto: new press), p. 96.

7. *La Presse*, 22 November 1969.

8. Press release, Montreal Labour Council, 23 May 1962. Available in archives of council. Author thanks André Messier for kind assistance.

9. Quoted in Claude Masson, "L'ex-maire de Jacques-Cartier, J.-Léo-Aldéo Rémillard, de nouveau dans l'arène politique," *La Presse*, 24 October 1968.

10. Catherine Breslin, "La terreur dans la banlieue," *Le Magazine Maclean*, March 1962, p. 19.

11. Quebec Police Commission, CECO, *Rapport Officiel: La Lutte au Crime organisé* (Ottawa: Editions Alaine Stanké, 1976) p. 155.

12. "Waste et Laidlaw s'emparent de 75% de la collecte des déchets," *La Presse*, 11 December 1984.

13. Jean-Benoit Nadeau, "L'industrie de l'ordure, c'est une question de gros sous," *La Presse*, 26 August 1989.

14. Andre Noel, "Le groupe SNC et al. gestion des déchets," *La Presse*, B3, June 22, 1990. Cited in Aaron Freeman, *Smokescreen: Incineration on the Island of Montreal, A Report on the Economic and Environmental Track Record of Foster Wheeler*, Quebec Public Interest Research Group, October 1991, p. 23.

15. Jean Denis Girouard, "La Régie Intermunicipale de gestion des déchets au bord de l'éclatement," *Journal de Montreal*, 10 June 1992.

16. Jean-François Gazaille, "La Régie dépense 1.3 million pour la promotion de l'incinérateur de l'Est," *La Presse*, 10 June 1992.

17. "Incinerator deal nearly set: Mayors," *Gazette*, 3 July 1991.

18. Louis-Gilles Francoeur, "Le 'tonnage minimal' consenti au nouveau centre de tri de Montreal préoccupe Quebec," *Le Devoir*, 17 December 1990.

19. *Waste Not #78*, cited in Aaron Freeman, *Smokescreen*, p. 9.

20. David Blow, "Kindred spirits battle facilities," *The Post-Star*, 27 October 1991.

21. *Greenwich Citizens Committee, et al* v. *Counties of Warren and Washington Industrial Development Agency et al.*, In the U.S. District Court Northern District of New York, Albany-Malone Division, Complaint.

22. Press release: "Citizens SLAPP Back, File $32 Million Civil Rights Suit Against Warren and A State Agency For Violation of Constitutional Rights."

23. David Blow, "Barber, partner sue plant foe for libel," *The Post-Star*, 24 January 1992.

24. Blow, "Barber, partner sue plant foe for libel."

25. Blow, "Barber, partner sue plant foe for libel," and David Blow, "Waste management says it won't drive others out," *The Post-Star*, 2 November 1992.

26. Blow, "Barber, partner sue plant foe for libel."

27. Press release: "Citizens SLAPP Back ..."

28. Press release: "Citizens SLAPP Back ..."

29. *Waste Not* #195. For more on the Hudson Falls project also see #78 and #196.

30. David Blow, "Plant to again take downstate trash at lower cost," *The Post-Star*, 4 March 1992.

31. Blow, "Plant to again take downstate trash ..."

32. Freeman, *Smokescreen*, p. 27.

33. Girouard, "La Régie Intermunicipale de gestion des déchets au bord de l'éclatement."

34. Louis-Gilles Francoeur, "Feu vert déguise à un incinérateur municipal," *Le Devoir*, 29 May 1992.

35. Jean Denis Girouard, "L'AESEQ cherche à limiter les dégâts," *Journal de Montreal*, 29 May 1992.

36. Nadeau, "L'industrie de l'ordure, c'est une ..."

37. Louis-Gilles Francoeur, "Les déchets des Québécois, l'industrie des étrangers," *Le Devoir*, 31 January 1991.

38. "Les multinationales du déchet alarment les ecolos," *La Tribune*, 15 February 1991.

39. Jacques Gingras, "Les municipalités essuient un échec," *Le Nouvelliste*, 10 January 1991.

40. *Le scandale des déchets au Québécois,* Manifeste du Front Commun québécois pour une gestion écologique des déchets solides, Montreal, 1992.

41. Brigitte Trahan, "Les mesures d'expropriation vont bon train à Saint-Etienne," *Le Nouvelliste*, 24 September 1990.

42. Henry Aubin, Paule Beaugrand-Champagne, Carole Beaulieu, Jean-V. Dufresne, Louis Falardeau, Guy Lamarche and Armand Saint-Jean, *Questions d'ethique, Jusqu'ou peuvent aller les journalistes?* pour La Federation Professionnelle Des Journalistes Du Quebec, (Montreal: Quebec/ Amerique, 1991) p. 10.

43. Henry Aubin et al., *Questions d'ethique*, p. 10.

44. Rita Legault, "Swiftly-formed coalition pressured governments to stop," *The Record*, 31 March 1989.

45. Michel Girard, *La Presse*, 27 May 1991.
46. Jim Sibbison, "Revolving Door at the E.P.A.," *The Nation*, 6 November 1989, 527.

Chapter Eleven: As Long as It Rains

1. President Suharto's role in massacring Indonesian Communists must give pause to local activists holding strong views on WMI's proposed West Java co-venture. The 1965 slaughter was said to have assumed such grotesque proportions that the CIA described the operation as "one of the ghastliest and most concentrated blood-lettings of current times." For background on the 1965 installation of President Suharto see Joel Bleifuss, "The First Stone," *In These Times*, 14-17 July 1990, and Eric Nelson, "Down under East Timor's blood and oil," *In These Times*, 18-24 December 1991.
2. *State of Wisconsin* v. *Acme Disposal et al.*, Complaint, 28 September 1962.
3. *A Critical Analysis of the San Diego County District Attorney's Final Report on Waste Management*, 28 May 1992. Prepared by the Los Angeles office of O'Melveny and Myers. The Report concludes that the "insinuation in the District Attorney's Report that Waste Management, operating in the environment it does, has maintained a secret relationship with organized crime dating back to 1962 is irresponsible. We have seen nothing even remotely linking Waste Management and organized crime."
4. Edwin L. Miller, Jr., District Attorney, "Waste Management Inc.," *Final Report*, March 1992, p. 22.
5. "St. Ed talks major trash," *Times Advocate*, (Escondido, California) date unknown, and Edwin L. Miller, Jr., District Attorney, "Waste Management Inc.," p. 57.
6. "St. Ed talks major trash," *Times Advocate*.
7. See Walter Lippmann, "The Underworld, Our Secret Servant," *Forum*, January 1931; and "The Underworld, a Stultified Conscience," *Forum*, February 1931.
8. Jock Ferguson and Michael Keating, "Organized Crime invading toxic-waste field, U.S. panel told," *Globe and Mail*, 22 December 1980.
9. Julia Flynn, "The Ugly Mess at Waste Management," *Business Week*, 13 April 1992, p. 76.

10. Leland Montgomery, "Down in the Dumps," *Financial World*, 23 June 1992. Also see Abraham Briloff, "Recycled Accounting: It Enhances Waste Management's Earnings," *Barron's*, 6 August 1990.

11. Leland Montgomery, "Down in the Dumps."

12. "The View From Deutsche Bank: What The World's Top Banker Sees Ahead for Key Global Economies," *Barron's*, 18 November 1991, p. 24.

13. "The View From Deutsche Bank," p. 24

14. *Guy Hunt* v. *Chemical Waste Management*, In the Supreme Court of Alabama, Case Nos. 190-1043 and 190-1044, Brief and Argument of Appellant Guy Hunt, p. 51.

15. *Guy Hunt* v. *Chemical Waste Management*, p. 45.

16. *Guy Hunt* v. *Chemical Waste Management*, p. 46-47.

17. The PAHLS Alliance's address is 102 N. Morgan, Suite A, Valparaiso, IN 46383, U.S.A.

18. *Cumberland Farms, Inc., et al.*, v. *BFI, et al.*, Master File No. 87-3717. Plaintiffs' Memorandum In Opposition To Defendant's Motion For Summary Judgement.

19. Jeff Bailey, "Waste Disposal Giant, Often Under Attack, Seems to Gain from It," *Wall Street Journal*, 1 May 1991.

20. William Greider, *Who Will Tell The People: The Betrayal of American Democracy*, (New York: Simon and Schuster, 1992), p. 44.

21. *El Pueblo Para El Aire Y Agua Limpio et al.*, v. *Chemical Waste Management Inc., et al.*, U.S. District Court, Northern District of California, Civ. No. c 91 2083 SBA, First Amended Complaint For Injunctive and Declatory Relief, 13 September 1991, p. 2; and Jeff Bailey, "Waste Disposal Often Under Attack, Seems to Gain From It," *Wall Street Journal*, 1 May 1991.

22. *El Pueblo Para El Aire Y Agua Limpio et al.*, v. *Chemical Waste Management Inc., et al.*, p. 2.

23. Michael Janeway, *The New York Times Book Review*, 5 July 1992, p. 1.

24. See Jonathan J. Hutson, "How Clean Are The Titans of Trash?" *Broadcaster*, 5 July 1989; and "Broadcast, Titans-0," *Broadcaster*, 2 August 1989.

25. Mathew Reiss, "The Garbage Broker," *The Village Voice*, 26 November 1991, p. 33.

26. Jeff Bailey, "Some Big Waste Firms Pay Some Tiny Towns Little for Dump Sites," *Wall Street Journal*, 3 December 1991.

27. Keith Schneider, "Rules Forcing Towns to Pick Big New Dumps or Big Costs," 6 January 1992.

28. *Report of the Task Force on the Ontario Environmental Bill of Rights*, Ministry of the Environment, 22 June 1992, p. 17.

29. Bureau de Consultation de Montreal, "Towards Integrated Waste Management — A Project of the Ville de Montreal." Brief Synopsis of the Public Consultations, June 1992, p. 11.

30. Bureau de Consultation de Montreal, p. 8.

Index